TRADITION FOR THE FUTURE

MIRRIT BOUTROS GHALI

TRADITION FOR THE FUTURE

Human Values and Social Purpose

THE ALDEN PRESS   OXFORD

1972

© 1972 MIRRIT BOUTROS GHALI

Printed in Great Britain by Alden & Mowbray Ltd
at the Alden Press, Oxford

Contents

Foreword   *page* 9

PART ONE—THE CHALLENGE   13

1. Political Trends   23
   1. TOTALITARIANISM   25
   2. WAR   31
   3. THE RULE OF LAW   34

2. Trends in Human Sciences   40
   1. DETERMINISM   40
   2. THE SOCIAL UNIT   44
   3. SOCIAL GOALS   46
   4. METHODOLOGY   47
   5. BIOLOGICAL DISCOVERY   49

3. Technological Advance   54
   1. THE ENDS OF TECHNIQUE   55
   2. TECHNICAL NECESSITY   58

4. Overpopulation   62
   1. INCREASING ORGANIZATION   69
   2. INCREASED SOCIAL STRIFE   70
   3. DEPRECIATION OF THE INDIVIDUAL   70
   4. DETERIORATION OF ENVIRONMENT   72

5. Intellectual and Moral Trends   77
   1. LIBERATION   77
   2. VIOLENCE   83
     A. Individual Violence   84
     B. Group Violence   86

5

C. State Violence   *page* 89
3. THE STUDENT REVOLT   90
4. THE MEDIA AND THE ARTS   95
5. WHAT IS WORTH WHILE?   103

6. Conclusion of Part One   109

PART TWO—THE ANSWER   119

7. The Human Values   125
1. FREEDOM   131
    A. Information   134
    B. Social Pressure   135
    C. Education   137
    D. Planning   138
    E. Too Much Freedom?   139
    F. Totalitarian Freedom   140
    G. Statistical Prediction   141
    H. The Metaphysical Objection   142
2. JUSTICE   143
3. DIGNITY   145
4. QUALITY   147
5. THE FIELDS OF APPLICATION   149

8. Change and Technology   152
1. PROGRESS OR IMPROVEMENT   153
2. THE ATTITUDE TO TECHNIQUE   157
3. THE WAY AHEAD   160

9. Policy and Administration   166
1. FEDERALISM   169
2. RESPONSIBILITY OF POWER   174
3. PERSONAL AND SOCIAL RIGHTS   179
4. REPRESENTATIVE RULE   183
5. CIVIC RESPONSIBILITY   185
6. SOCIAL SERVICES   188

CONTENTS

10. Population Policy   *page* 191
    1. BIRTH CONTROL   192
    2. FOOD PRODUCTION   197
    3. OPTIMUM POPULATION   198

11. World Community   204
    1. THE WIDENING GAP   204
    2. INTERNATIONAL SOLIDARITY   211

12. Education and Instruction   224
    1. SOCIAL DISCIPLINE   225
    2. CONTENT OF CULTURE   229
    3. KNOWLEDGE AND SKILLS   235

13. Conclusion of Part Two   243

Epilogue   256

Notes   261

Index   283

Foreword

ON HUMAN VALUES and social purpose most things have been said, much earlier and much better than is commonly realized. But principles that are not constantly affirmed are forgotten. Ideas become stale not because they are no longer true, but because their expression has not changed with the times. Basic ideas remain basic, but they must be defined in the style of each age. Fundamental values must be reasserted in terms consonant to present conditions. Circumstances change and situations evolve, and social purpose is mistakenly supposed also to have to change, when the fact is that means and methods have to change, because the means that were adapted to previous circumstances may no longer be effective in the new circumstances. But because social ends are submerged by an endless surge of new desires and new excitements, the means are taken for ends in themselves and social purpose is lost. Each generation must think out how fundamental values apply to new circumstances and new situations, and find out how the new means created by technological advance or heightened social consciousness may be used to realize those values and to attain the social ends deriving from them. Never is this re-thinking more needed than in times of rapid change. Otherwise no meaningful priorities remain to guide the way to the future, and men become unconscious puppets or willing slaves of forces that they did not have the wisdom to appraise or the energy to control.

Persons and societies are studied and dissected in a thousand social laboratories, their modes of operation are tirelessly scrutinized and exposed, every detail of their behaviour is painstakingly noted and recorded. Yet despite the volume and quality of this research, it seldom reaches to essentials, because there is little understanding of the fundamental human values to give it depth, direction, and

9

significance. Social relations, social functions, social institutions are considered without constant reference to the fundamentals upon which human society must be based. The basic values are thus pushed into the background. They insensibly become blurred in people's minds, while derivative goals and desires become the ever-changing focus of attention. There comes a time when a civilization is threatened with debasement because its vision of human order is fading, a time when a society faces disintegration because the sense of purpose that gave it life becomes dimmed and uncertain.

This book is an attempt to define the permanent and fundamental values of civilization in this time of crisis and swift social change. When human rights are denied to the majority of mankind; when totalitarian rule is spreading and freedom's ground is shrinking; when democracy is threatened from within, by declining civic sense and narrowing channels of communication; when overpopulation strengthens the assurance of hunger and famine, and the probability of strife and war; when violence increases in all countries and weapons of war are ready to unleash apocalyptic destruction; there is indeed cause to worry about fundamental values. A mark of our age is the anxious and self-conscious observation that produces so many warnings about so many things. Coming from one who is not a participant in European or American affairs, this warning is placed in a perspective somewhat different to the usual perspective in the advanced countries. It aims to present a brief survey of human affairs that will include the rich and the poor nations in an integrated world view.

So this book tries to look at fundamentals and the broad lines of their application to everyday problems, great or small, personal or social. It will appear simple for people conversant with philosophical analysis of social evolution and for those who actually have to cope with the practical difficulties of social affairs. But basic ideas and perennial principles are simple, even if their application in theory and in practice is a complicated and an arduous operation. Their expression can never be strikingly original. When they are exhumed out of the limbo to which they are often relegated, when they are considered apart from the theoretical and practical superstructure that each age in turn has to build upon them, they appear so elementary that they are apt to be passed over in an examination of the complexities of modern society. Yet they remain the foundation upon which all is built, and without which everything falls.

*   *   *

This case for human values as social ends may seem overstated, alike for those who take the human values for granted and for those who think that they are no longer relevant to this age, but understatement would be the greater fault. The scope of this essay is broad and comprehensive, and the approach is inevitably speculative and controversial. These pages are proposed as an agenda of ends and means for study and discussion. The urgency of their matter is good reason for ringing the bell loud, and possible overemphasis may stimulate thought and enquiry. Indeed, as these pages finally go to the printers, I reflect that much time has passed in writing them, and events have moved very fast. Statements now seem to me too qualified, expression too mild, too measured, too lacking in a sense of urgency. However, it would be self-defeating to try to bring them up to mark. No writer could hope to keep up with the present rapidity of change and, at the same time, preserve the balanced expression without which readers cannot be expected to consider ideas and conclusions.

Addis Ababa, Cairo, Lausanne, 1967–1971

PART ONE
THE CHALLENGE

We have left undone those things which
we ought to have done; And we have
done those things which we ought not
to have done.

Book of Common Prayer

The Challenge

IT IS HARD to admit that the feats of science and technology are the only original and commendable achievements of our age. Human beings cannot without damage restrict their aspirations to machines and gadgets. They cannot put all their hopes in science and technology. Yet this is where we appear to be heading in our priorities and our cultural aims. Notable accomplishments have been made in the fields of material progress, but the price is high. The scope of human action is expanding at an accelerated rate. The universe is opening before us and we are probing deep into the secret of matter and of life itself. We can recognize that we are living in a remarkable age, but we must also recognize that we may be losing our sense of proportion. We are being induced to deny our experience and our inherited wisdom in order to follow the superior knowledge of the cybernator and his computer. We are being led to a breach with our past in order to enter some hazy and constricted future. Our vision is narrowing when we have the means to see farther and more clearly. Our range of thought is contracting at the same time as our scope of action is expanding.

The 20th century is the century of electronics and nuclear fission, of daring surgery and wonder drugs, of thinking machines and space travel. But it is also the century of the most cynical denials of human values, the most brutal aggressions against human rights. Two world wars, the most destructive in history so far, with the ever-present prospect of a third even more destructive, do not grace the picture of our age. And the picture is further marred by the decline of the individual and the rise of totalitarian societies. It is made ugly by incredibly massive massacres of Armenians, Russians, Jews, Biafrans, Bengalis, of countless others in every continent. Slaughter and butchery of men, women and children are continuously repeated in thousands or tens of thousands or hundreds of thousands all over the world. Which then is to be taken as criterion for this century, technological progress or human values? If technological progress, it is naturally the most advanced, as the 21st century will surely be the most advanced in its turn. But in terms of human values, progress is discouragingly slow and uneven.

Our grandchildren will look back at us as we look back at our grandfathers. Our rockets and computers will appear as clumsy as steam locomotives and flickering gaslights. Science is based on the collection and storage of information from generation to generation. We can take justifiable pride in playing our part in the accumulation of knowledge, but we must remember that we appreciate past civilizations not by their technological achievements—which must be lower than ours, just as ours must be lower than those to come—but by the quality of society, the orderly freedom of thought and action, the creations of the literary and the plastic arts. We must be concerned that, in our obsession with science and our fixation on technique, we do not leave the fundamental values of society to wither away.

Modern technology resounds to the glory of the human mind. Its benefits are undeniable and undenied, but we are delivering our human values into its blind and uncaring keep. We are abdicating our responsibility and renouncing our liberty by trying to make it carry the weight of society. This can lead nowhere but to disaster. Let us not be too impressed by the giant we have made. Let us not think that, as gods, we have created him in our image, so that we can trust him with our priceless human tradition. Our descendants will create other giants, with even greater power to build and to destroy, but our future and theirs depends on our capacity to manage this one. Our generation more than any other is responsible to show the way to employ the giant of technology for the betterment of society.

*   *   *

Society is for human beings. It is established by them for their own needs and it may not be subverted and used against them. Its aim is the satisfaction of the individual by the development of his physical, his intellectual, and his emotive capacities, by the exercise of his creativity, his desire for quality, his quest for perfection. Society cannot be an end in itself, nor can it have an end that is not the good of its individual members. This fundamental truth has never been denied in the tradition of Western civilization, but the difficulty has been at all times to define the values that derive from it, and to ensure that these values are paramount in the order and operation of society.

I admire human beings. I respect humanity as a whole, and certain persons in particular. I have little admiration for aught else. The inconceivable immensity of the universe does not humble my littleness nor does it move me to thoughts of high endeavour, but I admire the intelligence and tenacity of my fellow-men that have made possible the venture into outer space. I am moderately interested by the incredible complexity of matter, by the ever smaller elements which in their unexpected mobility make up its character and its features, but I am impressed by the ingenuity and perseverance of my fellow-men who are probing ever deeper into its secrets. Perhaps the elements of matter will prove to be unlimited in their smallness as the universe may be unlimited in its boundlessness, but both are senseless and unaware and I cannot derive from either a sense of value, a knowledge of what is good and what is bad, nor a sense of my destiny nor a reason for my existence. Only in my humanity and in that of my fellow-men can I find answers to these questions.

Our finite persons are placed between the very small and the very large. They are frail and short-lived, but the energy of life and love runs strongly within them. They are conscious and aware, and nothing can be said to exist but through their awareness. They are the descendants of untold generations that found themselves in a hostile and unthinking world. There were no pointers to the requisites of social grouping, of experience and knowledge. Primitive men—in the midst of constant hunger and permanent insecurity— slowly thought out the principles of freedom and justice, of dignity and quality. Nothing around them taught them these concepts, which they elaborated through their understanding of the respect each one owed to and expected from the other in their small communities. Other attributes, that are also precious for human beings, we share to some extent with animals, life itself to begin with, then health, strength, agility, and even in some small measure reason and intelligence and love. Because of this sharing, men must also have respect for animals, and indeed for all of nature; and it is for lack of this respect that the ecological threat is growing. But the values that are the foundation of civilized society have no counterpart whatever in anything that nature can show. Nature is totally alien to freedom and justice. Neither minerals, plants, animals, nor the infinite cosmos have any relation to dignity or quality.

In saying that men created these concepts, the intention is not to deny those who believe that they were revealed. To those who are sustained by this belief I would say: 'Man alone was chosen for divine revelation, and these principles should be even more sacred for you than for others who do not share your faith.' But there are many who do not share this or any other faith, and for them the worth of men in having created these high concepts of society must be greater. Spiritual and religious considerations will be omitted in these pages, not because they carry no significance for the human values, but because they have become alien to so many people. In a book too short to draw more than the bare outlines, it may be wise to avoid arousing the irrational reactions that mention of the spirit calls forth in those who, in the name of rationality, no longer recognize its existence. There is no place here to answer them, and it will be enough to remain at the level of social principles without basing them on spiritual ground and transcendental religion.

Perhaps no society has ever reached in practice the standard of these concepts, but all societies may be judged *solely* by the degree to which they approached them. That men seldom live up to the fundamental values which they established for themselves cannot be reason to despise them or to deny the relevance of these values. Rather should one be impressed by the general respect for principles, by the decency of the average human being, despite the example of nature engaged in an unceasing movement of degradation and erosion, of pulling down and destroying; despite man's own dark, primitive fears and his deep animal instinct to kill for dominance, for excitement, or for need; and despite evil and selfish leadership that too often depraves and corrupts a society, and makes a mockery of human rights.

Technique, people say, has progressed faster than man. Science of Matter has advanced so far ahead of Science of Man that, while his material power to build and to destroy has become immense, his rational and moral guides to thought and action have not improved. His values are no longer fit for his technique. The remedy is to devote more time, money and effort to the Science of Man, so that an appropriate combination of behavioural and biological manipulation will improve men by adjusting them to the New Society, and may eventually produce something like supermen, consistently calm and rational, subject to neither anguish nor doubt, not troubled by dreams or disturbed by passions . . . divine in fact, or merely mechanical. This is nonsense. It is the same man astride a mule or inside a rocket, and he needs the same basic values in the one and the other position. There is no reason why he should be different, nor indeed is there cause to wish him such as behavioural and genetic experimentation may make of him. His dreams and his passions no less than his reason and his intelligence have elaborated the fundamental values upon which culture and civilization are based; and to maintain culture and civilization while solving the human problems posed by technological progress, it is enough that these values be maintained to inform society and to guide individual thought and action. How to uphold these values when they are in danger of being lost or ignored, how to recapture their sense when it is apparently dimmed by accelerated change, how to replenish their content when it is being drained by seemingly unopposable trends, these are the essential issues of our time.

In a primary sense values can only be human, inasmuch as they are always defined by human beings for human beings. In this sense, the term 'human values' could be a redundancy. But here we speak of an appreciation of worth and import that considers the individual human being as the pre-eminent factor of society, and his development and satisfaction as the paramount end of social order. We are thus referring to these values from the perspective of their substance and content, not from that of those who define and hold them. In this second sense it is legitimate, even necessary, to speak of 'human' values, as there can be social values that are inhuman or anti-human. Such are the deification of race or state, the assertion that the development of a social entity is more important than that of its individual members, that the satisfaction of a social entity (if such a thing were possible) must supersede that of the individual person. This is why the term of human values is used as the central theme of this essay, namely the values that derive from the understanding that the individual human being is the fundamental factor of the social order.

Human values are thus the social principles which are founded on the basic premise of the autonomy, the worth, and the dignity of the human person, on the fact that individual human beings are the reason and the end of society. This is a very old truth, and it is not less true for being old and clouded over by the passing ages. Society —to paraphrase a famous saying—has no existence but through individuals, by individuals, for individuals. The values of freedom and justice, dignity and quality are the principles of civilized society because they are the rules devised by men to preserve each other's worth and to respect each other's persons in their relations with one another. They are the absolute foundation of morality. They are the foundation of human rights, and of the duties which are their counterpart. There can be bad societies, in which these principles are ignored or denied. There have been bad societies in the past and there are bad societies in our day. There is now the threat of a very bad society in the advanced and affluent countries.

A chain is only as strong as one of its links, and tradition may be likened to a chain in which every generation is a link. The tradition of culture that keeps a society going is generally only as strong as one human life-span, and often much less than that. It can be broken if a generation loses sight of the fundamental values because of political revolution, military defeat, or changing environment. In orderly, powerful and prosperous nations, revolution or defeat may not be likely, but the impact of change can be as effective in weakening and breaking a tradition. Every generation is responsible to keep the ends of society in view, to reaffirm and re-define the human values in changing circumstances. Never has this responsibility been greater than it is now, face to face with population growth and technological advance. Do the changing circumstances threaten civilization? If not, our age is a happy one, and we can take confidence in our future. But if the ends of society are threatened and its principles undermined, an arduous, a formidable reappraisal must be made, in order to control population increase and to make technology the servant of human values. This is the challenge to the present generation.

* * *

The challenge to civilization is probably greater today than at any other time in history, first, because the danger confronts a much larger number of human beings; second, because it is more insidious and pervading, as it touches every element of the person and every activity of society; third, because the direction taken by the generations now living will affect the future of humanity for as long as we can or dare foresee; fourth, because the evolution of the more powerful societies of the North Atlantic may well fix the design for the whole world; and fifth, because the penalty for failure will be more intolerable than at any time before, while the reward of success will be more precious than it has ever been. Basically the challenge is that the fundamental premise of the human person as the sole end of society is ignored or denied. The principles that proceed from this premise, and that define the ends and means of civilized societies, are threatened by the juncture of relatively recent developments, mainly connected with accelerated increase of population and advance of technology.

These developments appear to obscure our understanding of the human values and to sap our faith, our purpose and our hope for the future. Most men and women in these times feel frustrated and helpless. Confounded by the rising tempo and widening range of national and international problems, confused by violent and seemingly disconnected reactions to these problems, dismayed by spreading disorder, by disintegration of their mould of living, many are led to think that humanity is faced with circumstances so different from any in the past that its traditional inheritance is out of date and its old experience of no avail. 'The sphere of knowledge has grown so vast, the power over nature has become so complete, that a new humanity is in formation. A "mutation" is occurring. Radically new answers are required and they must be sought in pragmatic responses unencumbered by inherited values and ancient principles.' This is the worst mistake that can be made, for it removes us even further away from the only adequate guiding lines in the present difficulties. The need is now for awareness of fundamentals, coupled with clear thinking and confident action. A review of some main political and cultural trends will bring out in clearer relief the underlying factors of the present momentous juncture in human affairs. It will also show that the threat to civilization lies not so much in the urgency and gravity of the problems, as in the fading of fundamental principles and basic values, and the resulting confusion of ends and means.

I

Political Trends

THERE WILL BE little of economics in this book. The bias on economic factors as the prime motives of human activity is such that philosophical and political factors are apt to be discounted. But progress or stagnation in every field of human activity, including the economic field, depends primarily on philosophical outlooks and political systems. Once basic physical needs are met (and this is an accomplished fact for the advanced nations) men and women are led by deeper motives towards further goals (such as power, security, fulfilment, recognition, charity) that derive from their values and their priorities. Economic success is only one of the means for attaining such goals. *Homo oeconomicus* is a narrow view, as misleading as other exclusive abstractions into which human beings are supposed to fit. Thus it is important to bring out in the first place the values upon which a civilization is founded and to clarify the priorities that constitute the frame of politics. Another reason for touching only incidentally on economic factors is the wealth of information available on every aspect of economics, so that the reader may be considered as acquainted with the economic issues relevant to the topics of this book.

The word *capitalism* is not used in these pages, while *socialism* and *communism* are used mostly in the sense of a political system of government, seldom in a sense related to ownership of means of production and other economic features. The impact of technology and population growth on national societies varies according to differences in political regimes and cultural standards much more than according to differences in economic systems. These appear to be tending towards a sort of unification. On one hand, the widening field of social solidarity and growing social complexity enlarge the scope of state intervention, and bring the 'capitalist' countries well into the realm of planned economy; while, on the other hand, the failure of communist economics is forcing a return to erstwhile heretical notions of decentralization, individual incentive and consumer satisfaction, thus reducing to some extent the scope of state intervention in the communist countries. This drawing closer may be related to the evolution of the formerly basic issue of property: the widening ownership of corporate ventures in the West begins to take on some characters of public ownership, while dawning independence granted to agricultural and industrial enterprises in the East starts to give them some of the features and modes of operation of Western corporations. In both cases, the rise of a technocratic managerial class may be observed.

The difference between Western and Eastern nations does not lie in the gradually blurring distinction between their production systems. Continued use of capitalist and communist as terms of abuse in the running propaganda duel between East and West points to a lack of imagination and perception on both sides. The real difference lies where it has always been: in the social and political distinction between democratic and totalitarian government, in the viable balance—which the former preserves and the latter denies—between individual rights and community cohesion, in the legal guarantees of democratic rights, in the understanding of fundamental human values. The West may now be degenerating inasmuch as it yields to the temptation of ignoring these values or emptying them of content, while the East could be regenerated inasmuch as it comes to recapture their meaning. In the present juncture, the basic issue for East and West alike, and indeed for the whole world, is to protect fundamental values, with the social principles and the political priorities that derive from them, against the challenge of growing overpopulation and pervading technological outlook.

Eastern Europe may one day return to a true sense of the human values as the only principles of civilization. The trend is manifest, despite the heavy Russian hand on restive satellites. The Russians themselves may not long be able to maintain the hard line in their own country, even if they gain time by renewed activity in power politics designed to take people's minds away from internal problems. Sooner or later, Europe will be unified in social and political outlook, but it is not yet clear at which point the meeting will be. It could be that the people of Eastern Europe will make it across the dividing line. It would be sadly ironical if they found people in the West settling down to a neglect of human values hardly different to that from which they emerged. This is a disquieting possibility, for the Third World no less than for the advanced countries. Such a prospect could be what incites so many people still to put more hope in 'socialism' than in 'capitalism'. Perhaps they think that the former is proceeding, however slowly, towards a better understanding of human values and social priorities, while the latter appears to them to be on the way to lose that understanding.

The philosophical thought of Karl Marx greatly contributed to widen and deepen the notion of human solidarity, and Marxist humanism remains a main source of inspiration for modern humanistic views all over the world; but Marxist economics were quickly disproved, both by theoretical refutation and by the results of practical policies in the West, and Marxist politics always made the fatal mistake of assuming that the ends justify the means. Collectivism and communism are generous dreams for a humane society, but the means employed to bring them into social reality, to embody them in political structures, invariably turn them into totalitarian nightmares of suffering and disappointment worse than any 'capitalist' excess. These dreams and any dreams for a better society cannot come true unless they respect the basic priorities in their practical policies and their institutional applications.

The main trends that constitute the political challenge to fundamental values and priorities may be grouped under the headings of totalitarianism, war, and the rule of law.

I. TOTALITARIANISM

The urge for domination and power is one of the instincts against which civilized man has to fight. It is encouraged by the fact that society cannot exist without authority to regulate its operation, and it is thus one of the oldest reasons for denying freedom and justice. Ancient and modern history is replete with tyranny, when a man or a group of men set themselves by force over other men. The pattern is much the same in every country and every age.[1] In the democratic process of government, the urge to command is canalized and refined, so that in theory and sometimes in practice those most competent to lead are voluntarily placed by their fellow citizens in the posts of command. In our age, democratic government operates in the advanced and affluent countries. In many other countries, some less developed form of popular participation operates under an authoritarian or a paternalistic rule, whereby the people or some of the people are granted a share in defining policy and taking decisions. This share is often small, and sometimes illusory, but it is better than no share at all. At least it may give some training in the freedom of expression and responsibility of action which are the necessary conditions of democratic institutions.

In some of the more retarded countries, the despot (individual or group) is well in evidence. This must not be taken lightly. The arsenal of weapons by which a dictator may arm himself against his people is growing. People in countries where freedom of thought and expression is taken for granted do not realize the situation of those who are denied this freedom. Pundits of London or Paris who often said that democracy was no good for retarded countries, that a dose of dictatorship was needed for such countries to progress before they could accede to democracy, were deceitful or foolish. If human values are to be defended as being the basis and the benefit of civilization, they must be defended everywhere. The exercise of a right can be learned only by exercise, and by making mistakes; it cannot be learned through the denial of that right. The time a country spends under a dictator is wasted, except for the roads and the buildings that appear to be the only positive legacies of dictatorial regimes. It is lost time because such regimes paralyse all possibilities for improvement of society, when it does not actually corrupt its institutions and deprave its members.

The totalitarian state is very different from ordinary despotism and it is a more elaborate and dangerous way of rejecting human values and denying human rights. It is constructed on the foundation of a political theory which, in order to be justified, must command every element of individual and social life. It is thus a total system because it must control not only attitudes and actions, but also thoughts and emotions. It must eliminate all individuals and groups who are not devoted in mind and body to the state considered as the personification of the political theory, as well as individuals and groups who are considered to be inferior in the light of the political theory. The state is the important element in the system and individuals are allowed to live only as units of the system and servants of the state. Nazism and Stalinism were the outstanding and terrifying examples of such a political dogma pushed to its logical extremity. Once the basic premise of society is rejected, once the individual as such is no longer important, human beings are stripped of their worth and dignity. They become objects, interchangeable and expendable units. They can be scrapped as so many useless parts of machinery. Nazis under Hitler like communists under Stalin acted with logic and method. The kulaks in Russia were opposed to communization and millions of them were liquidated. Jews were considered as inferior to 'aryan' nazis and they were exterminated to the tune of five or six million. What is a million more or less if the suffering and agony of man, woman and child is counted of no importance?

Besides physical extermination by death and near extermination in work camps and concentration camps, there is degradation of the moral environment that contributes to the quality of life. This applies as much to the South African regime, where the democratic organization of the ruling minority does not make it less totalitarian for the subject majority, as to the more common totalitarian regimes of the communist or fascist varieties. Such regimes are possible because of the pliability of human beings and their capacity to adapt to practically any circumstances short of outright starvation. People get conditioned to a deadening of mind and soul under totalitarian regimes provided that they have no other picture against which to compare their predicament, so the various curtains are put up to prevent comparison that could awake criticism and dissatisfaction. There are indeed minorities in the most affluent nation in the world who live in a degraded environment with a comparable constriction of mind and soul. Maybe the existence of such unfortunate minorities in America is more scandalous than the similar position of people in totalitarian states, because a depressed minority in an affluent majority naturally evokes more resentment than a generally depressed level elsewhere. The fact remains, however, that there is hope for depressed minorities to rise up to the average American level within the established system, while it does not appear possible for people in totalitarian states to enjoy a better moral environment without a radical change of their established system.

Hitlerism and Stalinism, as well as the lesser 'isms that ape them, are not survivals from a barbarous past. They are not simply more perfect expressions of despotism such as the world has known from ancient times. Despite all that is written and said about these dreadful visitations, their real message is not often squarely faced, perhaps because many people are unconsciously afraid to realize their full implications. Historically their rise may be traced back to the French revolution or to other violent impositions of creed and dogma in modern times, but they are new—really new—in their deep and overwhelming drive towards total organization. Far from being survivals of the past, they are forerunners of a possible future. They are prefigurations, necessarily imperfect, of systems that will be established again in more efficient (and perhaps less openly brutal) ways if the fundamental values are not more strongly affirmed in the advanced countries that provide, for better or for worse, the pattern of the future for themselves and for the rest of the world.

These inhuman systems were not designed in backward countries which might be supposed to have an insufficient tradition of civilization. The most terrible was conceived and operated in the centre of Europe, which led the world in philosophy and science for many hundreds of years. It was worked with machine-like efficiency and machine-like indifference to human values in the country of Goethe and Beethoven.[2] The nazis were not bloodthirsty savages slaking atavistic rage to kill; the gas-chambers of Auschwitz in 1941 had little in common with the human pyramids of Nishapour in 1221. They were intelligent people searching for efficiency. Their means were excellently contrived, beautifully efficient in mechanistic terms. Only their ends were bad. They were acting with the logic of madness. They were insane, and the real meaning of insanity is to be out of touch with human values and human reality.

Fanatics who are granted the favour of trying out their theories on a society deny the exercise of human rights in their time in order to establish the system that is to ensure those rights in the future. They think, if their purpose is honest, that their ends justify their means. They do not realize that wrong means destroy right ends more surely than the impossibility or failure to achieve those ends through the right means. Russian communist leaders of the early thirties (assuming that they were not thinking only of how to remain in power) sacrificed millions of human beings to achieve their design to make human beings happy. A monstrous arithmetic thus develops: so many frustrated in this generation to make so many fulfilled in the next, a number despoiled of dignity and hope in order that a greater number should later enjoy a secure and a decent life. This computation is akin to that of a chess player or a military commander: how many men must be sacrificed to gain this position? How can I improve my kill-ratio? The new utopians[3] at the keyboards of their computers are much of the same mind as regards the importance of an individual. Human beings become subject to numbers, to proportions, to statistical averages. Human values are mislaid in the process, and the real ends of society are forgotten.

The present crisis in human affairs, some elements of which are reviewed in following chapters, creates an atmosphere more consonant with the spread of totalitarian than democratic government. No nation, however liberal and advanced, can say 'this cannot happen to us'. The balance of a society is very fine. The madness is always round the corner. Chauvinists and Jingoists, or extremists of any denomination are always ready to take over. Emergency laws such as the McCarran Act in America and similar legislation in most of the democratic countries are easily enacted and easily misused. Concentration camps are quickly established. People can be confident of the future only if they affirm, with clearsighted awareness and unswerving determination, their human values and their social ends. Moreover, totalitarian organization was a product of the machine age even before computers and cybernated equipment;[4] with technicists left to push ahead undirected and uncontrolled, the totalitarian tendency receives potent impetus and, at the same time, assurance of efficiency such that no revolt will be possible any more.[5] Hitlerism was destroyed by military defeat and Stalinism was reversed by a reaction which took place after the death of Stalin, but in the more efficient totalitarian state of the future, if it is ever established, there will be no defeat, no revolt, no reaction because by then the whole of humanity will have been absorbed into the all-encompassing system.

Liberal democracy (or free democracy: the redundant adjective is required because of the current confusion of words and meanings)[6] is a rare plant, hard to raise and easy to destroy. If the ground where it grows is allowed to become eroded and sterile, by lack of foresight and sound judgment, by slackness and corruption in administration, by a premium put on material values, by an abdication of the thinking and humanist elite, a hardier plant must take its place, such as a desert bush with spikes on its rough and resistant bark and little sap left for the green leaves of culture and the flowering of human values. When a democracy is faced by external attack, it has to tighten up its operation for the pursuit of war. When it faces internal difficulties brought on by its own deficiencies, the remedy is sought in a strong government and this usually means in these times a military government. When there is a serious threat of a collectivist take-over, which inevitably heralds a totalitarian system, the only answer appears to be another sort of totalitarian system to resist the take-over, but when it is in fact the only possible answer, it means that the sickness of democracy has spread so deep that it can no longer survive. Examples of this process are numerous in our generation.

The various totalitarian systems do not all indulge in torture and massacre, at least not to the same degree, but they are all oblivious of human values, deadening to mind and soul. The communist regimes rave against the fascist dictatorships and these rant against the communists. In their opinions on such regimes, people in democratic countries are guided more by ready-made ideas and hackneyed expressions than by an awareness of the meaning of civilization and a concern for its values. The free press does criticize dictatorial regimes in general, but it lays the accent against the 'rightist' or the 'leftist' types according to prejudice or sympathy, economic or political interest. It does not expose with enough force and sincerity the deficiencies that, in its own countries, erode the soil in which democracy found its nourishment. Engrossed by the day-to-day play of politics, absorbed by financial and professional competition, subservient to the fashion of a merely fact-finding role, the democratic press tends to neglect the useful comparison between what happened in less fortunate nations to bring them under totalitarian rule, and what happens in its own countries that could ultimately put the free nations in a similarly unfortunate position.

2. WAR

The requirements of defence and attack in time of war reduce the respect for human values; these are not denied, but they are put aside as secondary to survival, and it is not always easy to recover respect for human worth and dignity when peace returns. That it should ever be deserving to kill human beings must weaken regard for human life. To be sure, self-defence is the often-invoked basis for the morality of avoiding death by inflicting it on another but self-defence, except in guerilla warfare, is no longer direct and obvious. War also imposes controls that tend to remain after peace returns. It makes people used to some reduction of human rights, their's and the rights of others. The degrading effect of two world wars has been considerable in this century. A third world war, even if survival were granted, would accelerate the reduction of freedom and the depreciation of the individual.

Philosophers of small stature have held that war ennobles human beings and that it is the supreme expression of the vitality of a nation. True, battles are often the setting for dedication and comradeship, the occasion for admirable acts of courage and abnegation, but everyday life also provides settings and occasions for men and women to exercise these virtues. War does not ennoble but rather degrades human beings unless they are of strong moral fibre, and warfare has lost even the lying appearance of pageantry and gallantry with which it was once disguised. Only very recently in the history of humanity has war been recognized as an unqualified evil by civilized societies, though this recognition is not preventing war, but it was recently also that some European governments asserted the nobility of fighting in order to gain more room to live. There are still defenders of the natural character of warfare who hold that, if it is an evil, it is at any rate an unavoidable evil.[7]

31

Since the earliest beginnings war was total. The vanquished who were not killed in battle became the things of the victors, to be despoiled and put to death or taken into slavery. With growing social specialization (warrior caste, mercenary troups, standing armies) a distinction appeared between military and non-military personnel. This distinction reached its highest point in the so-called civilized wars of 18th-century Europe when, theoretically at least, warfare was waged by rulers and their armies; while civilians were non-participants, safe from the physical impact of war unless they happened to be in the path of an army or near a field of battle. Total warfare in its modern national form returned with the wars of the French revolution. In the 20th century, increased dependence on economic backing of the war effort and development of long-range artillery and aerial bombardment brought the horrors of war back to nonmilitary populations in their cities and their homes. This culminated in the nuclear bombs that destroyed Hiroshima and Nagasaki in 1945. Since then it is manifest that warfare has become total to a degree that, if the present arsenals are opened, it will certainly lead humanity to complete degradation, and perhaps to extinction.[8]

We are already accustomed to the idea of total annihilation. Young people now have to accept this possible future as part of their reaching adult status. This appears to be a basic, though seldom expressed, cause of their revolt against society and their desire for a better social order. They despise an order in which their elders are preparing their regression and degradation for lack of vision and moral courage. They do not take pride in the knowledge that we can now make explosions comparable to those of the stars in the firmament. Nuclear bombs are proliferating like deadly weeds and lethal microbes. Soon the smallest state, the most irresponsible dictator will have an A or an H bomb with which to start an atomic war and end civilization. And can we entrust our future to the belief that governments of the larger states are wiser and more responsible? They are certainly not proving their wisdom by their mad nuclear competition, with the French government intent on taking part in the atomic race even though far behind. Is it a consolation that atomic weapons are now outlawed by mutual agreement in outer space? One is tempted to say that outer space is just the place for them: it is on this overcrowded Earth that they must be eliminated and destroyed.

It is hard to view the Geneva disarmament talks, with meetings now running in the hundreds, as anything but a sinister game, even taking into account the presumed goodwill and sense of duty of the patient participants. However, some progress now seems possible. The most limited agreement would of course be better than none but, until nuclear weapons are destroyed, the threat of nuclear warfare will remain the major factor that weighs upon the future of humanity regardless of whatever treaties are signed and undertakings solemnly sworn. Perhaps something encouraging will emerge from the SALT talks, but the most probable outcome of the intricate atomic *danse-à-deux* between U.S.A. and U.S.S.R. is just nothing but more armaments. There is only one reasonable question for each side to ask of the other: what are your terms for complete destruction of nuclear arms, tactic and strategic, IRBMs and ICBMs and MIRVs and all? If there is a readiness to give and take with this as starting point, there will be ground for hope, and time to force all other governments to destroy their nuclear arms. If there is no readiness to discuss on this line, then each of us may as well come to terms with his or her own anxiety or despair for the future according to individual character and attitude towards life.

The apocalyptic violence of nuclear bombs is said to be a deterrent to their use in war. In the absence of any other reason for avoiding catastrophe, we can only pray that this one is real. But wars with conventional weapons (bazookas and TNT and napalm are now conventional!) will not be abated as long as the world remains in its present critical juncture. These wars are here with us now and we see how destructive and how unavailing they are. In terms of suffering each human being bears his own pain. It makes little difference to him whether he dies of a conventional or a nuclear explosion, of a knife in the guts, a shrapnel in the chest, or radiation in the blood. It makes no difference to those who loved him whether he was killed in a world conflagration or in a minor war. There is also the ever-present possibility of a conventional war suddenly developing into a nuclear blaze. Besides nuclear arms, chemical and biological weapons of calamitous potency are being perfected. Once

B   33

a weapon exists, there is no guarantee whatever that it will not be used.[9]

A false notion of economy and finance presses for maintaining a state of war in order to prevent the slump that is mistakenly supposed or dishonestly declared to be the inevitable result of a return to peace. The economic use of war is another durable fallacy. Our 'expanding economy based on waste and war has only two ultimate outlets: rubbish heaps and ruined cities' (Lewis Mumford). War is the greatest waste maker of all and so it helps to keep the wheels of industry turning, but to no purpose relevant to a better life for men and women. War does indeed speed up scientific and technological progress, but the advance it brings is seldom the best suited to social improvement. In any case, if the advance were so urgently needed, it could be achieved equally well at much less cost by a peace-time effort. With its illimited waste of resources and its deleterious results on morals and politics, war is one factor that prevents maybe for always the Good, the Great, the Golden Society of men's dreams.

Wars will continue until an equal concern for fundamental values shall be shared by all people on Earth. At present this is obviously nothing more than a pious hope.[10] But perhaps the concept of absolute state sovereignty will finally give way, in the not too distant future, to an understanding between nations whereby disarmament will become a reality. Maybe the two most powerful governments in the world will realize that their reasons for mutual fear and suspicion are less powerful than their common interests. The advantages that they are busily pursuing against each other are as nothing compared to the advantages which would be their's and the world's if they came together. They could effectively impose peace and they could co-operate in solving the tragically pressing problems of the poor nations and underdeveloped countries. This is a vision and a realistic aim to inspire thinkers and statesmen in U.S.A. and U.S.S.R.

3. THE RULE OF LAW

The rule of law is a much respected principle of Western civilization and it is generally considered a criterion of civilization. Basically it means that the authority of society is held by persons appointed by the people, directly or through their freely elected representatives; that these persons take no action that is not based on law and precedent; that laws must be approved by the freely elected representatives of the people; that no precedent can be established other than by courts of justice appointed according to the law; and that nobody can be punished for contravening the law without due legal and judicial process. Its content is wider in the Anglo-Saxon tradition than it is in the Roman. The latter tends to insist more on the principle that no action may be taken that is not in accordance with a published and intelligible law, and less on the method by which the law was established and whether it was freely established by a democratic process. Without the rule of law there is no guarantee of freedom, of justice, of dignity for the individual. No society may or indeed does deny the rule of law, but in many countries it is a travesty whereby the whims of tyranny masquerade as the rule of law. Law is thus emptied of content and it is turned against the human values that it no longer protects. Few things are as important as to be aware of the real content of the rule of law and to be watchful for any reduction or debasement of this content by subversion or by outright denial.

1. The most frequent subversion is that the government of a country is not appointed by a majority of the people or that it retains power after the majority has ceased to support it, and that laws are not approved by freely elected representatives even though they may be clearly phrased and widely published. In such cases the rule of law does not exist. It would be easy to list here how many sovereign states can now boast a freely elected government and how many nations would maintain their governments and their laws if free elections were held. It is enough here to recall that freely elected governments are a shrinking minority in the world and that totalitarian regimes are spreading, but that all the advanced nations have freely elected governments. Seizure or retention of power against the will of the people is an obvious subversion of the rule of law and one that is hopefully easy to avoid for the Western democracies.

2. A less obvious subversion, which often takes in foreign visitors, is the travesty of democracy by which its form is preserved while it is emptied of substance. Elections are held, but freedom is absent

from the process. Legislation is discussed by the elected, but it is an impotent discussion. Laws become the immediate expression of the wishes of the governing person or group. They become in reality administrative decisions and regulations, which incidentally is the reason why they are changed so frequently in dictatorial countries, but they are published in proper legal form. If the maxim still holds good that hypocrisy is the homage that vice renders to virtue, it must be admitted that vice is prevalent, though virtue remains just strong enough to claim the hypocritical deference that is all it can obtain. The travesty of democracy is a diverse and many-hued costume. One-party systems, single electoral lists, pre-selection or screening of candidates are simply more polite ways of subverting democratic institutions than plain forcing or cooking of votes. However, in some countries that are far removed from real democracy, the travesty may keep the idea of freedom alive and, with the idea, the hope of acceding to democratic operation of government.

3. A new departure is the 'blanket law' designed to give the executive the equivalent of a blank cheque to take action. In some cases, permission of parliament or what stands for a parliament is sought in order to give government the sanction of a democratic process for arbitrary action. Full powers are 'legally' granted to guard against political plotting or economic sabotage, or other similar excuses, and the measures taken—however inhuman they may be— are then supposed to have received previous approval from the people. In other cases, even in democratic countries, sanction for the executive's liberty of action is sought because the problems involved are considered too difficult for a full and open discussion. This new tendency may be observed in Europe more than in America. Growing complexity of national and international problems makes it hard to impart sufficient information to public opinion and to its representatives, and it makes the passing of legislation a lengthy and tedious process. The executive becomes impatient and persuades the legislature to abdicate part of its responsibility by approving blanket laws couched in terms so general as to cover practically any action that circumstances may render advisable. 'Pleins pouvoirs' and 'delegated legislation' are other names for this practice which is an insidious subversion of the rule of law, and one against which

free societies must carefully guard. This problem will be considered from another angle in Part Two (see pp. 183–188).

4. The rule of law, as the protector of human values and individual rights, may be subverted by the preponderance of collective aims and by inhuman laws and regulations. This process is so well known in totalitarian countries[11] that there would be no need to mention it here were it not taking an unexpected twist in the democratic countries, because of the difficulties involved in administering and controlling increasingly overcrowded and complex urban agglomerations. More and more must administration provide for large numbers (so large that we are expected to believe that only computers can cope with the effort); less and less can administration look after individual cases and examine infringements of individual rights. Administration thus really becomes a governing machine.[12] Unless the utmost vigilance is exerted, the rule of law can be vitiated even in democratic societies by the fact of having to deal with very large numbers of human beings. This threat must exercise the close attention of all who understand social ends as based on fundamental values. Decentralization, with local government developed down to the smallest possible unit with the largest possible competence, is one obvious solution, though hard to realize in overcrowded cities. Another solution is to set up easy and flexible recourse institutions and procedures for redress against administrative decisions at every level, as well as public officers such as the Roman tribune or the Scandinavian ombudsman to seek out injustice and to ensure redress even where no recourse was made.

5. In last analysis the protector of human values is the judiciary. As long as it remains independent, there is nothing basically wrong with a country, even if there are glaring faults in its repressive process from police to prisons. Of the vigorous democratic institutions of the U.S.A. the judiciary is the most alert, the most independent, the most concerned with human rights. It is more concerned than the executive, primarily occupied with executing policies and enforcing decisions, and the legislative, in which so many different interests and points are necessarily represented. It has given clear and forceful proof of this concern on more than one important issue in recent years. In Western Europe the judiciary may have a less

independent attitude than in America and Great Britain, it may be more inclined to apply the law with exact justice than to temper its application with equity and fairness (probably because of the difference between the Roman and the Common Law approaches) but it is nevertheless as strong a bulwark for democracy and human rights. While in countries where the judiciary is under the control of the executive, where it is not scandalous nor even unusual that judges are instructed on the judgments they are to give, the rule of law is gravely impaired. There is no redress for administrative infringements of individual rights and personal freedom, especially as competence of judiciary courts is systematically reduced in order to enlarge the competence of administrative courts, the function of which is more to ensure that people observe regulations than to protect them against arbitrary authority.

*   *   *

For many persons, especially of the younger generations, expressions such as the Rule of Law, the Due Process of Law, Proper Legal and Judicial Process are losing their meaning. Like other important notions (democracy, freedom, justice) they are distorted and debased, deliberately by clever propagandists or unconsciously by woolly thinkers. The rule of law is a basic notion of civilization and a fundamental condition of civilization. It must not be allowed to vanish into a meaningless catchword or a vaporous truism. According to the traditional dignity of their profession, jurists are the defenders of individual rights and fundamental values. But many are now sliding down the behaviourist slope, so that their main object becomes to adapt juridical theories and formulas to immediate needs rather than to preserve perennial principles in changing circumstances. They become technicians concerned with means and ignorant of ends. Like technicians in other fields (nuclear specialists, biologists, economists, sociologists) many are not adverse to let the governing power, administration or business, make what use it wills of their knowledge and intelligence. This is not a reference to the shameful prostitution of jurists in totalitarian states, but to the tendency in democratic countries to lose sight of the principle that the human values are the only ends of society and to the fact that some jurists appear to be falling in line with that tendency.[13] This trend towards expediency and immediacy of solutions even at the expense of fundamentals is a serious challenge to all members of the legal professions. It must be their care to unmask the deceptions whereby arbitrary force masquerades as law and to resist the pressures that distort the principles and deplete the content of law.

2

Trends in Human Sciences

SOCIOLOGY WAS PERHAPS handicapped by coming late, for it has apparently not been able to defend its position against the physical sciences as well as the older human sciences have done. Inasmuch as it is permeated by the concepts and the methods of the sciences of matter, sociology has tended to retreat from a humanistic and normative stand to a purely fact-finding attitude (like the press, as remarked above, but with less excuse than the press). Most sociologists believe that they should discover and describe only what is. They hold firm to the mistaken principle that their scientific status does not allow them also to discover and describe what should be. A sort of neutral rationality was long considered as the highest intellectual position, though it induced a dangerous ambivalence towards moral and ethical issues, a paralysing indifference to fundamental values, a sterile scepticism that was exhibited as proof of worldliness and modern enlightenment. There is now a definite trend away from this attitude in favour of greater involvement in ethical issues (surprisingly enough among scientists more than humanists) but sociologists appear still to be confined to neutrality and non-involvement, with a pseudo-scientific dread of values and value judgments.

I. DETERMINISM

Determinism was ingrained in man's early social achievements and it remained a basic though unconscious feature of ancient civilizations. Later, when the Western tradition began, when its values were elaborated on the Eastern shores of the Mediterranean—in the bold explorations and brilliant intuitions of Greek philosophers, in the dogged faith and indomitable spirit of Hebrew prophets—determinism did not disappear, but it became a conception to be accepted or refused. Since then it has not lacked ardent supporters and articulate votaries. Natural selection, biological evolution, economic necessity, historical process, dialectical materialism are modern expressions of the sense of inexorable fate which has always haunted men and in which some have found refuge and consolation. Despite their real or supposed scientific character, these theories when applied to human affairs and social change are a regression to a primitive stage and a rejection of the heritage of Western civilization. Determinism is the deadly foe of human values because it is the negation of man's freedom to choose his social ends.

In the present social content two aspects of determinism should be considered: first, that individuals are entirely conditioned by their environment as it is provided by society and, secondly, that society is entirely determined by natural forces and inevitable historical and technological processes. Such theories have been so often expounded and discussed that there is no need here to enlarge on the subject. When it is not a political ideology to further the desire for power, determinism is a refuge for the weak in spirit. 'Man being materially determined, there is no place for heart-breaking aspirations, no need for exhausting freedom, no call for agonizing moral choice. Adjustment becomes a sufficient condition for satisfaction and conformism the greatest social virtue.' The cause of determinism is strong and its arguments not without weight. In last analysis, however, they only prove that man is up against great difficulties and that the exercise of free will and responsible choice is no light matter. 'Freedom is completely without meaning unless it is related to necessity, unless it represents victory over necessity.'[14]

Determination exists in the sense that the movements of inanimate matter and unconscious life are not random. They follow a pattern which depends on the nature of things and the interaction between them. If nothing comes to modify this pattern, they remain determined by it. Movements can be defined and the future position and character of the thing under examination may be deduced with a measure of accuracy depending on the extent of knowledge. Nothing can modify this pattern except the act of a free and conscious will. For man himself and for the societies he forms there is no determination because he is free to act, either alone or with his fellows, and thus to impart a new direction to social movement or at least to

41

change the pattern of his own life. To say that we are determined is to reduce ourselves to the unconscious life of amoebas or insects, to bring us down to the level of inanimate matter. It is to degrade ourselves for no purpose, unless as an apology for weakness of spirit and cultural decadence, an excuse to put down the heavy load of freedom and responsibility that is our honour and our pride.[15]

When determinism is part of philosophical attitudes, religious dogma, or political theories which teach that men must sweat and suffer in order to promote the predetermined evolution, a basic contradiction is manifest: either the future of society is so determined that it cannot be changed, so that there is no need to make efforts in order to bring it about (personal sacrifice for the Calvinist, total obedience for the collectivist, revolution for the Marxist, hard work for the tenant of mechanistic society); or else the future really needs these efforts to make it come true and, if that is the case, it cannot be so determined that we have no choice of another future if we design one more in harmony with human aspirations. Why work for something that is coming anyway? Sensible persons would prefer to work for something more desirable which will not come if they make no effort.

Determinism has taken a new lease with the advance of technology. It is now reinvigorated. New arguments derived from the prevailing mechanistic and mathematical views have come to relieve the older arguments based on philosophy and history. When certain historians discourse on the determinism of increasing organization, when some mathematicians ride high on geometrical progressions and exponential curves applied to human affairs, there is no stopping them. There exists no doubt a terrifying possibility of society being reduced to the soulless organization of post-historic man in his technicist ant-hill or bee-hive, but according to modern determinists we should make no effort to avoid this unpleasant fate because we cannot escape it. And they add that our ideas about human values will change, because we will be conditioned and adjusted, so that we will be content with our fate and even imagine that we have chosen it of our own free will.

Determinism does not always imply an evil fate. There is also an optimistic determinism that holds out the assurance of a pleasant destiny. Such was the idea of progress prevalent in the West until the second third of the 20th century: it promised that improvement of society would automatically follow scientific discovery and technological advance. Such also is a belief in recurrent cycles, so that things get so bad that they must get better, that out of Evil Good must eventually come, that the present low ebb is sure to be followed by a high tide of culture and civilization. On their side, Marxist-Leninists have their brand of optimistic determinism, as far removed from reality as the Western brands. But whether it promises good or condemns to evil, determinism is always a negation of human freedom. It erodes the will and it weakens the sense of responsibility. It induces a passive acceptance of present conditions instead of an active resistance to negative attitudes and destructive trends.[16]

When determinists are forced to recognize that men do have the means to shape their future, they counter that a society is incapable of defining its will and directing its action in time to avert that which is going to happen. Thus they imply that even if it has the means, it does not have the ends and therefore cannot take an action based on choice. In this they are unfortunately not far from the mark as things look nowadays. In the distinguished but not ample literature directly concerned with the future of society in this technological and overpopulated age, there are two significant features common to all authors, humanists and scientists alike: one is the sombre picture of a social organization increasingly removed from human values and the other is a sense of impending doom from a process that seems well-nigh unavoidable because of the extraordinary energy that would be required to check it or reverse it. All know that human beings can be masters of their future, but all feel helplessness and near despair at the magnitude of the task and the indifference or incomprehension of the majority of people. However, this awareness of danger in a thinking minority is a start towards the vision of a more desirable future. 'We must find in ourselves the purposes and plans we have so far sought to derive from the machine.'[17] Organization and technology are means and must be given a finality. We, the human beings, are the 'givers of finality'.[18] We must beware that we do not abdicate our responsibility and turn away from the challenge.

2. THE SOCIAL UNIT

The notion of society as an organism independent of its constituent units has been used by social thinkers since antiquity. This organic theory of society has been considerably developed in modern times, in order to grasp the increasing complexity of social organization, but the individual thereby tends to recede out of sight. Some theorists consider that the constituent parts of a social organism are the various groups and sub-groups (political, administrative, economic, cultural) formed by human beings. Such groups (parties, corporations, unions, associations, institutions, etc.) are thereby personalized and become citizens in the first rank, thereby relegating individual persons even further out of sight. Others take a biological and even an anthropomorphic view. They endow society with a body composed of various organs, the cells of which are the individual men and women, and with a mind for which they invent a social psychology. As if society had an organism other than the organisms of its individual members and as if there could be any psychology in the proper sense but that of the individual.

These notions help research as long as they are kept within the bounds of a useful fiction, but the fiction tends to become reality in the minds of social theorists. The 'cells' of society tend to be considered as non-individuated and practically interchangeable units. The interest of many social scientists now appears to be more with society considered as an autonomous entity than with the human being in society. The values, the desires, the suffering of the individual become matters beneath their concern, to be left to the ministrations of the psychiatrist and the medical practitioner. Some sociologists help in this way to reduce the relevance of the human values and to throw a shadow over social ends. And if they remark that their professional concern is with society, so that they cannot be criticized for giving it all their interest, the answer is that sociology is the science that studies men in their relations with other men, not their relations with something autonomous and independent of individual human beings that is called society.

Collectivities neither think nor act, despite the verbal short cuts by which we personalize them, such as 'the Government declares', 'the Company agrees', 'the Union refuses'. These current expressions insensibly influence our thinking. A collectivity is represented by individuals who are chosen or who impose themselves to act in its name: it neither agrees nor refuses, but the individuals who represent it agree or refuse. A collectivity neither suffers nor can it be satisfied, except in the sense that a large proportion of the individuals composing it are suffering or satisfied. In various senses society is indeed an entity with a character or a structure different to the individuals who compose it, but it has no existence apart from those individuals. It obviously influences them, indeed they would be nothing without it, but this simply means that a human being is nothing if he is deprived of relations with other human beings: the concern of sociology should be with those relations. A baseball team or a commando group is something different from its members considered separately, but it becomes a useless or a dangerous fiction when it is considered as an organism apart from them, yet this is precisely what so many sociologists appear to be doing in their studies on society.

There is no such thing as a collective social conscience. There is no culture existing as an entity independent of individuals. A society is bound together by ideas and these ideas are contained in the narrow compass of each human head; they are not floating about in the air and they have no existence outside the minds of human beings, even when they are printed in books or stored in computers. Cohesion and homogeneity of society depend on the scope and the quality of these ideas, and on the proportion of individual members of that society whose minds accept the same ideas. Civilization and culture dwell in the heart and the mind of each individual person, and they have no other abode. Progress and decadence of society are movements and changes in the hearts and minds of the individuals composing that society. Men, not societies, are the only autonomous and conscious entities on Earth. Creation and selection of ideas, by which a society may exist and develop, are exclusively individual processes. Values and priorities have no meaning unless related to the individuals who hold them. When this is forgotten, creativity dies, civilization dries up, and a society crumbles into dust or it crystallizes into some mechanical and lifeless form.

It has been aptly said that the personalization of society results in the de-personalization of the individual, that the complexity of collective organisms is compensated by the simplification of human types,[19] that the reduction of human diversity gives rise to sub-human uniformity.[20] The results of these developments are manifest: rising importance of collectivities and decreasing importance of individuals considered as parts and components of the masses, increasing indifference to human values and pursuit of goals that reduce the worth of the individual and the dignity of the person. All this is happening before our eyes. It does not need acute observation or penetrating perception to realize the danger that springs from social attitudes increasingly indifferent to the individual and to the fundamental values that are exclusively the values of individual persons.

3. SOCIAL GOALS

Fundamental questions are not often asked, even less answered. Perhaps questions and answers are so obvious that there is no cause to examine them, or could it be that they are too difficult for the ordinary run of public or private discussion? I suggest that they are seldom asked because those who should ask them and propose the answers are not in a position to do so. Consider for instance the very fundamental question: what is the purpose of society? All would no doubt agree that it is somehow to make human beings satisfied and fulfilled. But if we go on to ask what social goals a nation must set itself in order to accomplish this purpose, who will answer? Politicians, philosophers, economists and non-specialists, in fact anybody and everybody can have, indeed should have, an opinion on social goals, for what is more important than to know what one wants and where one wants to go? But this is just politics! Of course it is. Then who will co-ordinate the various perspectives of social goals and study them for presentation to public opinion and political bodies? Why, that is the role of sociology. . . .

But sociologists believe that their field is bound by the constricted limits of precise observation and factual description. Their scientific status is supposed to rest on neutral rationality and to prevent them from making value judgments, even from holding value opinions in their professional capacity. 'Pure' sociology is the same as 'pure' art: it must not be sullied by hopes and emotions and aspirations. To reach reality must be the aim of all science, but the reality of human relations is different from the reality of inanimate matter, and it does include the values and aspirations of human beings. Thus sociology is out of touch with the reality it seeks when it follows the physical sciences in confining itself to what can be seen and quantified and experimentally tested. Some economists have succeeded in breaking out from this confinement and to realize that such human factors as hunger and poverty and despair must also be their concern, that they must make a choice of values in order to propose economic policy that will improve living standards. They have graduated from studying only what is to studying also what should be.

The Greek fable of the philosopher who fell into a hole because he was too busy looking at the stars may be capped by a modern fable of sociologists who did not see the stars of human aspirations because they kept their eyes too firmly fixed on their feet. Sociology has no future if it continues to confine itself within the limits that are the legacy of the 19th century, but it has a great role to play for the future if it breaks out of its stifling and constricting limitations. Alienation from society, youthful violence and disorientation, drugs and suicides: there are enough social ills in this overpopulated and technological age to persuade sociologists to leave aside academism and neutrality and to become involved in the fundamental issues of these dangerous times. They can be assured that their status, be it scientific or political or social, will thereby be greatly enhanced. Here also is a challenge that must be faced.

4. METHODOLOGY

Confronted by rising complexity of the technicist society, by ever increasing numbers of individuals, economic and social planners often appear to have their understanding dulled and their sensibilities blunted. To facilitate their work and to give it the scientific form that is now fashionable, they adopt the methods and the tools that have proved outstandingly successful for the physical sciences. The mathematical language of modern technology, the quantitative mode of thought, tend to set aside the elements of human living that cannot be expressed in mathematical formulas and quantitative terms. Only by a steadfast concern with moral values can the influence of these methods be overcome, and this concern is not easy to maintain when social goals are not clear. 'If human values are abstracted, the social sciences become irrelevant or worse.'[21] Blinded by the desire to follow in the wake of the physical sciences, many sociologists and economists succumb to the temptation to see individuals as things, not persons, as units that can be manipulated with pencil and paper or computer taping. They are thus led to deny the very reason for their studies and the only justification for their work: the human values which it must be the purpose of society to preserve and to cultivate.

There is a possibility that the individual may become beneath attention in research and planning, except on the medical or psychiatric plane, to be delivered into the hands of psycho-technicians for conditioning and adjustment when he goes wrong. The language of totalitarian manipulation of the masses is unaccountably permeating democratic societies and it is debasing the values that are the foundation of Western civilization. Some sociologists and economists appear to have risen so high that they cannot be bothered any more with the qualitative characters of the individuals composing the societies that are the objects of their studies. Too little background education and general culture, an ignorance of history and philosophy, preoccupation with technical skills and an obsession with the methods of physical science, a near total dependence on statistical techniques, all this has so much elevated their view that they would now need, as the physical scientists, a microscope in order to perceive with detached curiosity the individual particles of social matter.

This picture is a manifest exaggeration. It is also unkind for many honest men and women who are doing their job as best they can. It does not take into account the few eminent minds in these fields. But it stresses a point that must be made. Other sociologists appear to have graduated from social science in order proudly to establish themselves as social engineers, while the social sciences are becoming the behavioural sciences, perhaps as obeisance to the paramount position of technology in our time.[22] Behaviour responds nicely to conditioning, especially if moral values and normative judgments are eliminated. Naturally new methods and techniques adapted from the physical sciences are useful and often necessary additions to the tools of the human sciences, but they must not be allowed to colour their outlook and to change their purpose. The time is ripe for a humanist reaction, but humanists have become diffident and shamefaced in the technicist society. At least it is encouraging that some scientists, who contributed to the development of mathematical machines and automated equipment, have become aware that with the generalized use of these advanced tools grows a mentality disengaged from the human values.

5. BIOLOGICAL DISCOVERY

More than in his primitive past, man now stands naked and defenceless. Naked, because his protective mystery has vanished and little remains secret of his inner being; defenceless, because it has become more easy than ever before to destroy him in his body and in his mind. Now, more than in other times, his only vesture is the respect of man for man, his only defence a mutual recognition of worth and dignity. For the humanist concerned with human values, this is an additional reason to reassert those values as the principles of society. For others, who have lost sight of human values in the passion for power, the impotence of determinism, or the excitement of technological progress, it is an added inducement to treat human beings as interchangeable, adjustable and expendable units.

For many people the worth and dignity of the human person appear to be reduced because the veil which surrounded it is torn apart, its bio-chemical elements analysed, the operation of body and mind laid bare. This is an immature reaction, like that of a child who has taken a watch apart to see what makes it tick. The pieces lie before him and he thinks: 'Is that all it is?' When mention is made of hallucigenic drugs or electronic stimulation and their effect on the human person, the first reaction, even with cultured and perceptive people, is the same as that of the child: 'Is that all it is, that it can be so easily manipulated?' There is a sense of disappointment, of reduced dignity, of shrunken stature. This may be a remnant of an ancient sense of mystery, of the tremendous quality of that which is hidden, of the extraordinary character of the unknown compared to the familiar and ordinary features of the known. The veil of mystery has indeed vanished. We look at each other with new awareness, like a grown-up son who suddenly realizes that his parents are like himself, who senses as akin to his their human weakness, which had been hidden under the mantle of authority and age.

Manipulation of body and mind grows ever more daring. Some of the new techniques are an unqualified good, such as deep surgery of heart and brain, mending and even replacing organs and parts of organs in the body. But many, particularly those concerned with genetic manipulation, with chemical or electronic control of the brain, are fraught with immense danger. As with other techniques, biological breakthroughs can bring benefit or harm according to whether the purposes of those who make use of them are good or evil. But even when the ends are surely good, there is a price to pay. The greater the apparent benefit, the greater may be the price, even if it is not claimed at once. It is unwise to consider the benefits of biological discovery as outright gain and it is dangerous to forget that they may be poisoned gifts.

Most people agree that new moral rules are needed to guide decision and action on these and other problems of our time. But they seldom consider that the moral rules required are new only in the sense that the fundamental values and priorities must now be applied to new fields opened up by science and technology, not in the sense that these new fields require a different morality, based on other values and priorities, to be somehow elaborated in the welter of accelerated change. In a thoughtful and thought-provoking book,[23] Fourastié remarks that science transfers some problems from the domain of morality to that of technique, while at the same time creating new problems for the domain of morality. An example of the former may be found in various disorders of mind and body leading to anti-social and anti-human behaviour, which can now be treated and sometimes cured, and which can therefore be transferred from the court of law to the hospital. Examples of the latter are genetic manipulation and control of mind processes: they must be submitted to the morality based on the fundamental human values, and this requires careful examination and wise consideration.

New ethical and legal problems deriving from recent advances in the life sciences are highly complex. Full information is needed for debate and discussion at all levels. The press plays its part in providing information, but cultural and political bodies in every country should make it their duty to collect and disseminate such knowledge as will allow conscious and reasoned choices. The latest discoveries in biology bear immense importance for the institutions of society (family, school, church, state) and, more deeply and basically, for the fundamental values. It is essential to have an understanding of social priorities and a real consensus on the minimum content of the principles of justice and dignity and freedom. Otherwise debate would be of little use because there would be no common measure for evaluation and discussion would not lead to practical conclusions.

Nuclear fission was developed as a military secret without consideration for human values. Its first application was not the peaceful harnessing of power but its apocalyptic unleashing to destroy human beings and life itself. Must leadership, political and cultural, again make the same sort of mistake and unthinkingly follow the same perilous path? Experimentation for manipulation of body and mind must be brought out into the open. Public opinion must understand the scope and the implications of present biological research, to realize its expected benefits and its certain dangers. All paths are not good to explore nor all roads to open up. Some absolute limit is required for biological experimentation regardless of the benefits, real or imagined, that may be foregone through this limitation. Does this arouse the shade of Galileo? Does it awake echoes of the old outcry against dissection of human bodies and vivisection of animals? Even so, the decision must not be allowed to go by default. Everybody must take sides on this issue. The advanced society must not be taken unawares and placed before an accomplished fact.

A caricature published in Prague in September 1968 showed a customs official lifting up the top of a traveller's head to see if he had any unauthorized ideas in it. The technical ability to find out the ideas in a man's mind and to extirpate them if required is already to hand, to be used if the forces of regression and evil gain the upper hand. It must be realized that technique can provide the means for the most monstrous projects, the most fantastic nightmares to come true. 'They can't get inside you' says Julia in *1984* but she finds out that they can. A state will be able to invade and to destroy the innermost being of the human person. By mass media and direct electronic impulse, it could achieve absolute control over the body and mind of every man, woman and child. The governing authority will have the instruments whereby to inject its ideas and its will into every subject, so that they become as cells of the body or parts of the machine. It can still the consciousness of every individual and put its own consciousness in its place (or, in McLuhanese, it can 'programme the total sensory environment to achieve the analogical sense ratios that constitute private consciousness') so that all the people shall behave as one person. These are the evil dreams of 20th-century totalitarians and they are no longer impossible dreams.

We understand with a clearer perception than before that the human person is a delicate and finely contrived organism, resting on the quivering balance of complex elements constantly responding to internal and external solicitations. The most precious things are often the most vulnerable and the most fragile, and this is more true for individual life than for anything else in the universe. That the body may be stilled by a blow or a bullet does not make it less worthy of being preserved from disintegration; that the mind may easily be broken or deformed does not make it less worthy of respect; that the person may be degraded by a few drops of LSD does not make it less important or less precious. This is a further chapter in the knowledge of ourselves and our fellow men. We must integrate this knowledge with our values as we have, or should have, integrated all our previous knowledge with our values. A clearer sense of human frailty must make us more concerned with the ends of society. That we now stand defenceless before one another must strengthen our feeling of kinship. Nowhere is the challenge to civilization more threatening than in this field that concerns the essence of human beings and the very foundation of human relations.

* * *

Knowledge is now measured by the quantity of facts uncovered by research, and the only 'original contributions to knowledge' (an expression much in vogue in university circles) are those that add new facts—of any description—to the immense amount of facts already available. Thought and meditation, with a view to synthesis and integration of the whole picture, wherein facts may assume their proper place, are not considered to be research conducive to knowledge, and they are therefore not worthy of academic interest and encouragement. As repeated to satiety, this is a practical age, 'an era of doers rather than thinkers and sayers', and we must above all get our facts right for the immediate purpose with which we happen to be concerned. Fractionation of knowledge is part of the general mode of overspecialization which underrates wisdom and ridicules common sense. But, at the present stage of human development, the wide-angle lens for an overall view is more important than specialized research and pinpointing of facts unconnected with any but the nearest and narrowest sequence of events. There is need somehow to leaven the undigested orgy of factual knowledge that weighs so heavily on our understanding of the world and our problems. This leaven should be provided by the human sciences, the sciences of man, as sociology and its allied specializations are sometimes proudly called. But this would entail a reversal of the present overpowering trend towards practicality and fractionation of knowledge, a widening of the present narrow horizon of thinking and doing. It would also entail an understanding of the human values that make most sociologists shy away like so many frightened horses.

3
Technological Advance

THE POWERS AND THE LIMITATIONS (some people would apparently be prepared to say the character and the psychology) of the machine, whether mechanic or electronic, permeate every aspect of society and every field of human activity. From the start of the machine age there has been a tendency to respect the 'nature' of the machine more than that of man, and to submit to its 'values' even at the detriment of those of man. Those who did not think in this way were called impractical philosophers or retarded reactionaries, while those who would not act as servants or slaves to the machines were branded as revolutionaries or saboteurs. The same attitudes call forth much the same responses to this day in West and East, in democratic and totalitarian countries alike.

After all, human beings are there anyway. They have been there for a long time and they are nothing new. They come cheap, in ever increasing numbers. They are difficult and unruly. And now, with growing automation, they are becoming more of a liability than an asset for social engineers. They do not have to be made. No man has made another man, except by the sexual process of reproduction (women's reactions to the machine may become the same as those of men if ever the time comes when they will not have to bear their babies), while the machine is made by man, with great expenditure of effort and ingenuity. It is his handiwork and his creation, more than his children, and he is inordinately proud of it. Beautiful and efficient machines are more precious for the new barbarians than ever gold and rubies were for the old barbarians, who sometimes put them above human life.

Scientists and technicians deserve, and obtain, our grateful appreciation. It is a truism that machines have brought immense benefits and enhanced man's dignity by increasing his power. If they have become in many cases a threat to the human values, the fault lies not with them but with those who use and misuse them. From the cobbler's awl to the system analyst's computer, tools and machines are useful if they are put to useful ends. They can also be put to nefarious or dangerous ends: the awl may be pushed into the next man's neck and the computer may be the instrument of totalitarian administration. The fault that should be recognized by all and that must be corrected is that we do not define the real values of society, which technology can serve. It is also a truism, not less true for constant repetition, that in increasing our means beyond the wildest dreams of past generations, we have lost sight of our ends.

I. THE ENDS OF TECHNIQUE

Machines have a rhythm of their own, which is not that of man or animal. The user must submit to this rhythm, as he submits to that of the animal when he uses it. But there must be no compulsion to use the machine if its rhythm conflicts with the human ends of society, if its operation reduces the relevance of those ends. The machine moves in accordance with the immediate purpose for which it is designed and it must be given a direction, an end. An automobile cannot be let loose on the present highways or a gun left to point itself without a target. Yet it seems that this is what we are starting to do with mathematical machines and automated equipment applied to administrative problems and social engineering: the operators, now on the way to becoming no more than component parts of the equipment, are not given long-term ends which they must further and respect while providing the means to short-term goals. They are not bound enough by fundamental values because they have not been sufficiently instructed in them by their education or by the political and intellectual leaders of society.

Naturally operators of the new equipment (technological and intellectual) applied to social problems have service to society and the good of human beings as their aim. But because they have lost sight of the ends of society, they are occupied with short-term results which may or may not coincide with those ends. They are concerned with developing skills for success in the present state of things, but unconcerned to know whether the present state of things should be changed or improved, or whether the skills should be put to better use. Social policy, as expressed in the behavioural sciences and exercised in systems designing, operational research and other innovations borrowed or adapted from the physical sciences and military experiments, is degenerating into sophistry, that is, behaviour without regard to truth, to the normative guides to action, to the ethical question of good and evil.[24]

Supporting this trend is a persistent strain of pragmatic philosophy, to the effect that knowledge is true or action is right only when 'it works', when its 'cash-value' can be determined. This pragmatism is useful in the sense in which the success schools of the Sophists were useful, and it is well adapted to a mechanistic mentality. But if a nation's philosophy does not rise above this pedestrian level, moral vision is lost and we cannot hope to keep in sight the ends of civilized society.[25] We cannot hope to give a direction to our future. We cannot even think of a more desirable future than the one that is awaiting us. We give in to the fatalists and determinists by acting exactly as they advise and foresee. We adjust ourselves to the state of things as they are, however unpleasant they promise to be. Instead of trying to change them, we condition ourselves to accept them. It looks as if the new way of tackling social problems in the advanced countries, particularly problems connected with advancing technology, were to adapt individuals to live in society as it is and as it will be, even at the price of depreciating human values. Europeans have remarked on the 'fatalism' of American sociology, but they tend to follow the same road. The trend which ought to be reversed is thereby accelerated.

Social engineers adapt their systems to society as it is, as civil engineers plan their highways to conform to the contours of the land. But in this comparison, civil engineers enjoy two advantages. The first is that they know the end of the road, because they have been told where it is to go. Their concern is to employ their means—the curves and gradients, bridges and tunnels—towards their ends. The second advantage they enjoy is that, although they must be efficient in their means, they must also preserve values that have nothing to do with efficiency, by avoiding the destruction of a historic site, the demolition of an artistic monument, the spoiling of a beautiful view. While social engineers, in their self-imposed limitations and narrowness of outlook, do not have these advantages. They do not realize that their means often contradict their ends, because they have not been told what their ends must be, nor have they been enough warned that efficiency in social organization must not be won at the expense of freedom and dignity for human beings. They take their means for their ends but they are not the ones to blame. The ones to blame are the leaders of society, those who have been elected to positions of trust and responsibility or those who possess greater knowledge and superior perception, and who keep silent through diffidence or indifference.

In America as well as in Europe some indeed are aware and some are concerned, but they are not energetic enough or numerous enough to reverse the dangerous trend. This is not a proper position for the most advanced and prosperous nations, that are moreover setting the pace and determining the future for the rest of the world. This is no advance of civilization. It is not redundant here to say human civilization. Civilization by definition can only be human, but a social organization is now in process of formation that is less relevant to human values, less attuned to the human person, less concerned with the individual. We shall continue to call it civilization, because we have become used to think of civilization in terms of material produce and mechanistic operation. It will no doubt be a very efficient set-up. It will take its inspiration from bees and ants and termites. Such a conception of civilization is unworthy and degrading.

'Not perfection of man, but the perfection of things is the aim of contemporary society.'[26] The common mistake is to equate civilization with machines and gadgets. 'Civilization has no justification unless it involves the improvement of human beings, not the improvement of the tools they use.'[27] This idea ought to be present in every person's mind and it should become a basic principle of education. Civilization implies above all a set of values, and machines have no relation to values. Automated and cybernated to any degree, they are still the efficient slaves of whoever operates them. They can equally well be the servants of real civilization or abominable degradation. 'The future offers very little hope for those

57

who expect that our new mechanical slaves will offer us a world in which we may rest from thinking. Help us they may, but at the cost of supreme demands upon our honesty and our intelligence.'[28] Honesty and intelligence, energy and drive, are now in urgent demand among all those who have not forgotten that human values are the foundation of civilization. The need is now for thinking and awareness, not tranquillizers and constant distraction.

2. TECHNICAL NECESSITY

A new sovereign is enthroned, as jealous and autocratic as the state. It has its unquestioned arguments, which are its reasons of state. They are called efficiency and technical necessity and, like reasons of state, they can be invoked to deny human rights and to justify useless, wasteful or criminal measures. Technical necessity has a definite and a limited meaning, that is, to do or make something efficiently it must be done or made by one way and not by another. A jet engine operates in one way and an electronic circuit functions in another way. They each have their technical necessity: a jet engine cannot be made to run on electric current, or an electronic circuit on petrol. If we want to ride automobiles we must have proper roads and if we want to fly in aeroplanes we must build runways. If we cannot do without SST, we must bear the bangs. Technical necessities are indeed unavoidable at a given time; they cannot be turned, except by new advances in technique.

But the argument is used out of place. It is employed not only to justify the means for a given aim, but to justify the aim itself. To be sure, it is a technical necessity that we have to bear the bangs in order to enjoy SST, but do people need or want SST as much as that?[29] It is indeed a technical necessity that men and women be adjusted to computerized public administration and conditioned to mechanized social systems, and social engineers and behaviourists are engaged in designing the processes for adjustment and conditioning. But the real question is not in this primitive logic. It is to know whether it is a necessity to use such new tools and equipment for public administration and to modify a traditional attitude towards social organization. Is this required for economy or because of lack of employees? Will it improve people's condition? What is the compulsion and what will be the benefit to the individual men and women who compose society? In truth, there is little benefit that bears relation to the human values, no compulsion save that it is Technical Progress, the new article of faith, the high aim of the technological society: if a thing *can* be done, it *must* be done at any cost. We are putting our pride in technical achievements, probably because they are less arduous than social betterment, less hard than spiritual improvement, and because they entail no heart-searching, no laborious choices, as do social ends based on human values.

Primitive agricultural tools, the first techniques for clothing and sheltering, early methods of recording facts and ideas, of measuring geometrical forms and figuring numerical operations, these were the fundamental achievements. They allowed the establishment of society and they helped the elaboration of the human values. Much later, with scientific discovery, the power of matter was harnessed and the machine age began. Machines grew ever more complex and efficient, up to the recent development of self-governing systems. But now we cannot but see that the advance of technique exacts a heavy price for its 'deceptive sweetenings of existence',[30] because it imposes its organization on society and its rhythm on human beings. With accelerating progress, after the stage of providing for the necessities of life is passed, the cost of technique—in human terms—increases, and its benefits—also in human terms—decrease. There appears to be a stage of diminishing return for technique in society and we are approaching, or we may already have reached the point where it takes away more than it gives.

Naturally, technological advance is always needed because important aspects of human development depend on continued progress, and because some of the harm wrought by hasty and careless advance (such as pollution and deterioration of environment) must at this stage be remedied by further advances in technique. Nor can the ominous problems of overpopulation be solved without progress in food production and birth control. But this is not a vicious circle, as some would have us believe, and the need is not indiscriminate. Continued technological advance is required in the fields where it can improve the human condition; it must be arrested where it is inimical to human values and it must be directed to those avenues which lead to the satisfaction and the fulfilment of men and women. As a general rule, this could sound too theoretical to be a guide for action, but it can be practically applied to all cases if there is some consensus on the meaning and content of the human values, together with more careful consideration of the results to be expected from investments in scientific research and technological application.

Investments in technique are judged by factors of cost and return, but the cost that is examined is only the internal financial cost and the return is likewise estimated only in money (when it is not simply in prestige for the state). They are seldom examined in the light of the human cost and return, the cost to satisfaction and fulfilment of individual human beings, the return to the dignity and the quality of their lives. Social cost-accounting is lamentably deficient. Were the account properly made, so that all the relevant factors were included, it would become clear that standards of living (in the sense of easy and generalized access to the necessities and the amenities of life) in the advanced industrial countries are in fact considerably lower than the levels indicated by the rise of GNP and the increase of consumption. The people of these countries are less successful and less fortunate than suggested in exclusively material and quantitative terms by the levels of efficiency and productivity which they have attained. The meaning and content of efficiency and productivity must be enlarged in order to include the moral and qualitative terms that they now exclude.

*　　*　　*

There should always be time to stop and take breath, to think more clearly, to find out where we are heading, and to consider if that is where we want to go. Some persons are qualified to think competently and to speak with authority on present and future, but all should be concerned. In the U.S.A. more than in any other country, society has given an elite the means to meditate upon its problems. Up to the present, it recognizes their right to think freely and their duty to express their thoughts as conscience bids them, but this may change. It is already an act of courage, fraught with material prejudice as well as social censure, even for great scientists and humanists, to oppose current trends, especially if they presume to touch the taboos of efficiency and technological advance. It may be too sombre a view, but it is neither a flight of fancy nor an impossible eventuality that this could be one of the last generations with the ability to think freely and the environment within which freely to express their thoughts. One of the last generations perhaps, even in the Western world, who still enjoy the dignity to be responsible for their actions; who still possess the means to shape their future and the future of those who follow; who still have the desire and the strength to affirm that the human person is the basic factor of social organization and that the human values are the foundation of all that we may aspire to name civilization.[31]

Some of those whom I like to think of as the moral and intellectual trustees of civilization have become aware of the confusion and conscious of the danger. Some of the younger rebels against society also appear, in their own baffling way, to be moved by the same awareness. But awareness is only a start, and many are aware who consider scientific and technological advance as an uncontrollable movement, with little relation to quality choices or moral priorities. From this position they go on to lament the movement or to devise the least noxious ways of adapting to its rhythm. It is easy to see how wrong this position is, how a clear-sighted view of social ends must condition the means to those ends, especially science and technology. Social scientists in particular bear a heavy responsibility. The human values are in their care and they fail their duty if they do not assert them forcefully enough. They can be assured that their opinions and their advice, co-ordinated as far as possible by permanent institutions, will deeply influence their generation and prepare the way to a better future than the one that is so clearly delineated in present trends.

4

Overpopulation

THIS IS THE OTHER of the two most important developments of our time. Of all the changing circumstances in which human values may be rejected, none is more ominous than the unprecedented multiplication of human beings on the face of Earth. *Without the impact of overpopulation, none of the problems touched upon in these pages would be as dangerous or as urgent.* Increase of population and progress of technique are inherent to the evolution of human societies, but the combined acceleration of both has created an immensely critical juncture. Of the two factors, the most potent is overpopulation: without it, technique could not exercise such a pervasive influence on social patterns, and the benefits of the machine would not be overshadowed by its threat to human values.

All through history, poverty has prevented a general application of the principles of freedom, justice and dignity. It is the same now in most of the poor countries. Scarcity and want impede the realization of the human values, by denying the primary body needs that are no longer objects for concern in the rich countries. Pressure of population on resources is already intolerable in many parts of the world, and its effects are felt morally and materially by all men. The human values become less relevant when the body cannot obtain the food, clothing, shelter and medical care without which it cannot flourish. True, great virtues may be generated, such as patience and resignation, and on a higher plane austerity and asceticism, but—admirable and worthy of respect as they are—they are hardly the virtues of an economically advanced society nor do they help human beings to improve their material condition. However, although the population explosion is—after war and peace—the most talked of problem of recent years, there is no consensus on its full implications which are not, even now, sufficiently recognized.

The factors of the problem are well known and they lend themselves to statistical definition and reasonably accurate forecasts. It is generally accepted that the number of human beings will be doubled in the next thirty years or so: it is now about three thousand five hundred million and it will be six or seven thousand million by the turn of the century. Projections for the 21st century are diligently pursued into impossibly large figures, but these are more like student exercises in elementary statistics than serious forecasts. The forecast for what is left of this century is enough to exert all the wisdom and energy of mankind. Population will go on multiplying, even at decreasing rates, until impossible densities are reached, after which it will not increase any more. Natural population control, at its most harsh and brutal, must inevitably take over with wholesale disease to bring less births and more deaths. It is important to estimate the impossible densities and to consider when they are expected to be reached in various parts of the world. But there are as yet no well-founded answers to this essential question, neither in the sense of food scarcity, nor in that of physical overcrowding, nor from the perspective of deteriorating quality of individual and social life.

There are other questions not less essential for which the answers must be found: What are the prospects for each country or region to provide for something like double their present population at an acceptable standard? What is now, or what will be an acceptable standard for various human communities? Can the more prosperous nations isolate themselves from the anguish of the others? What will be the impact (social, political, military) on the prosperous nations of suffering and despair in a great portion of the world? Assuming that some pooling of wealth and sharing of resources may be achieved, what could be the prospects for the world as a whole? Can the resources of the advanced countries make up for the deficiencies of the poor countries as well as provide for their own increases of population? How would resources be transferred and what would be the effect of these transfers on the rich countries?

The present trends are very clear: considering that half of mankind is barely at subsistence level, that population in the underdeveloped countries is growing faster than food production, that erosion and building are taking land out of cultivation faster than land reclamation is replacing it, that the world *per capita* average of food production is falling, that the average standard of living is dropping in many underdeveloped countries, it becomes obvious that for the majority of countries there is very little hope—in the foreseeable future, that is, up to the end of this century—of providing for the expected growth of population, let alone at an acceptable standard. The prosperous minority will have enough to eat, if they can hold on to what they have, but not enough left over to alleviate the hardships of the majority or to supply its needs.

At present, about 50 per cent of humanity does not get enough to eat, while over 10 per cent cannot escape the grip of famine. 'In developing countries, at least one person in five is starving, one in three suffers from undernourishment in proteins, and three in five from malnutrition' (FAO report). These proportions are certain to increase before the end of the century. Malnutrition and starvation remain the greatest killers of all, more than any other disease. They cause the death of one in every four human beings. When they do not kill, they maim and incapacitate. Those who survive prolonged undernourishment are generally damaged for the rest of their lives in their physical and their mental capacities. Their resistance to disease, the aptitude for learning, their capacity for work become gravely impaired. This is another of the vicious circles of underdevelopment.[32] The future of the poor nations, already overburdened by increasing unbalance between resources and population, is further threatened by failing strength and vitality of their new generations.

Every year, thirty million tons or so of cereals are transferred from the developed to the poor countries, but the problem is not only one of distribution: it is a problem of absolute scarcity. Every human being would suffer from malnutrition if all the food resources in the world were equally distributed. To provide an adequate diet for every human being today, present food resources would practically have to be doubled. 'It is abundantly clear that mankind will have great difficulty providing an adequate diet for 3.5 billion people by the year 2000, and that providing a proper diet for 7.0 billion by that time is out of the question. . . . Only the most determined disregard for biology, physics, human behaviour and economics permits any other conclusion.'[33]

This ominous note seems to be contradicted by the encouraging start of an agricultural renewal in some Asian countries (apart from China of which little is known). More government care for agriculture, better training of agricultural specialists, increased availability of fertilizers and, above all, new high-yield, early maturing, fertilizer-responsive, widely adaptable varieties of cereals are the main factors of a substantial increase in productivity (the so-called green revolution). This in turn is starting a chain of beneficial economic and social reactions in the countries concerned. Given the required government support and wiser economic policies, a similar improvement could be achieved in African and Latin American countries. Some of the reactions, however, are ecologically detrimental, mainly through excessive use of pesticides and fertilizers, and they will lead to lasting damage in the long run. There is also the possibility that food production may to some extent displace industrial crops as these lose ground to synthetic materials. Other, more imaginative means of augmenting food production are being explored, such as synthetic proteins and improved sea harvesting.

But there is no contradiction between these encouraging beginnings of agricultural renewal and the dark prognosis for the next thirty years. Agricultural progress, if it continues to spread, will provide a measure of precious time to help stave off more famine and to slow down the birth rate. If this time is not used to the utmost, if extreme and urgent efforts are not exerted to damp demographic growth and stabilize population, as well as to improve food supply while restoring and maintaining ecological balance, it will not be possible to avert intense suffering in many countries, and catastrophe on the national and the international scale. As things are going at present, it does not look as if the necessary efforts will be forthcoming. Famine and despair are bad counsellors, and modern weapons are plentiful. The last third of the 20th century promises to be more difficult and more pregnant with disaster than any previous period.

* * *

As for the advanced nations, their future is projected with continuously sustained economic advance, unceasing technological progress, and soaring curves of GNP. There is talk, quite learned talk, of the perils of affluence,[34] and this sounds incredibly unfeeling and parochial to people concerned with the perils of poverty. Present growth is taken as perpetual and undeviating, and little effort is made to think how and when it must eventually stop or slow down. Even serious writers often reason as though the developed countries were standing alone. They do not appear to realize the impact that the underdeveloped countries are sure to have, are already beginning to have on world affairs. Despite the evidence, there are voices to say that 'the age of plenty has come and the dismal science is out of date. Production will soon be limited only by consumption. Unlimited energy with automation and cybernation are turning work into a luxury for the gifted few, while forced leisure will become the new yoke of the common man. This is the new millennium and we must quickly adapt to it'. There is perhaps nothing fundamentally untrue about this picture, but it is not for tomorrow or for after tomorrow, or for any time at all if present economic and technological trends are not reversed. A more likely development is that the advanced nations will not be able to maintain their 'private enclaves of affluence',[35] their high material standards, and even their democratic institutions in the face of increasing poverty of the poor nations.

The affluent society depends on unequal distribution of the use of natural resources. In the present state of technique, there is simply not enough of such resources for world population as a whole to reach a tenth part of the American standard. Insufficiency of foodstuffs for an adequate average world diet is one illustration of this fact. Another may be found in the consumption of mining products. The U.S.A. for example, with 6 per cent of world population, use 30 to 40 per cent of the world's supply of non-recurrent resources. Their spectacular economic and technological advance would not have been achieved, nor could it be maintained, without the use of this high percentage of available materials. Part of these materials must be imported into America and this is a prime factor of American policy.[36] In the same way, the prosperity of other industrially advanced countries depends on the use of natural resources in proportions exceeding the proportion of their population to world population. 'If all the other nations were suddenly to use as much energy as the U.S. does, energy resources would disappear in eighteen months' (Rogers Morton). The same holds true for most other natural resources. It follows that the promise of prosperity for the underdeveloped countries, if only they learn the advanced nations' skills in technology and management, is a practical impossibility and a deliberate deception in the present state of technique, a mirage that promptly dissolves in the light of reality.

It also follows that the advanced countries will encounter more difficulty to obtain the material and energy resources that they require in order to sustain their economic development. Doubling of world population in the next thirty years will be accompanied by an important change in its composition. Today the underdeveloped countries account for two-thirds of it, but they will include four-fifths of it at the close of the century. This will intensify the impact (both economic and political) of the poor nations. With their rapidly growing population, however slow and inadequate their development may be, it must augment their consumption of natural resources and make it harder for the rich nations to satisfy their needs. Countries poor in natural resources such as Japan and Great Britain (however advanced they are) and countries whose standard of living depends on imports of essential raw materials such as U.S.A. (even if their domestic resources are plentiful) must experience a slowing down of their economic progress and a fall in their standard of living.

This probable development does not mean that the gap between available mineral resources and the promise of plenty for the whole world must remain for ever. On the contrary, there are limitless sources of basic raw materials in the sea and the air, and even common rocks. Starts have been made in this field, such as the extraction of magnesium from sea water or the fixation of nitrogen from the air. Nuclear fission or fusion will provide equally limitless sources of energy. There will be enough for all when technological progress will make it possible to exploit these sources of material and energy to full advantage, but this will take time, and time is what we have least in the present critical juncture. It does mean, therefore, that forecasts of continued economic expansion in the advanced countries must be uncertain, at least until new materials are elaborated and new sources tapped, and—more importantly—until a reasonably stable balance can be achieved between the rich and the poor nations. It also means that, unless a more civilized international order is established to avoid waste of resources in armaments and war, there will be a further impoverishment of the poor nations and a slowing down of the rich nations' advance.

Nothing but real international solidarity can bring safety and progress out of the present ominous drift. Revived isolationism and stronger defences will not be sufficient protection for the advanced nations, because the others will have less to risk in trying to overthrow a precarious international structure. Disparity between nations is becoming as explosive as the disparity between classes was when it led to violent revolution in many nations, as the disparity is now for minority groups in several countries. In effect, it is more explosive because the government of even a poor country will have the weapons of international revolution: not the stones, knives and guns of popular uprisings, but the nuclear, chemical and biological arms that will soon be in every arsenal, recklessly to be used when the bad counsellors hold the reins. The rise of dictatorial or totalitarian governments for administering the economics of scarcity are a result of the increasing difficulties of the Third World. Military regimes have become the political panacea of this age. There are fewer democratic nations and they comprise a falling proportion of total world population. 'Their weakness is that they must too often deny themselves in order to survive.'[37] When in mortal danger, the consensual rules of democracy give way to totalitarian command, and the human values are put aside in the process.

*   *   *

As directly relevant to the main theme of this book is to consider what the effects of overpopulation and overcrowding could be on human values even if a nation were assured of sufficient material resources for its growing numbers. Assuming that the advanced and affluent nations will be able to provide for the poor countries as well as for their own increased numbers, or that they will want and be able to dissociate themselves from the rest of the world, what will be the effect of rising numbers and increased density on the content of the human values and the understanding of the social ends of civilized society.

I. INCREASING ORGANIZATION

There is a direct relation between population and organization. The more closely human beings are located in a given area—however plentiful their resources and however committed to freedom their social order may be—the more friction will be generated, and the more authority will be needed to contain its expressions and to repress its explosions. Increasingly strict laws and regulations are required for authority to operate in overcrowded areas. They are likewise required to ensure that each individual has his or her fair share (but not sufficient share) of space and privacy, and such other amenities as overcrowding may allow. Accelerated population growth is expanding the urban areas, and the time is near when the overwhelming majority of human beings will be agglomerated in large cities. Previews of the Eastern, the Western and the Central 'megalopolis' in U.S.A. (Boswash, Sansan, Chipitts) are already familiar to planners and technicians. The same sort of gigantopolis is being planned for London, Tokyo, Mexico and other inflated cities. Few town planners and architects can or dare raise their eyes above the immediate means with which they are involved, to see that their remunerative talents for designing housing machines are helping to prepare a much reduced life for human beings.

There is no need to labour the point, except to remark that the quantitative society is not necessarily a result of advancing technology or totalitarian institutions, that sheer mass of numbers must inevitably produce the same cultural paralysis, the same social disintegration, the same rejection of human values as the most mechanistically designed organization. The city was the cradle of civilization, to which it gave its name. It is depressing to think that the grave of civilization may be the giant town of the age of technique, the cosmopolis (Spengler) threatened by internal disease and spreading cancer even more than by nuclear destruction. Social engineers act logically in striving for total organization as they foresee that over-population, if allowed to progress unchecked, will make it a necessity. But this could only be, at best, a delaying action to postpone the time of disaster, a cure as deathly as the ill that it aims to remedy. Besides the disavowal and the destruction of the spiritual gains of civiliza-tion, the rejection of human values that is implicit both in social disintegration and in the total organization required to control it, the material gains of civilization must also be wiped out as the resources of the planet are depleted by senseless exploitation.

2. INCREASED SOCIAL STRIFE

There is also a direct relation between population density and social strife, and it is expressed in two basic reactions: the first is that mere proximity sharpens the feelings of dislike and inflates the occasions for dispute between social groups; the second is that keener com-petition for livelihood exasperates the causes of discord and conflict. Even in the nation that has preserved in its own country the greatest respect for human rights, this respect is beginning to break down because of overcrowding: the animosity displayed against lawful immigrants to England from the East and the West Indies is dis-graceful and disquieting. It is a pointer to the social strife that must be the result, on a much greater scale, of overpopulation in every part of the world. Aggressiveness increases with proximity. Popula-tion growth, far from encouraging better understanding between ethnic, cultural, religious or economic groups within national com-munities, will exacerbate the underlying or occasional animosity between them. Racial prejudice—and with it disorder and violence—is certain to increase with overpopulation, in advanced and in de-veloping countries alike. This situation will require from governments far better leadership and from public opinion far greater wisdom than now exists.

3. DEPRECIATION OF THE INDIVIDUAL

Depreciation of the individual—of his rights, his dignity, his worth —follows the increase of his numbers in a group, when that group has grown too big in relation to the space, the material resources, and the social institutions at its disposal. This is due to two direct causes. The first is simply the fact that an individual becomes one of a very large number so that, unless he has a superior character, he is less important than he would be as a member of a smaller group. His impact on the social environment becomes feeble or inexistent. He becomes one of the masses. The other cause is the amount of organization, as already mentioned, required for an overcrowded area. The constraints imposed on an individual become more close and more strict, his privacy is invaded, his personality is crushed and sand-papered by constant shoulder to shoulder rubbing. And— again, unless he has a superior character—he loses many human traits as he melts into anonymity. It is a distressing paradox that the more human beings there are in one place, the less humanity they have; the more closely they are crowded, the less humanly they behave. With growth of population and urban overcrowding, it is doubtful if there can ever be a Great Society, whatever the degree of technological advance and material affluence.

These effects are partly avoidable. Besides the basic recourse to slowing population growth and dispersing urban conglomeration, they can be offset in some measure by a more imaginative approach to social problems, a search for solutions more attuned to human values than the blueprints of social engineers and systems designers. This is another field where sociologists appear to have abdicated their responsibility, by holding that their scientific status lies in studying things as they are without going on from there to study what they should be. More political and administrative decentraliza-tion, local community life comprising more aspects of human activity and more occasions for individual realization, better in-formation and more contact between people and government at all levels: there are ways of keeping meaningful social activity out of the reach of mass-planned and soul-destroying organization. This will certainly be at the cost of some efficiency, but we can allow ourselves a blasphemy against the new social god by saying that there is now enough efficiency in the affluent society. The notion of efficiency has overstepped its own fruitful field of material production into fields— individual and social, intellectual and affective—where it has little useful service to offer. Efficiency also has its limits, which it must not be allowed to cross.

4. DETERIORATION OF ENVIRONMENT

We find peace in nature, in unspoiled nature as inhabitants of the advanced countries call those areas which they have not yet ravished and despoiled. It is the peace of being away from overcrowding, of enjoying a leave from social urges and stresses in the company of stones, plants, animals—things inanimate or insensible or unthinking. We need rest from constant awareness of other human beings, hopefully to become more aware of our own being. We need relief from wariness of all but the closest relations and friends. It is a saving grace of our times that most of us still find rest and beauty in unspoiled nature, probably because we know no other forms and movements, except those that are created out of man's thought and are therefore urgeful and restless. All city dwellers, adults and children alike, need the relaxation and recreation that only communion with nature can bring them. But unspoiled nature is shrinking fast under the onslaught of urban and industrial development. Living earth is smothered under asphalt and cement at an increasing rate. This is most manifest in Europe, but even the huge spaces of the U.S.A. are becoming reduced and overrun to an alarming degree.

Urban congestion was generally considered to be a result of economic advance: because of increased efficiency of primary industry and development of secondary and tertiary industry, farms and villages are depopulated and cities are overcrowded. But, for quite different reasons, the poor countries are going through a similar process: hungry people leave the overpopulated countryside to search for a livelihood in overcrowded towns, where they swell the ranks of the out-of-work and out-of-hope. Chicago and Cairo, Los Angeles and Bombay, Paris and Calcutta are swelling at comparable rates. The major factor of the urban concentration that spreads like a dropsy over the face of Earth is population increase. With the improvement of transport and communication, large towns will become a sign of underdevelopment and poverty, while the affluent communities will spill their ecumenopolis (C. A. Doxiades) with less concentration over the remaining green spaces, leaving their poor in the congested and decaying cities.

Highly articulate voices are raised in anxiety at the decadence of human values in the immense and amorphous urban agglomerations of our time. Lewis Mumford's *The City in History* (1961) is a detailed analysis and comprehensive synthesis of the folly and danger of modern urban concentrations. Little could be added to this brilliant and well-documented study. In practically all the large towns of the world, in Europe no less than anywhere else, the 'monumental slums of the 21st century' are now being built, in the form of immense bird-cages or bee-hives, constricting body, mind and soul. The expression of urban deserts is all too apt: deserts, because there are no trees and green life; deserts, because there is no place for children to play in safety; deserts, because the loneliness and segregation of overcrowding destroy the warmth of neighbourliness and the mutual interest of community life. How much overcrowding can human beings stand? There is no objection to trying it out on mice in laboratory experiments, whereby they become afflicted with sharply increased mortality, miscarriages, diseases, neuroses, homosexuality and cannibalism. But a no less fruitful field for research is ready in overcrowded towns all over the world, in rich and poor countries alike; and it is well to keep in mind that human societies respond to values different to those of mousey societies, so that the human values will be destroyed long, long before the same physical results of overcrowding may be observed in mice and men.

For the visitor from abroad no less than for Americans, New York City is an object lesson in the detrimental results of size and overcrowding on every factor of living and every aspect of social relations. A well-known architect is reported to have said: 'Size can mean healthy growth or cancer. In New York, it's become cancer.' But he was wrong, as the growth of a town can never be healthy after a certain level of numbers and density has been reached. It is always cancer. Paradoxically, the *per capita* costs of urban services (transport, power and water supply, food distribution, sewage and garbage disposal) instead of falling when distributed over greater numbers, actually start increasing after a town reaches a limit of size and concentration. Beyond this limit, expenses rise sharply, while amenities fall no less sharply, and it becomes a fool's game to go on living there unless there is no escape. Also, the very complexity of the system puts it at the mercy of any chance breakdown or malicious damage, so that millions of citizens may be instantly deprived of water and food and light, and even mobility. Besides the material factors of dirt and noise, pollution and discomfort, there are the social factors of loosening of community ties, and rise of violence and group friction. Increase in the rate of crime follows increase in the city's size. Strikes and slow-downs by teachers, police, firemen, sanitation workers and other essential services (even grave-diggers!) reflect fading civic sense as a result of deterioration of the physical and social environment.

The historical benefits of city life are wiped out by this deterioration. All those who can flee the congested centres do not hesitate to go out in search of a better moral and material atmosphere. They find that overcrowded transport and exhausting commuting are not too high a price to pay for the relatively purer air and better human relations of residential suburbs. The richer taxpayers thus leave the city to its poorer citizens. This development compounds the city's difficulties, as revenues decrease while demands on social services increase; it has become a pressing problem for all large towns, for New York no less than for others, and it calls for drastic and imaginative solutions on a national scale. The largest and richest (but not rich enough) town in the world is setting the pace for all inflated towns, and in its thorny problems the others can observe the fate towards which they are advancing and examine the deficiencies that they may hopefully try to remedy. What will be the quality of life in the urban conglomerations of the near future, many of which are expected to hold twenty or thirty million people before the end of this century?

And where urban development is not actually spreading, man-made pollution of the good earth, of the air to breathe, the water to drink, and the soil to till takes an increasing toll of plant and animal life. Lake Erie and Lake Geneva are equally poisoned and dying, because of urban sewage and industrial waste, and even the seas and oceans begin to show warning signs of man-made poisoning. Large-scale accidents have given this problem a new urgency, with radioactive sterilization of the erstwhile fertile land of Palomares in Spain, spilling of chemicals to kill fish in the Rhine, of gas to decimate sheep on the slopes of Utah hills, of oil to spoil sea life on the coasts of South England and Southern California. Such spectacular events make headlines, but there are countless and unceasing instances of pollution that do not rate a mention in the news, and their combined effects make up a formidable and rapidly growing threat to the ecology of our planet.

Deterioration of environment in town and country is finally causing real alarm. The danger for human health, the threat to the ecosphere, as well as desecration of natural beauty and dying out of wild life, have aroused widespread complaint and a beginning of action. Pollution of air and water has become a political issue that must be taken into account by public administrators and industrial corporations. Public opinion in most of the advanced countries is now sensitized to pollution; it is becoming ready to accept the impositions that are required to prevent its spread and to remedy the harm that it has already done. Japan appears recently to have taken a lead with a series of tough anti-pollution laws enacted in 1970. The Japanese have started to compute the price of anti-pollution policies, both as an added charge on public funds and as an increase of industrial costs, and to evaluate the extent to which this expense is expected to reduce the rate of Japan's economic expansion and income growth.

*   *   *

Such are some of the effects of overpopulation on the human values and the quality of life, even if material sufficiency (or even affluence) is assured. These effects can already be clearly discerned in the rich countries, where they are more visible against the background of apparent prosperity. In the poor countries, they are relatively less visible against the general background of poverty and underdevelopment. However, it is hard to foresee how far and how fast the deterioration will proceed, and to what extent it may be arrested and, hopefully, reversed by appropriate remedies. If present trends continue, it is certain that long before population density becomes impossible in the physical sense, it will become intolerable in the moral and intellectual sense; the human values will be squeezed out

75

of the social system well before the physical limits of density are reached. Before the resources of technology for feeding, clothing and sheltering human beings become insufficient, the overcrowded society may well have lost its claim to civilization and culture. It is no doubt encouraging to note that realization of the pollution threat has come relatively fast, but the fact is that the realization is forced on people by the exponential increase of ecological damage, as it is compounded from the interaction of technological advance, economic growth, and population increase. From what appeared to be small beginnings not so long ago, the damage grew very fast indeed, and it goes on growing at a rate that makes it imperative to enforce urgent and energetic measures. Also, deterioration of the physical environment touches the daily life of all people, even of those who are insensitive to spiritual and intellectual considerations; it is therefore natural that practical concern for the present threat to civilization should begin with the material factors. But the threat is not only physical, and the moral pollution of society poses a much greater challenge to humanity, as it is so much harder to define and to remedy. There will be better hope for the future when the threat to the fundamental values is also realized as an object for urgent and practical concern. In reality, the physical, the moral, and the intellectual factors of the present social disruption are closely linked, and they will not be remedied until a saner philosophy of life provides the basis and the impulse for wiser, more humane, and more co-ordinated policies.

5
Intellectual and Moral Trends

THESE INTERACT with the factors reviewed under the preceding headings. They cannot be quantitatively assessed nor is it easy to define them, but there is a sufficient body of factual information to allow a picture to be drawn. This picture may be unconvincing for people who accept facts only when they stand out in undisputed relief, preferably supported by graphs and figures. Lord Kelvin, the 19th century scientist, said that 'you do not understand anything you cannot measure'. A logical sequel of this shallow mode of thought is the obtuse remark attributed to Stalin: 'The Pope, how many divisions has he got?' as much as the quantitative and rationalistic thinking now in fashion. Despite such authorized opinions, intellectual and moral trends do set the direction that the future is taking, and an attempt must be made to analyse them or at least to explain their causes and their effects. These trends may be observed from many angles. A selection of the most representative must be made if one is not to wander about in interminably discursive description. The choice unavoidably depends on personal experience and opinion. The following headings appear to comprise most of what is important in these trends for an understanding of the challenge to civilization that arises from the present juncture in human affairs.

I. LIBERATION

Among many possible labels for our time, it could well be called *The Age of Liberation*. The liberating process started in earnest with this century and it has borne on every feature of the human condition. Women are liberated from ancient social handicaps and youth from parental and social constraints. Colonized and dependent people are nearly all liberated from foreign colonizers and exploiters. Libera-

77

tion from class and caste is progressing and the right of minorities to be free from majority oppression is generally admitted. In all countries, the generations now living have become more sensitive to human rights and they react with greater force than in previous times to discrimination of any kind. As for liberation of sex, it is no doubt the most discussed and the most spectacular, but not the most far-reaching aspect of this trend; sexual permissiveness will apparently not be as salient an element of social change as could be expected.[38] Finally, and also importantly both as effect and contributing cause in this overall trend, literature and art are liberated from most of the rules and restraints that were considered necessary for literary expression and artistic creation.

The benefits of liberation are manifest. An increase of freedom and justice for the individual and the recognition of human dignity for all races and peoples are impressive achievements. Even if only a small portion of humanity actually enjoys the benefit of the recognition, it is a greater portion than before and it should continue to grow unless disaster overtakes Western civilization. The removal of handicaps that were fundamentally unfair and harmful, the acknowledgment of the need of men and women for self-expression and self-fulfilment, the elimination in principle of discrimination between human beings for ethnical, racial, cultural, religious or any reasons other than individual worth and merit, the abandonment of unfruitful academism by artists and writers, all these aspects of the liberation process manifestly constitute an improvement in social and cultural outlook and they contain a promise for real betterment of the human condition.

But the process is now overstepping the limits of usefulness and reason. Rejection of restraints has passed the stage where it acted to correct injustice and to free latent or repressed capacities. The discipline inherent to body, thought and action, the balance essential to social order and personal endeavour are also considered, for 'advanced' or 'progressive' opinion, as restraints to be rejected. Liberation becomes an obsession that must be pushed to its ultimate conclusion, and you cannot be considered progressive unless you are determined to settle for nothing less than *total liberation*. The beneficial breeze that blew away unfair constraints is

growing into a gale that threatens to carry away some of the requirements of civilization and to reduce much of what makes the quality
of life. The cleansing stream that washed away unhealthy restraints
could become a torrent that tears down the discipline inseparable
from social order and destroys the fundamental values of human
beings.

All principles and rules can be pushed to extremes that become
logically absurd and practically harmful. To be nourished is good,
therefore the more we eat the more health and strength we gain, so
let us be gluttons; or, conversely, to eat little is good, therefore the
less we eat the better our health and strength will be, so let us starve
ourselves. Such elementary examples of the fallacy of pushing an
idea to its ultimate consequence are not different from the fallacy of
total liberation. Liberation is good, so the more we are liberated from
any sort of rules and restraints the better we and society will be.
There is a wind of excess blowing, that is the negation of measure.
The words of a French Dominican priest, 'the world is dying of
measure and it will return to life only through excess', reveal an
outlook that appears to attract many people, generous, ignorant, or
self-seeking. The condition of civilization remains measure and
balance, the proportioned exercise of human faculties in a human
environment. Balance is the condition of freedom as it constantly
implies a choice, while excess leaves no room for choice or for
freedom and individual rights. Measure and balance exclude neither
strength nor energy. Rather does a temperate society require of its
members more energy and more strength of mind than the unbridled deportment of extreme progressivism (or extreme conservatism, for that matter). Not unexpectedly, a balanced and independent
attitude in thought and action is hated by all totalitarians, revolutionaries and radicals, the political and the intellectual alike.

Revolutionaries are traditionally bent on establishing a new order
by violent upheaval, but many present-day revolutionaries appear
to have no new order in mind, only the violent upheaval. Many
members of the 'New Left' are apparently committed to the destruction of present institutions in the advanced countries by a rejection,
in the name of liberation, of the very notion of social discipline and
a personal standard of conduct. They are blind to the fact that

liberation from the fundamental conditions of civilized society is no liberation at all, but a regression to something that is contradictory and auto-destructive. If every sort of restraint is rejected, even the discipline of conscious thought and purposeful effort, there remains for a man to become no more than a random particle of social matter, a unit in the mass, guided by no aims of its own, by 'nothing save spontaneity, immediacy of response, and the obliteration of all stabilities'. The condition thus reached becomes anti-human and anti-social. Total liberation, the denial of personal and social discipline, the rejection of all authority, even that of learning or reason or morality, lead to nihilistic emptiness of life, impoverishment of art and literature, and by direct lines to totalitarian or technocratic rule.

Hippies are as innocent nihilists who want to retire from society. They must not be judged by the few criminals who infiltrated their numbers. Caught in the contradiction of a movement that rejects all rules, even those required to fulfil its aim of escaping from the rules, they become pitiable drop-outs, the waste of the advanced society, and they hurt only themselves. They would not be waste and they would not hurt themselves so, were they not such determined hedonists and were they more like the ascetic hermits and the purposeful monks who also retired from society in their time to people the deserts of early Christianity. But some of the aims and beliefs for which the hippies made their stand will no doubt remain, however confused, as part of a new attitude towards life. Society may be better, and it will certainly not be worse for their apparently short-lived movement. Not innocent at all are would-be destroyers of society, such as the anarchists who were in the forefront of the Paris disturbances in May and June 1968. Anarchists (I refer here to the bomb-throwers, not the articulate and rather attractive theorizers) are a familiar phenomenon in the last hundred years or so, and these are new only inasmuch as they subscribe to the slogans of the day. Total destruction rhymes well with total liberation, and they are quick to hitch on to generous if ignorant group movements in order to further their own brand of political revolution. Thus they add a dangerous dimension to current trends.

As innocent as the hippies are painters and sculptors who also appear to run away from society in the name of liberation from constraint. Some turn to abstract shapes or minimal forms of 'ultimate purity', far removed from the complexity of life and social reality. These shapes and forms are supposed thus to gain a reality of their own, so they are called real art or art of the real. But this new reality, despite the publicity it enjoys, appears to most people singularly poor and uninspiring. Its simplified forms and lines are akin to machine drawings and building elements. It often seeks to compensate irrelevancy by sheer size or it introduces mobility of form and light to make up for incapacity to convey life and effort, thought and emotion. But the attitude is indeed to convey nothing of human reality and it appears to lead to a dead-end with little possibility of development.

However, this is but one aspect of contemporary art, which is lively and diverse. There is a warning in the work of contemporary artists who, in common with artists in every generation, express the character of their time. On canvases immense and bare, or in broken colours and tortured features; with enormous blocks of inhuman form or geometrical shape; with obscure or trivial montages of every possible material; in tinkling and twinkling movables of metal, water, light and sound; are faithfully expressed the existentialist immediacy of life deprived of absolutes, and the emptiness and anxiety and fear of our souls. It is irrelevant to say that contemporary plastic arts are satisfying or disappointing. That is not the point. Each person, unless a specialist in art technique or expert in art trade, has his own likes and dislikes, generally rooted in hard-to-trace subjective experiences. The point is that artists—in the whole range from the best to the average and down to the mediocre—reproduce in their respective media the picture of our time, a transparent and striking preview of things to come.

Another aspect of this trend may be observed in some 'advanced' writing, especially in poetry. The liberated writer and poet tries to capture an inner voice, independent of social relations. This plausible aim also leads to a dead-end, because of its rejection of the discipline of thought and its intended divorce from life and social reality. The inner voice is not that of conscious thought, but of random association of concepts and automatic assemblage of images, caught as if in a dream or a drug-induced state. It appears unable to produce other than 'collages' in words, similar to the 'poems' that are put together at great speed and in unlimited numbers by suitably programmed computers.[39] The liberated writer is also prone to use expressions that were traditionally considered to be unprintable. The four-letter words which help some authors to air their complexes, to assert their personality, or to court publicity, are not as bold or as shocking as they would have them. They are merely childish and in bad taste, like spitting on the floor or picking one's nose. Independence of mind and liberation of thought are not expressed in terms that add nothing to vigour and clarity. Between genteel talk and barrack-room scurrility there are middle paths that young and not so young rebels should have no difficulty in treading. Between mealy-mouthedness and schoolboy scatology there is a wide range for sensible expression and good taste.

Admittedly, these are matters of secondary importance but they are relevant inasmuch as they help to define present trends. Other examples could be given, such as recent theatrical experiments, psychedelic films, happenings and other products of emancipated art. They would also show that it is self-defeating to strive for artistic expression without the discipline of thought that is indispensable to all endeavour.[40] These unrestrained believers in liberation, hippies and nihilists, *avant-garde* artists and poets of a certain type are only a fraction of the relatively cultured people in any country, but they are representative of a significant trend of thinking and feeling in the Western world. There is not much harm in their experiments and the affluent society can easily pay for their keep, but one cannot help wishing that so much energy and goodwill were put to more rewarding purpose.

More important and of greater significance are developments in education, where liberation from restraints has also been beneficial up to a point. A degree of permissiveness in bringing up boys and girls is required but—as always—it is a question of keeping a measure between ultimate bounds. A civilized society must have moral principles that derive from the fundamental values. Much is wrong in a community if education does not lay stress, openly and explicitly, on the good and the true, on the duty of individual commitment towards human beings and the claims of dignity and integrity in personal relations. The notions traditionally expressed by these words tend to be shrugged off by the not-so-young progressivists, while the youngsters appear to be trying confusedly to recapture them. It is a distressing fact that these principles of civilization are less familiar to the new generations and that they are being emptied of content by would-be liberated and emancipated revolutionaries.

A code is required for relations between human beings; rules are necessary for autonomous individuals to live and work together; principles of conduct must be followed for each one's dignity to be upheld and each one's integrity to be respected. In other words, there is a discipline inherent to society. If the notion of liberation extends to this discipline, it becomes an absurdity, nonsense that only the very young, the very ignorant, or the very wily can propagate. Thus total liberation is a myth because it is impossible and an illusion because, were it possible, it would immediately become enslavement. To be liberated from the discipline inherent to individual life and social co-operation would be to become like a dry leaf that is blown about by each passing breath. Nothing leads more surely to enmassment and totalitarian rule.

Real liberation, that is, the application of the principle of freedom, requires the restraint of discipline. Democracy is a liberation from despotism and totalitarianism because it has its own discipline that guards personal liberty and freedom of expression as much from mob rule as from police oppression. But the discipline of democracy is also being shaken by the wind of excess that blows over the advanced societies. It is also something to be thrown off for the simple minds that conceive the notion of total liberation. They find willing allies in those who want to establish an anarchic or a despotic regime. And such unholy alliances are called progressive, though they are regressive movements aimed at overthrowing democratic institutions and trampling underfoot the values elaborated in the course of men's laborious rise to civilization.

2. VIOLENCE

The same winds of excess fan the spread of violence in the advanced countries. Violence appears to be nature's main instrument for maintaining a balance between living organisms and the use of force has always been part of human relations, all the way from cavemen to sophisticated denizens of skyscraper cities. But a constant aspiration of mankind has been to replace coercion by consensus. Improvement in this line of endeavour is embodied in ethics and law and social institutions, and further progress could have been expected with spread of instruction and rise of living standards. Instead, a most perplexing trend of these times is the increasing propensity to violence in conjunction with advanced forms of economic and social organization. This regression is compounded by an apparent rejection of any limits to physical and moral coercion. Even when a resort to violence is condoned or unavoidable (such as in war and in rebellion) there are limits—fixed by an understanding of human values—which may not be transgressed without a debasement of civilization. Such limits are beginning to be recognized in principle (Red Cross conventions, war crimes responsibility, reprobation of genocide), but practice lags far behind. In fact there is now, perhaps more than in previous times, often no restraint to the frenzy for coercion and destruction, no degree of cruelty and atrocity at which revulsion from the attack on human dignity would stay the hand of violence.

This trend is manifest in all contemporary forms of violence, by individuals, by groups, or by governments. Individual violence is usually called crime and it springs from hate, greed, passion, or plain devilry and madness. It thrives on secrecy and it is undone by publicity. Group violence is severally called riot, revolt, rebellion, insurrection, and it proceeds mainly from political or social causes. It cannot be hidden, and part of its effectiveness lies in publicity. As to violence in the name of the state, when it denies justice and human dignity, it can proceed as much from the reasons of individual crime as from those of political interest. There are cases that fall between these categories, such as political assassination and gang crime, but the distinction based on the authors of violence is on the whole more instructive than distinctions based on the various types and methods of violence.

A. *Individual Violence.* Every nation has its share of murder and assault, robbery and peculation but, until recently, crime was not a really pressing problem in any country, advanced or retarded, demo-cratic or totalitarian, with the exception of U.S.A.[41] In fact, over the last hundred and fifty years, there was a reduction in the rate of crime. This was clearest in Europe and it was probably a result of greater affluence and greater tolerance; the two appear to be comple-mentary up to a point, especially in relation to crime against property, as improvement of the standard of living makes crimes due to poverty less prevalent and less threatening, and therefore less severely repressed. But the trend has been reversed, mostly in the highly industrialized countries, and the rate of crime is rising since World War II. This regression is obviously linked with spreading urbanization due to rapid population growth, most of which takes place in cities or gravitates towards cities. This point was mentioned in the preceding chapter. A great part of this recent increase in crime consists of juvenile delinquency, which is emerging as another sign of what appears to be a disintegration of the advanced societies. All the way from theft to murder (with drug addiction and sexual promiscuity as contributing causes) crime by the young adds a new and particularly disquieting dimension to the crisis in social in-stitutions.

The reasons seem obvious: permissive education; the example of violence all around; the devaluation of moral ideas and ethical rules, the denial of absolute criteria for good and evil, indeed the current rejection of such notions as good and evil; all these are reasons enough to incite surprise at the number of criminals, particularly adolescent criminals, not being greater than it is. The trend to violence is exemplified and stimulated by the tales of cruelty and pain to which so much of our time is devoted, on television, at the cinema, and in countless cheap novels, as if the daily reports of massacre and torture from all over the world were not enough to quench the thirst for blood. The adventures of hard-riding and sharp-shooting heroes of the American West are untiringly retold in a score of languages. Crime books and films seldom point to a moral. Strips, comic and not so comic, lay the accent on force. A current of savagery and brutality is running wide and deep. Part of an outlaw's or desperado's appeal no doubt lies in his tragic self-assertiveness, so far removed from the everyday life of more or less adjusted citizens, but the urban mugger and killer does not have even this spurious quality, and it is a telling exposure of a scale of values that personality should be expressed—and recognized—in a capacity for violence rather than a higher order of thought and action.

But incitement to violence is less harmful (there are always violent individuals who need no incitement) than the decadent thrill of vicarious sadism and masochism that so very many people find enjoyable and satisfying. Little boys are incapable of realizing other people's feelings, but adults finding entertainment in stories of pain and cruelty have sluggish imaginations and dulled emotions, and this is precisely what is happening to the mass public of TV and cinema. Sex on show has a limited field and it quickly becomes a surfeit, while sadism (more or less linked with sex) has a practically unlimited field in degree and variety. The entertainment industry is cashing in on instincts that men have traditionally tried to control and, with the help of the mass media in every home and hall, it is playing its part in desensitizing men and women, and pulling them away from the humane attitude that is a main condition of civilization. We are unlearning the value of human life. The mass media induce familiarity with violence, alienation from pity and charity and compassion, so that lack of feeling is accepted as ordinary by adolescents and adults, and violence as inseparable from human relations. Growing coarseness and inhumanity is excellent groundwork for the fall of democratic society and appropriate preparation for the rise of totalitarian mass conditioning, which can exist only if individuals lose their concern for the community and their feeling of solidarity for one another.

B. *Group Violence*. It is surely a significant fact that social grievances and the violence they provoke are now more manifest in the advanced countries than in the others. Group violence spreads in the United States with the increase of prosperity and the same may be observed in other affluent nations. Reasons for this trend are hard to elucidate out of the welter of raucous expression and intemperate action. Various factors may be considered. For instance, public voicing of grievances and the attendant use of violence could be related to the lesser tyranny of government in democratic countries. Not one of the twenty or thirty thousand participants in the 1971

May Day contestation in Washington was reported killed, while Poles, Czechs, Hungarians and East Germans have been mowed down by the hundreds to put an end to protest. Kent State in America remains an isolated occurrence, and the extreme indignation it provoked is proof abundant of its exceptional character. Protest is less dangerous in democratic countries and this is one reason for its greater frequency.

Another factor could be a more sensitive awareness of individual rights in the advanced nations and, with that awareness, a faster and more decisive refusal of what appears to deny those rights. It could also be that greater literacy and better health provide more direction and more energy for complaint than would be available in the poor countries. From these angles group violence, if it is not too disruptive, could be a symptom of social sanity rather than infirmity, and the restraint manifest under authoritarian regimes could cover an insidious spread of social and political disaffection that would be less harmful were it vocal and visible. Not many people would hold this view.

A less obvious reason for the spread of violence in advanced countries could be some correlation between reduction of material causes for complaint and increase in moral grievances. The moral grievances can emerge because the necessities of food, shelter, education and medical care are ensured for the great majority. Or the correlation could be compensatory: as men cannot be satisfied, reduction of material causes for complaint must be compensated by an increase in grievances for moral causes. The correlation could also be more foreboding, in the sense that the moral grievances (dissatisfaction, dehumanization, alienation) arise out of the very conditions required for increase of prosperity (advanced technology, mass production, accent on consumption). The problem of mounting violence would thus be in some way inseparable from material progress. If such an explanation were borne out by research and experience (and many believe that it is a valid explanation) it would be a valuable if disquieting pointer to the future.

Group violence is a pressing problem in many of the advanced countries. It is a threat to democratic government because it disdains democratic operation and it provokes violent and undemocratic reaction. Besides incitement by trained agents, it is generally due to disappointment with the political process. 'Only violence then is capable of bringing neglected problems before public opinion, of forcing authority to move towards a solution, and eventually—should it prove too hard to make it move—of overthrowing a social establishment or political regime.' To say that there exists a general feeling of disaffection in many Western countries (especially in the U.S.A.) and real frustration and discontent for certain groups within those countries is to say the obvious and therefore little that is significant. The degree of success of a social organization may be defined by the proportion between the satisfied and the unsatisfied, and this proportion also defines, to some extent, its degree of stability. What is significant in many of the advanced nations, but especially in America, is that the proportion of the dissatisfied and frustrated appears to be growing instead of being reduced, and that they become more vocal and more active.

There are specific causes for the increase of group violence in various countries. Such are for America economic and cultural discrimination against poor minorities and the pursuit of an unpopular and unsuccessful war. Such are for some totalitarian countries the lack of basic freedoms and the insufficiency of basic supplies. In many underdeveloped countries and poor nations, the lack of employment for the educated few and the disappointment of rising expectations incite people to disaffection and rebellion. But there are also—more importantly—general causes for rising dissatisfaction and they may be found under the preceding headings. Rationalism and materialism moving to extremes, debasement of the quality of life in many fields, increasing possibility of total annihilation, there is no need to recapitulate. The technological age is not keeping its promise and people are naturally resentful. But a further point must be stressed. In times of rapid change, men and women must either know their basic values and guiding principles or they must be guided by leaders and counsellors whose opinions they respect. Now, principles and values are confused and real leadership, intellectual or political, is conspicuously absent. The dissatisfied and the unfulfilled have lost a knowledge of the fundamental values of society, though they do have a sense of their loss, and they do not find in their leaders the grade of morality and devotion, vision and intelligence, courage and energy that is required in the present juncture. The professional politicians of democratic government are faltering badly, but only the deluded would welcome totalitarian regimes to put an end to confusion by imposing their organization. This is the dilemma facing many groups who are not content to remain passive and they sometimes seek to resolve it by a resort to violence.

As a social and political lever, violence is hard to control. It feeds on itself and it spreads in ways that end up far removed from the original grievances. The battle escalates, often with the help of hangers-on and opportunists who have their own axes to grind. Disorder and destruction follow. Freedom is denied in the name of freedom and democracy is subverted by the call to better democracy. Much is lost that is good and true, fertile and promising. The final advantage is always to change over immobilism; the longer the battle, the more drastic the solution and the greater the losses. We speak here of the play of forces, even violent, in a reasonably balanced and temperate society; there is no play of forces when total explosion or total repression are effected by unmitigated brutality, of which there are examples enough in contemporary events to sicken the most hardened. Violence may often be the only way and, in a civilized society, changes can be effected by force without crippling loss of values, lives and production, but only if there is a thorough and a general grounding in the fundamental values and priorities, so that they acquire precedence over other interests and constitute the limits that neither side will transgress. Such a grounding is possible through education. It is a weakness of Western culture that it neglects these fundamentals now that it is threatened by so many destructive trends.

c. *State Violence.* Totalitarian government, as remarked above, is more successful in preventing violence. This is due to its greater repressive force and to its practical monopoly. As they become prerogatives of the state, murder and robbery are called political purges and social appropriations. They are nationalized along with other interests in the public sector, thus restraining the private sector from undue indulgence in such practices. While to maintain a façade of freedom, shows of group violence may be staged by the Popular Movements Brigades with carefully planned spontaneous demonstrations, nicely graded from plain marching and slogan chanting up to the ritual baiting and burning of foreign embassies. This is not to say that there is no state violence in democratic countries (police brutality is an unfortunate and often dangerous fact of life) but it is incomparably less in scope and degree and it is effectively tempered by freedom of the press and recourse to the courts.

A distinction must naturally be made between state violence towards other national communities, properly called war, and state violence within the national community, called by the various names devised by political duplicity. War has been briefly considered as well as tyranny and oppression. Violence exercised by the state against its own subjects is mentioned again under this heading only because it is part of the overall pattern of violence and because it is spreading with the spread of absolutist regimes. Communist countries are firmly in the grip of totalitarianism, but there was hope that the emerging nations could escape it despite the overpopulation and underdevelopment that make their present so hard and their future so bleak. This hope is not being realized, perhaps understandably, and the greater portion of these nations is lapsing under authoritarian rule in one form or the other, generally that of military dictatorship. This applies to most of Latin America, Africa and Asia. India remains a notable but an insecure exception. Even in the democratic countries, state violence grows in direct proportion to the violence of groups whom the institutions of democracy do not satisfy any more.

3. THE STUDENT REVOLT

Student revolt is a salient aspect of the general trend of violence. It erupts all over the world and student movements have become a feature of social unrest in most countries. Their frequency and force appear to be growing. In some instances they have grown into full social and political revolt and nothing points to an abatement in coming years. Their import in the context of human values can hardly be overestimated, as they are so closely related to intellectual and moral trends in the Western, the Communist, and the Third Worlds. Any opinion on their future course cannot be based on other than personal reaction and individual insight, but it is possible to define the place of the student revolt in the complex problems of this age and to consider its significance for the present challenge to civilization.

Students have always been among the first to oppose conservatism and political oppression and to speak out in favour of the causes they believed to be just, whether connected with their interests or with wider human issues. In the 19th century, particularly after the 1848 revolutions in Europe, students began to participate in political activity as a group or a class. Often they protested injustice and contested unpopular power and excessive restraints in a generous if sometimes unthinking spirit. It must be considered as a tribute to this spirit that they often fought for lost causes. Students in many of the colonized and dependent nations played a similar role and they performed, at some risk and sacrifice, their share of duty towards liberating their countries from foreign yoke. They also generally did not fail to protest the home-made yoke when it turned out to be no less oppressive in some liberated countries.

College and university students of both sexes are naturally in the vanguard of movements for reparation of injustice and change of existing conditions. The contrary attitude would be unnatural in young people. They have ideals of freedom and justice, more felt than thought, more instinctive than reasoned, that experience has not yet tarnished or destroyed. They do not generally have to earn a living nor do they usually have dependents and responsibilities. They have come out of childhood, when so much has to be taken on trust, and not yet entered manhood, when so much must be taken as unavoidable. They see the shortcomings of society but they take its achievements for granted, not realizing the labour of previous generations that made them possible. Generosity coupled with ignorance of the facts or underestimation of the odds urges them to try to change what they think or feel is wrong. This has always been so. What then can be called new in the student revolts of recent years? Are they simply a continuation or is there a change of nature and direction?

The most important change is surely the growing proportion of young people of both sexes enrolled in colleges and universities. They now represent a significant percentage of total population in the advanced countries. The student class is homogeneous and constant in the features that set it apart from other groups: youth, a higher level of education, an attitude oriented towards change and typically critical of authority. It is thus a stable class in every country despite the transient character of its membership. Its capacity to influence social and political change is enhanced by the general trend of liberation from traditional restraints, so that the young become less inhibited and their elders more receptive to their ideas. The present accent on youth, on its supposed desirability above any other age, also encourages young people to have their say in social affairs. Bringing the voting age down to 18 years recognizes the fact that anybody old enough to go to war must be mature enough to have an opinion on the policies that send him there. The basis of participation in public matters is thus broadened, a result undoubtedly in line with the principles of a working democracy and the extension of the franchise across the older limitations of money, race, sex and age.

In developing countries the student class is no less vocal and influential, though it represents a smaller proportion of the population (a notable exception is Egypt, where the proportion of students is relatively high). What the student class lacks in numbers in emerging countries, it gains from the fact that it is more set apart by the privilege of having access to higher education. In some of these countries students have played a political role which their fellows in the advanced countries were not called upon to perform, and this has enhanced their stature. To have taken part in the liberation of their country from foreign rule is a service that is paralleled in recent years only by student action in totalitarian countries, especially in Eastern Europe, for the cause of democratic freedom. Students in the advanced countries, fortunately maybe for them and for their countries, seldom have such well-defined services to perform or such clear-cut attitudes to maintain. Perhaps this is a reason for the lack of definite aims that may be sensed in many aspects of their action, and for the consequent intrusion of destructive influences.

These factors help to explain the rising weight of the student class all over the world, but they do not discover the causes of the now generalized student revolt, particularly in the affluent countries. Some of these causes may be readily associated with the student condition, such as the growing size of universities, which makes the more sensitive students feel that it is no longer on a human scale and that they are treated as numbers or computer cards, the widespread complaints of insufficient communication between students and professors, increasing preoccupation of the faculty with non-teaching responsibilities, and irrelevancy of part of the curricula in the light of present problems. Such complaints are legitimately advanced by students and they deserve patient and honest examination. But this does not need a revolt. The example of Geneva University, where thoughtful and fruitful discussion was quickly set up between professors and students, should not have been hard to follow.

But the real reasons of the student revolt must be deeper than these specific causes. They are related to issues that are not the direct concern of colleges and universities. Some of these issues are easily identified in America, such as human rights and racial or ethnic discrimination, or the Vietnam war and the directives of foreign policy. There is no excuse to run down the generous spirit in which American students took up their cudgels for these issues or to demean the possibly beneficial long-term results that may be expected from their action. It was in a similarly generous spirit, but at real danger to themselves, that students in Hungary, in Poland, in Czechoslovakia, in Egypt and other countries demonstrated publicly against totalitarian rule and agitated for freedom of opinion and expression. Other reasons lie deeper in the minds and hearts of people in the prosperous countries. The general sense of alienation, of frustration, of loss of individuality, of vacuum of leadership, of lack of faith and ideals is stronger in the young and it arouses in them more active reactions than it does in their elders. They seem to be groping, in violent and muddled ways, for the values that would give meaning to their lives and hope for their societies. This appears to be the basic reason for the violence of the student eruption, though the immediate causes lay in more defined and identifiable issues.

From this lack of definition of their basic reasons and therefore of their aims springs the danger that hangs upon the student movements in the Western countries. There comes to the fore an urge to destruction in the name of emancipation, a breakdown of reason in the name of liberation, a rejection of democratic process in the name of a quest for identity or power, that discredit student movements for the majority of public opinion. Extremists, professional agitators and even paid agents of foreign interests seize the occasion to obscure even more the aims of the revolt while they fan its violence to further their own aims. This was manifest in the Paris student revolt of May and June 1968. This most spectacular uprising deserves attention because it was no doubt the least commendable in its aims, its methods, and its results. The disgraceful scenes of 'inliving' at the Sorbonne should not be allowed to influence a fair appraisal, but the most that can be said in exoneration of the students—or rather of the relatively small number who took an active part in the violence—is that their movement appears to have been taken over from the start if not actually instigated by professional agitators.

The originally declared aim of university reform, for which there is really ample cause in France, was quickly pushed into the background by a call to destruction in openly anarchist style. Contestation of every rule and every value in order to increase confusion; marathon discussions in seeming liberty or calculated chaos, but with the leaders in control; consistent refusal to take votes because, as one naively or cynically put it, 'the vote would be against us'; continued renewal of violence apparently aiming at nothing but destruction; constant resort to mob excitement so as to drown the voice of reason or charity; these were the methods applied during six weeks of unforgivable disorder in the full glare of publicity. For some Europeans, they recalled nothing as much as the start of the nazi call to hate and violence that ravaged a centre of Western civilization for full twelve years of this century.

What struck some observers even more than this blatant intrusion of the methods of regressive political regimes was the lack of generosity of the youthful and very vocal leaders of the uprising. They did not appeal in favour of the weak and the disfavoured, or intercede on behalf of the disabled and the aged (of which there are in France about three million in extreme poverty), nor did they express com-

94

passion for the unportioned and the starving in other countries. They repeated slogans that evinced a distasteful mixture of selfishness and presumption (such as 'we do not want a world where the assurance of not dying of hunger is exchanged for the risk of dying of boredom' or we must reach 'the zero point where everything can really begin')[42] and they were shamefully offensive to the middle-aged war veterans and survivors of the Resistance. All this is not in the tradition of the French people, their sense of measure and their feeling for humanity, and it may be expected or hoped that they will not again allow themselves to be so misrepresented.

This example of a cunning and effective take-over should persuade the majority of students, whether in Paris or any other university, the 80 or 90 per cent who do not participate in student movements, not to keep away any more. Only by full participation can they prevent the intrusion of extremists and professional agitators, and thereby exert a stronger influence for reform and change in an orderly and constructive manner. They should not make the same mistake as their elders, many of whom are wont to say—particularly in Europe —that politics are dirty or boring work and that they prefer to stay out and mind their own business. Such an attitude is a denial of democracy and a rejection of the principles for which people under totalitarian rule are often prepared to fight and sometimes to die. Salvation will come from involvement not isolation, participation not refusal: the involvement and participation of individuals co-operating as autonomous beings, not as units of masses that move in unison to calls of excess and unreason; autonomous beings who disagree within some bound of discipline and good sense, and who keep nevertheless together by a shared faith in the principles of civilization and a shared hope to make them come true.

4. THE MEDIA AND THE ARTS

Youthful ardour cools, and this is the normal course of most people's lives. Of the few who go on avoiding the overcrowded highway, some drop on the way as the waste and wreckage of society and some preserve their vision and perception into later years. These are the unadjusted who remain involved and committed, and do not try to escape human problems. Though few in numbers, they render greater service to society than the mass of those who conform to its trends. They express their awareness of these trends in more or less independent and forceful ways, in the political or the social field. In writing, in filming, their work is frequently original and creative in its commitment to human values. It is not hard to estimate the quality of contemporary portrayals of social comedies and individual tragedies, but difficult to foresee how they will evolve. Their taste is acrid but how to tell if it is the raw promise of maturity to come or the bitter fruit of a declining season? Now there are many to applaud their harsh protests, because they convey a still understandable message. But if society becomes fossilized in the uniformity of some technological system—and nobody can doubt any longer that this is one possible future—there will be none left to create, none left to understand and applaud.

Turning to less controversial fields than writing and filming, it must be noted that the theatre, ballet and music are enjoying a renewal of vitality and popularity. Even the totalitarian states encourage the performing arts, as homage to the culture that they suppress when it presumes to uphold the freedom and dignity of individuals. In Prague, in Warsaw, in Moscow, writers are hounded for the most discreet expression of intellectual liberty, but state-run theatres and concert halls achieve a high level of excellence. Thus the totalitarian government shows that it is not a rude barbarian while it maintains iron shackles on persons inclined to independent thought. In the Western countries, the vast increase in the performing arts may be a sign of increased affluence or of an improvement in the cultural standard of more than a minority of people. It could also be a healthy reaction against the soul-destroying triviality of the mass media and the cheap eroticism of the entertainment industry. In the developing countries, there is also development and improvement of the performing arts, both in traditional national styles and in modern international forms.

Another field with increased activity is that of recording and preserving the treasures of the plastic arts, great and small, including architecture. Never has there been so much collecting by individuals, by institutions, by governments. Museums are everywhere founded and enlarged, in West and East alike, in advanced countries and in the others. Exhibitions of works of art, antique and modern, are arranged on a grand scale. The work of discovering and re-restoring, registering and recording, compiling and collating proceeds in increasing detail. Description and analysis of the plastic arts attracts many specialists and there is an abundance of art publications. All this activity is good, even if it is not creative. It may be due to greater affluence, or it may derive from a greater awareness of culture now that it looks as though coming generations will not continue to enrich the arts and the humanities as past generations have done. It could even be due to an unconscious sense of impending change, so that this activity is like a stock-taking, an inventory of the heritage of civilization before the god of war and the idol of technology take their toll of human values and the creativeness which springs from them.

There have been times when great and essentially different styles of art co-existed in various centres of civilization, but the world is now becoming one in the cultural sense also. Even the plastic arts, historically so varied, are becoming uniform in style. There are indeed still some traditional arts and the charm of many a so-called backward country lies in the living quality of its local modes of artistic expression, but they are losing their vigour and creativeness. Some are kept alive as national witnesses, museum pieces or tourist attractions. Painting and sculpture are already universal, which means uniform. They all partake of a modern style, differently expressed by artists when they have talent but no longer different according to nations and regions. As for exhibitions of abstract painting, they are very much the same in every part of the world.

Architecture no longer has any traditional or regional difference, except strictly utilitarian adaptations to different climates. The ancient individuality of towns is fast disappearing everywhere. Only the achievements of older times retain the individual characters that still attract visitors and thoughtful persons. All the new quarters in all the towns of the world have practically the same aspect and the same design, and they are remarkably uninspiring and depressing. Uniformity is deplorable in cultural expression, but there is little to be done against this process of impoverishment, which dulls creativeness and blunts emotional and intellectual reactions. It is part of the system that reduces life and its fruitful diversity to logical unity and rational organization. In any case, it is the uniformity imposed by Western civilization. These often heard remarks are repeated here only in order to point out once again that if the Western nations allow their cultural values—the aesthetic values as well as the moral and the social—to become tarnished and debased, the whole of humanity will suffer the loss.

An encouraging sign could be the great increase in books, especially inexpensive paper-backs, both in variety of subjects and in numbers of circulation despite the development of broadcast and television. There is also an increase in periodicals of general or special interest, some of which attain a high intellectual or artistic level. The increase of printed matter is certainly due in part to improvement of the average standard of instruction and it seems to give the lie to prophecies of a decline in literate culture and the rise of a purely vocal and 'imaginate' culture. But this abundance of print must be seen in its true perspective. Books with some intellectual and moral nourishment, that is, not produced solely for entertainment like Westerns or detective novels or sex stories, are relatively less abundant and they do not command large circulation. For fiction, biography, history, a circulation of ten to twenty thousand is above average. For essays and studies (apart from the purely technical) the average is lower. There are of course outstanding works that are widely read, but they are infrequent exceptions. Even considering that each copy is read by a number of persons and that reprints prolong the life of books that withstand the test of time, the number of readers is small in relation to the multitudes of listeners and viewers, particularly because reading is unequally distributed between a minority who read much and the majority who read little. The present profusion of print cannot counterbalance the much greater profusion of broadcast words and televised pictures.

Children and people with little instruction prefer illustrated books because pictures supplement their lack of imagination. While educated persons generally prefer books without illustrations, as their more developed imagination does not need the help of pictures, but is on the contrary restrained by their limited outline and defined character. Unless pictures are shown for actual representation of objects or factual reporting of events, or unless they have high artistic quality, they may have an inhibiting influence on the image forming capacity, the creative activity of the mind. An image cannot express the richness of ideas and the variety of conceptual shades that may be conveyed by the written word. The foremost mass communication medium relies principally on the image to convey its message and it cannot convey anything but the simplest ideas. The printed word can stir the imagination because the reader has to translate the words he reads into his own mental language and associations, thereby exerting some creativeness in the process of understanding. While television leaves little to understand or to imagine by imposing, with insinuating potency, a simple but complete form made of shape, sound and movement. It gives little encouragement to originality in the sender or creativity in the receiver, and it tends to induce in its communicants not active participation but passive receptivity.

Social culture, save for an elite, is being shaped by the mass media, that speak the impoverished language of the technicist society, the *newspeak* of the future. The constant solicitations of the untiring and ubiquitous media, the permanent distraction and dissipation of thought, overcrowded work and recreation places, the tension of city life and the added fatigue of mechanized leisure—everything tends to stupefy all but the best minds and to induce in people a dazed acceptance of things as they are, or as they are going to be if nothing is done. Only a vigorous awakening of the advanced societies can reverse or arrest this trend. If consciousness is the foundation of culture, if awareness of fundamentals is the condition of civilization, it must be clear that the process of impoverishment of Western culture has begun.

Culture is expressed in thought (preserved in the records of philosophy and science, literature and history, poetry and music) and in the plastic arts (architecture, sculpture, painting and the other plastic media). Thought and art are thus the main expressions of a civilization and they are closely bound with the values of that civilization. It is now time to question whether human beings diminished by an unconscious rejection of the human values as the essential ends of society would continue to react with understanding and intensity of feeling to their cultural heritage. No less important is to question whether the fading of human values will not prevent the creation of works of art, literary and plastic, which are nothing if they are not expressions of mind and soul, except for some time only as a despairing protest against the new trends of society. From where can creativity spring when individual values and individual rights and individual personalities are squeezed out and rubbed away? What then will be the fate of the creative minority? Will there still be a creative minority? These are questions of extreme relevance to the future.

I am reluctant to use the expression of mass culture because its meaning is always confused and often derogatory. If mass culture means that culture should not be the privilege of the few but that all people should be as cultured as possible, it is obviously a good thing. But if it means that the people, the masses, must be fed a different, lower sort of culture, it is a bad thing and a subversive notion for democratic societies. Unfortunately the latter meaning seems to be the one generally accepted in these days. The larger the public, the lower the quality of the ideas proposed to their understanding and the more futile the entertainments provided for their recreation. Instead of aiming to raise the cultural level of the masses, the habit is growing of talking down to them in a sort of baby-speak and pidgin-thought. When the talking is done by the aptly named mass media, the standard becomes positively infantile. This observation applies more to America than to Western Europe where the quality is better. In totalitarian countries, the serious tone of constant indoctrination is a poor disguise for inferior cultural quality.

Marshall McLuhan proposes an explanation of this trend. The sole relevant fact is that people are subjected to mass communication media. It is irrelevant to enquire about the sense or quality of the message, to consider its intellectual and moral content, because the only meaningful reality is that the medium, especially television, shapes people's minds regardless of its message. In his *Understanding Media: The Extensions of Man* (1964), this author renders the service of pointing out the direction of the present cultural revolution by the mass media and revealing its paradoxical terminus: the better we can communicate, the less we can communicate.[43] Presumably, if communication becomes immediate (by direct impact on the mind, for example) there will be nothing to communicate, but it will be all right because 'the medium is the message'. Naturally values and ideals also become irrelevant as good and evil, freedom and dignity are words without sense in this preposterous atmosphere. It is fantastic that such ideas can be seriously discussed. Nothing is rational that does not take human values into first account. If it does not, it becomes the logic of madness, divorced from the reality of sensible people but creating its own insane reality. Therein lies the danger of this *dementia technologica*.

'Indeed, our cult of progress is in danger of imposing on us even more childish dreams of the future, the harder it presses us to escape from the past' (C. G. Jung). Infantile dreams of the future have their counterpart in infantile amusements of the present, such as the gambling machines before which so many mindless people appear content to cluster like midges around a light. Another thing to which the appellation of mass culture in a derogatory sense must be applied is what journalists have called the mythology of the 20th century, Super Man, Iron Man, Captain America or Captain Marvel. There is nothing wrong if small boys and girls find in their adventures, as recorded in the comic strips, an outlet for childish frustration in a parental and censuring world, but something is wrong if adults derive from them entertainment or solace. I hope that I do not tread on too many toes by denouncing such puerile symbolism. Are these impossible heroes and over-simplified figures a sign of the 'creeping childishness' (Toynbee), the 'terrible triviality' (Mumford), the 'overwhelming flood of feeble-mindedness' (Schiller) in which the advance formation of future society appears to be drowning? It is no consolation to see people in Western Europe responding with the same thoughtless interest to superman *à la Française* or *all-Italiana*.

However, the intellectual and emotional shallowness of the mass media, particularly in the U.S.A., is more satisfactorily explained by commercial, historical and technological reasons. Commercially, there is advantage in pandering to people's mental laziness rather than jolting them into consciousness. Puerile programmes, such as interminable guessing games, are cheap to produce and they induce an uncritical attitude in a passive audience, thus allowing easy insertion of commercials as pills in sugar coating. The remarkable technical accomplishment of television mostly serves to dissipate people's attention in trivial entertainment, when it is not used for deliberate distortion and deception as in most absolutist regimes. TV networks in Western Europe are generally state-owned and, maybe because the requirements of commercial publicity are out of the way or at least not a main consideration, they maintain a better cultural standard. Unless American TV networks agree to devote adequate time and effort to provide programmes with a higher cultural quality, it will be found necessary to set up a federal TV agency to provide an example of the use of mass media for something else than to dull the understanding and to numb the sensibility of their audiences. The recent success and growing audience of public TV is an encouraging pointer and it gives promise for improvement in coming years.

Historically, culture above the lowest level was the privilege of the gifted or the fortunate few. In the long fight for recognition of the people's rights, liberal education and general culture came to be regarded as a mark of privilege, because only the few with wealth and leisure or with powerful protection could aspire to acquire them. Now, although the fight for social rights is practically over in the advanced countries and although the best education and instruction are available for the many, popular prejudice against culture is presumed to be still alive. When the mass media began to penetrate into every home, they were made to speak the language that people 'in the mass' were supposed to like and understand. So the cultural standard of the mass media tends to be set deliberately low instead of deliberately high. But why not aim for a better cultural tone, a nation of mental aristocrats so to speak? If the prospect of reduced work and greater leisure is realized by technological advance, only an improvement in the general level of culture could provide meaningful occupation for all those who will no longer have the necessity of daily labour to fill their lives. In this improvement the mass media can play an effective role.

Finally, the puerility of the mass media is due as much to decreasing relevance of the fundamental values as to the increasingly technical instruction of men and women. What the technicist society appears most to require is specialists, suitably taped for their jobs, without redundant liberal education or unsettling general culture. So their leisure must be programmed to induce a suspension of thought in a passive vacancy, not an active urge towards new horizons in a curious and questioning spirit. If the technicist society is ever fully established, culture will decline in proportion to fading of human values and obscurity of social ends. Awareness of human values and fundamental priorities, the consciousness that is the foundation of culture must be reduced in a technicist operation of society. Unless the opposition between technique and human values is resolved by a proper understanding of social ends (and that this is possible constitutes the thesis of this book) human beings may all become 'outsiders in a world without values' or they will step down from the level of consciousness and awareness that is the honour, the burden, and the consolation of their human condition.

5. WHAT IS WORTH WHILE?

The most difficult task ahead is to recapture faith in an ideal, a moral vision and a sense of purpose. This needs, to begin with, the clear sight and firm comprehension that are qualities of awareness, so that it is required to show up cant and false sentiments, myths and illusions. Glory of war and conquest, deification of state or race, pretence to virtue and goodness, fanaticism in religion, historical necessity, excessive materialism, exaggerated formalism, academism and pedantry, all these attitudes and ideas and so many others are a façade that must be pulled down in order to show up the reality behind. To debunk such falsehoods and fallacies, to dispel such illusions, is a legitimate and a beneficial intellectual operation.

But debunking can be pushed to extremes. It can become a bad habit for intelligent people. It is apt to fall into mere scoffing and sneering, or it contributes to a sterile rationalism that impoverishes human beings. Rationalist writers of the last century, in France more than elsewhere, appeared unable to refrain from mocking respectable traditions and poking fun at human dignity. They cultivated a trend that is still recognizable nowadays, though it has been considerably stiffened and modified by positivist and pseudo-scientific thinking. It is easy and cheap to demean real sentiment, to deride disinterestedness and self-sacrifice, to dispel true beliefs and moral vision. Debunking thus overshoots its mark. The intelligent—when they are inexperienced and unsure, or too afraid of being taken in—fall into the rut of current-day rationalism, which is limited to correct reasoning, quantitative assessment, and materialist explanation, thereby excluding other ways of understanding and alternative modes of knowledge. They are the hard-headed and short-sighted realists, who seldom raise their eyes from the ground.

Behaviour is explained in terms of precise psychological cause and effect. The process that starts in instinct and experience and leads through thought (both concepts and sentiments) to attitudes and finally actions is explained on a plane that excludes spiritual worth and moral value. Motivations of the criminal and the disinterested, the generous and the selfish are put on the same level in order to reach understanding in purely mechanistic terms. When the mechanism of individual satisfaction is taken apart to show that it works in the same way for those whose motivations lead them to deny social discipline or to accept it, that it is the same process for the selfish and grasping, or the charitable and open-handed, there is no need to consider what is good and what is bad in such motivations. Everything is explained for rational persons without reference to ethical appraisal or moral judgment. In effect, nothing is explained because an essential part of the process is overlooked. To consider human motives and behaviour without relating them to moral vision and the notion of good and evil is to drag human beings down to the level of animals and machines, and to discard their infinitely complex possibilities for spiritual worth and energy.

With moral vision put aside, faith—all faith, even faith in the value of life—is debunked as an illusion, a myth that the age of reason does not need any more. Thereupon there remains little in which to believe, save the benefits of comfort and ease of body, the security of power and money, which things are good and worth striving for, but insufficient as the only ends of life. A successful career, a house and garden, with the gadgets of the affluent society, are respectable desires and workable aims, but they cannot be the only measure of men and women nor, once they are won, do they fulfil the abilities and the capacities of human beings. Without moral principles, without absolute values, there can be no hope for fulfilment because we do not know where fulfilment lies. Like Dante's poet in limbo, without hope we live in desire. The objects of our desire grow in variety, to be granted to many members of the rich nations, to be coveted and envied by the poor nations, but with this there grows a deep sense of dissatisfaction which is a source of alienation and suffering.

'I am a rational person. My mind is free of all those left-overs from primitive religion and ancient history. We live in the 20th century, with rockets and computers, and we don't have to carry that junk around with us. I am a realist and I see things as they are. I know what is good for me and I know what I want and I try to get it. I respect laws as best I can and I say let every man get on with his work and not bother with useless ideas and the world will be a better place.' This sample of modern pragmatism still applies to the great majority of average people. As a philosophy of life it is poor and trivial. It provides no anchor and no beacon in troubled seas. When simple pragmatists and self-styled realists sense that their world, which they thought they understood so well, is not functioning as it should, that it does not become better just because everyone gets on with his work, they are lost and ready for any reversal. They become part of the masses, easy material for activists and politicians, and they submit to totalitarianism of various sorts because they have no absolutes to fortify their understanding, no moral vision to direct their actions.

However, this sample may be somewhat out of date because there is the beginning of a change. For many reasons, some of which are touched upon in these pages (such as less certainty in science, that is, knowledge as apart from technique; the manifest failure of reason unsupported by moral vision to achieve political security and social betterment; the impoverishment of arts and letters that the more perceptive are able to sense) there is a trend away from 19th-century rationalism and 20th-century scientism which could be the starting point for something better. There is a re-thinking, a dawning recognition that there are factors more relevant to human behaviour, closer related to human fulfilment, than the aims and desires of material pragmatism. It begins again to be understood that reason standing alone is wrong, that reason is unreasonable if it denies emotion and a sense of the absolute in the human person. This would be an altogether beneficial trend were it turning towards the fundamental values that give meaning to life and purpose to society.

But the fundamental values appear hard to recover. The urge for change is inimical to inherited ideas and the revolutionary spirit wants only novelty, so the current dissatisfaction with material aims and desires fosters new attitudes and ideas rather than a return to basic principles. Liberation becomes a new shibboleth, to replace democratic freedom as a principle of Western society; an egalitarian attitude displaces the notion of what is fair and right, in a simplified caricature of justice; aimless spontaneity and immediate satisfaction are understood to be the proper cure for behavioural conditionment and the pressures of the consumer society; secular Christianity or Jesus freaks are advertised as the right way to bring old-fashioned religion to grips with modern problems; the overwhelming weight of the masses, the disordered vitality of the crowd are supposed to be compensation enough for the individual's loss of dignity. On the other side, the 1968 *Action Program* of Czechoslovakia's Communist Party, so brutally damped by the Russians, spoke of a return to democratic freedom, denounced egalitarianism, and extolled a humanistic socialism that could sound good to ears disappointed by the later brands of Western humanism. There is truly a great confusion in the world as to what are the values of society.

Values is a term much used and sometimes misused, but there is no other suitable expression. It would add to the confusion to invent a new word in order to express the meaning that this one has lost for so many people. Far wiser to re-assert the real sense of the human values, not as men's transient aims and changing desires, but as the standard against which to appraise ideas and actions, the touchstone for good and bad.[44] In substance, the problem of the advanced societies, and of the whole world in being, is the problem of *what is worth while*. What is worth living for, striving for, and perhaps dying for? What is worth the effort of doing the day's work, of keeping fit and alert? What will give meaning to our lives? What in hours of weariness and heavy heart will bring back a sense of confidence and good purpose? This is the fundamental question and most of us seem to have lost the answer. We must find it again or think out a better one if we can.

Besides those blessed with religious faith, related to that after-life that we all wish for without imagining what it could be like, a few have the answer for this life. They know that the human values are the worthwhile aims of human striving and the worthwhile ends of society. Some of these who know are active and disinterested, and it could be the small number of really disinterested and self-sacrificing men and women in every age that keeps humanity from perishing. Another minority recognize the existence of the problem but they do not have an answer, so they wander in search of something to believe in, to love and to respect, and they sometimes get trapped in dead-ends or lost in barren wastes. While the majority have little awareness of the question and do not even think of a reply because they are constantly distracted by things that are shallow and superficial. But a feeling of alienation is deep within them, as well as a disenchantment with established institutions, religious and political. The unending spate of new sects, cults, creeds, theosophies and scientosophies, the superstitions, amulets and ju-jus of the advanced societies, testify to the unsatisfied need for hope and faith.

Now, without mockery or irony, there is just one thing left to debunk. Now that old myths and illusions are dispelled, that we are emancipated from every restraint, liberated from everything, even from ideals to believe in and hope to sustain us, that we have only desires left to spur our daily effort, the time has come to turn away from the discouraged determinism, excessive rationalism, aggressive materialism, and obsession with technical efficiency that have spread a mental smog over all of us. These are also myths that cloud our understanding and fallacies that impoverish our spirit. Let us debunk them too. We can then turn to the fundamental values that may enable us to act humanely and wisely in these difficult and dangerous times. We can then recapture a moral vision and an image of the future for inspiration and guidance. This is the voice of reason, in its true sense of knowledge, logic and emotion together. It is also the voice of what is best in Western tradition. For the time being, it appears to have lost strength and authority. How do we give it allure and appeal? Can we rest with the hope that it will be raised loud and strong by the younger generations?

6

Conclusion of Part One

WE COME TO THE END OF THIS REVIEW. We have touched on many factors, each of which tends to undermine human values and to obscure social ends. They are primarily the challenge to the advanced countries, but they also threaten all civilization on Earth. These factors are considered separately for the purpose of analysis, but they are facets of the same problem; each appears more or less preponderant according to the angle at which one is placed to consider the present juncture in human affairs. Whatever the perspective may be, whether it be that of politics, administration or social organization, whether the main concern be philosophical, cultural or economic, the crisis is one. And it is a crisis for the whole world, though its scope and its effects are not the same in the advanced countries and in the others.

The expression of a crisis may be unacceptable to some readers, as it usually implies a quick outcome. In medicine, in politics, a crisis cannot last long and an issue, favourable or unfavourable, must quickly follow the point where the situation could not continue without a definite change for better or for worse. Even an economic crisis, if it is really a crisis and not just a difficult pass, is relatively short. While in speaking of a crisis of civilization, there is naturally no implication of a quick outcome. The elements of the crisis have taken generations to build up and, though the tempo of the build-up is rising, the present momentous juncture in human affairs cannot be resolved into a definite issue before the last decade of this century. Despite this, it is really a crisis because humanity is placed before two diverging ways—to maintain against every odds the fundamental human values as the tradition for the future, or to lose them in all but name as the drift of present trends is allowed resistlessly to gain momentum—and the signs are there to show that it cannot indefinitely remain in a middle path.

That it is a juncture of extreme gravity appears to be an accepted fact. Scientists and humanists, philosophers and historians, essayists and novelists, economists and even some politicians have no doubt that humanity is passing through a crucial period, the outcome of which could mean the difference between night and day.[45] The threat to human values, the confusion of social ends is felt by all. Each person reacts according to his or her particular character and circumstances. Those of more discernment and culture and those who take time to think are more aware of the threat and more conscious of its implications. Yet despite this general recognition of a momentous juncture, the urgent and fundamental character of the crisis is not sufficiently realized. 'We have failed even to comprehend the life-and-death nature of this challenge, and are leaving the response to chance' (Fred L. Polak).

1. In the advanced countries, the tangible benefits of technological achievements and material prosperity on one hand, the picture of orderly and democratic operation of government on the other hand, have tended to an undervaluation of the symptoms of danger and disease. Though the picture is clouding over, cries of warning—when they point to the fundamental nature of the threat—are still discounted by most people as the accustomed voices of chronic pessimists or disgruntled traditionalists. This remark applies particularly to the American scene where an unprecedented prosperity developed in an atmosphere of democracy and freedom. Despite the rupture of the Vietnam war, the mounting internal violence, the rising sense of frustration and confusion, a superficial view of the immense and vital panorama of the United States still gives the lie to pessimistic forecasts and gloomy visions of the future.

Yet the signs of danger are visible enough. The Negro problem, in the context of these pages, is *not* one of these signs. On the contrary, as a healthy claim to human rights it may be considered as an expression of concern with human values. The solution has progressed considerably in recent years. The questions at issue are well defined and the remedies, the only civilized remedies, are known. Strife is deplorable and violence is dangerous, but their significance must not be misunderstood. The basic decision has been taken by a responsible elite and the obstacles lie now in the execution. On one side, the difficulty is to bring the least enlightened part of the nation quickly enough to recognize the need to affirm human rights for all without discrimination and to accept the sacrifice required to make the recognition effective. On the other side, there is the practical difficulty of integrating (in a controlled movement fast enough to make up for the delay which led to the present explosion) depressed minorities into a social system that is itself in a state of crisis because of technological change and because of deep division on serious foreign policy issues.

Thus the Negro problem is a problem from the past, the solution of which has been much delayed. It is a difficulty for the present, not for the future. Its elements are defined by past trends and traditional attitudes, not by the trends and attitudes that begin to shape a future in which social priorities could be different, in which the human values—on which the Negro claims and the claims of other ethnic minorities are based—may be deformed or pressed out of existence. This is not to minimize the importance of the Negro problem for the United States: it is an essential issue and, if mishandled, it could break the American tradition and ruin the promise held out to coming generations. This is the great trial of the American people, greater than which they have not faced before. They will emerge from it either diminished in stature and repute, or squarely placed in the forefront of civilization, with the means to lead the world. There is reason to expect that the American people can pay the price and will make the necessary psychological and economic adjustments, and to believe that the Negro problem and that of other depressed minorities can be solved in the present understanding of the human values.

Indeed the symptoms of disease are less the painful sores of the Negro problem in the United States and similar problems in other countries, than the cancers of alienated youth, increased incidence of drugs and alcoholism, mental diseases and psychopathic disorders, mounting violence, mass killings and new types of criminals, brutality and sadism in literature and entertainment, excessive attachment to material interests, obsessive preoccupation with technology, deterioration of environment and depreciation of the individual, and the apparent indifference to fundamental values in a great number of those who are or claim to be leaders of Western culture. Social purpose becomes obscured in the very countries where economic abundance and political maturity should hold out the promise, indeed the assurance of full recognition of human rights and full satisfaction for human beings. These cancers may be small as yet, but there is no mistaking their malignant character, and they corrupt the deepest springs of all that can be called civilization. Above all, there is no vision of the future, no real faith in a good and a fulfilling tomorrow for humanity.

Fred L. Polak has developed, with great cogency and profound humanism, the thesis that a society and a culture are sustained by an image of the future, and that they disintegrate when the image dims and fades. For each successive period, this image is that of a future better than the present, a vision of human improvement, a dream of a better society. It is a fruit of creative imagination and it gives faith and courage to its generation.[46] But there have been no positive images of the future since World War I and the Great Depression. On the contrary, a wave of anti-utopias has come to 'project into the future a vision of society more dark than the deepest pessimism of the ancient world ever conjured up'.[47] These negative utopias, some of which have already become classics, delineate in unmistakable definition the 'dreadful natural terminus' of present trends,[48] the shape of tomorrow that today is even now taking on before our eyes. Science fiction (in the enormous mass of which some films reach extraordinary intensity and some books attain deep insight and literary excellence) is based without exception on the inhuman character of the technological future.

We do, then, have an image of the future, more clearly defined in the anti-utopias and in science fiction than at any previous time in the history of Western civilization, but it holds out no hope. It is a terrible and a repulsive image, and men recoil from it into the present that they know, that they want to prevent from getting worse. The most positive, the most constructive, the most hopeful minds of this generation do not get any further than plans to mend the widening breaches in the dykes, not to improve the lands beyond; no further than designs to mend the lengthening rents in the fabric of society, not to weave a better fabric. No one has a picture of the really better future that may be possible for humanity. A spirit of despondency and confusion, even fear and panic, is settling down on the advanced societies at the time of their greatest scientific and technological triumphs, as if to show that they neglected their basic priorities and placed their pride and their effort in things secondary and subordinate. Nothing shows up humanity's plight in the present crisis more than the lack of positive and hopeful visions for the future.

And yet it would be wrong to maintain that humanity has no ideal of hope in these troubled times. There is an ideal, a humanistic ideal that can be summarized in the ambiguous and undefined content of the idea of socialism. It includes different social approaches, all the way from the Swiss, the British, or the Scandinavian varieties to the socialisms of Russia and China with their satellites. The idea (and the word that expresses it) does not lose its magic, because it derives from men's deep aspiration to social justice (mistakenly but generally understood simply as equality). No charitable human being, indeed no intelligent person could declare that he or she is against socialism. All progressists, reformers or radicals, claim to be good socialists. As a philosophical concept for improvement of the human condition, it is a respectable ideal for everybody. As a political and economic system, it has taken on so many meanings, its historical realizations have been so varied that its practical ends and applicable means evoke no consensus. The content of socialism must be revised in the present crisis, in order that the human values upon which it is based may be brought again to the fore in its ends and its means, so that it becomes a constructive and a hopeful vision for the future.

2. In communist countries there is of course thought for the future but, as it has to conform to the compulsory official doctrine, it is apparently little interested in fundamental human values. In U.S.S.R. there are numerous institutes and associations devoted to social prevision, besides those that specialize in scientific, technological, and military forecasts. But all thought in this field is ruled by the resolutely deterministic and optimistic view of orthodox communism. Russian thinkers have to be guided by 'the theoretical thesis of dialectical and historical materialism, precisely the theory of

scientific communism, entirely utilizing the advantages of the socialist economic system which, according to soviet scientists, may ensure an efficient development of research in the field of social prevision at the level of the imperatives of modern science'.[49] Despite the jargon, the sense is unmistakable. On their side, communist science fiction writers paint a childish picture of a happy technological future, with little of the anxiety expressed by their Western counterparts. There is not much guidance for the present crisis to be found in the Marxist-Leninist outlook on the future, except perhaps as an example of what to avoid. A generation ago, the ills of Western society were already manifest and many thought to find in Marxism the remedy for bourgeois decadence. Now the ills have developed into an acute crisis, but it has become clear that Marxism cannot provide the answer.[50]

However, in several East European countries there is a new independence of thought which, while paying due homage to orthodox communism, proceeds to destroy most of its assumptions and implications in the effort to discover why communist countries are lagging behind Western advance. In Poland and Romania to some extent, but particularly in Czechoslovakia there are signs of a welcome change of outlook and attitude. Inasmuch as this intellectual movement recognizes that rigid socialism has stifled economic and cultural development, it implies a return to the human values that have been the principles of social progress. But in so far as it follows Western models, especially American, it is open to the danger of ignoring human values despite its declared insistence on a humanist view. In any case, after the Russian crackdown on the stirrings of liberalism, this movement will no doubt be arrested and the interesting contributions that it promised to make to studies of the future will not be forthcoming.

3. As for countries of the Third World, long-range view of their future is obstructed by their short-range difficulties of providing the bare requisites of living for expanding populations. When scarcity and famine are at the gate, human values are less an object of concern than human needs on the lower plane of bodily necessities. The long-range view is also prevented by the generally lower standard of instruction and social education, and by undemocratic governments

that restrict freedom of expression. In many of these countries, as under totalitarian regimes, the intrusion of political propaganda and administrative harassment is so pervading that it does not allow even an elite to rise above petty and daily renewed difficulties in order to consider larger problems with some quietude and attention. Reflection on the future thus appears to be practically confined to the advanced countries because (a) they provide the atmosphere of freedom required not only for expression but for thought itself, (b) their institutions grant some thinkers material aid and living conditions conducive to reflection, (c) they are nearer, so to speak, to the future and more immediately concerned, and (d) people of underdeveloped and totalitarian countries are faced by problems more urgent in their view and more nagging than those of a future that seems to them very far away.

Therefore, people of the poor countries are less aware of the problems of human values and social ends in the context of the future. They cannot be of much help in averting the dangers of a technology which they do not possess. They have respectable and often valuable social traditions, but these will not withstand the impact of Western civilization. Traditional patterns in all emerging countries are fast disappearing because their people look to the advanced nations for the know-how and the financial aid to feed their expanding numbers and raise their depressed standard of living. The new generations are mounting fast and they must somehow be fed and clothed, sheltered and educated. The race to keep abreast of population in the poor countries leaves neither time nor breath for anything else. Because of this situation, emerging countries cannot be expected to make an effective contribution to the fundamental problems of our times. The responsibility for this rests mainly on the advanced nations of the Atlantic community, because they have the means to discharge this responsibility, and because their values and their priorities—such as they are or such as they will be—will become the values and priorities of the whole world.

4. The deep concern in the present crises of humanity must therefore be for Western civilization, because no other civilization or culture can resist its impact and withstand its influence. This is not due to its higher moral and ethical position in its relations with

the rest of the world, but to its technological advance, its accumulated wealth, and its superior level of instruction. Arnold Toynbee wrote in 1950 that 'today the Western Civilization holds in its hands the destiny of the whole human race' and the truth of this becomes more clear with every passing year. It is vital that the advanced nations of Europe and North America preserve social ends based on human values. The poor nations need the help of the rich nations; and the rich nations cannot help themselves and the rest of the world without a deep re-thinking of their priorities, their ends and their means. If the human values are depreciated or rejected in the advanced countries—as it appears that they can be—they will be lost for the whole world.

A double criticism is certain to be levelled at this proposition, angry from some and patronizing from others. Readers from emerging countries will say that I am drawn by the powerful operation of the Western democracies and thereby blinded to the concern for human values that other cultures still retain: their often genuine (though different) forms of democracy, the warmth of human relations, tolerance and compassion for human weakness, the spirit of kinship and help among families and individuals. Western values are not the only values. Their social expression is too often hard and grudging, impersonal and unfeeling. . . . While others of the European or American scene, disenchanted actors or sceptical onlookers, will say that I am naïvely ascribing to Western democracies qualities that they do not possess. They will point out corruption and hypocrisy, crime and violence, the jungle of urban agglomerations. They will repeat the arguments so often expounded against the existence of real freedom and justice. They will say that, in my desperate search for something to cling to, I am clutching a reed that is already broken.

However, I do not think that I am blind or naïve. Of course human values are generally respected in the poorer and more traditional societies, where their individual expressions are often more sincere than in advanced and prosperous nations. These could benefit from the traditions of other cultures. In the past, there had always been beneficial influence of the East on the West. But in the present era, the values, the goals, the desires of Western civilization are inexorably permeating the emerging countries and re-shaping their traditional notions of person, family and society.... Of course, the picture of democratic government in the advanced nations is marred by undercurrents of pretence and corruption, but it remains the best or the least bad form of government. Western civilization is threatened in its fundamental principles but, such as it is, it remains the best hope for the future. No other form of society and culture appears to offer better hope, least of all the new totalitarian technocracy that is in the minds of many people of this generation.

This is why the evolution of Western civilization is of such vital import to the whole of humanity. Europeans and Americans are setting the pace and they are making the design for all other nations and peoples. Americans in particular have placed themselves in the first rank of power and prosperity. They have gone further than any other people on the road of technological advance and material prosperity. Up to the present, they have achieved this in a comparatively free and open society operating a liberal economy and a democratic form of government. But it is now clear that the human values may be denied or depreciated by technological development and population concentration, that social ends are already obscured by a mechanistic attitude towards social organization and a materialistic understanding of social good. Americans are thus the first to bear the open clash between material progress and human values.[51] They are in the front line to face this challenge and the basic issues of humanity depend on how they meet it.

PART TWO
THE ANSWER

Where there is no vision,
the people perish.
Proverbs 29.18

The Answer

EUROPEANS in the second half of the 10th century were alarmed by the approach of the year 1000. The end of the world was expected to come at that date. Many prepared in fear and exaltation for the last judgment, when the damned would be lost for ever and the saved eternally blessed. They saw destruction coming, but they also looked forward to a rebirth, a redemption, a new coming. Perhaps the old magic of numbers in relation to the first Christian millennium was responsible for the impression of impending doom, and the year 2000 may have connotations of the same sort for some of the living today, but they have no rebirth to pray for after possible destruction. In reality, it bears a more dangerous significance for humanity. The approach to the second millennium of the Christian era, which now numbers the passing years for the whole world, coincides with an unprecedented conjunction of circumstances, a crisis that is fraught with great danger and possible disaster for the human race.

Most of the recently established research and planning institutions in Europe and America have chosen the year 2000 as a convenient term of reference. Their forecasts of needs and resources are based on the expected evolution of population growth and technological progress up to the end of this century. Besides the psychological attraction of the round figure, this is a sensible choice. At the present level of forecasting and planning capacity, thirty years or so is adequate for long-term planning, near enough for the basic forecasts to be reasonably sure, far enough for a long-range programme to produce results. Moreover, it is an adequate period for education of public opinion, by honest information and open debate. It gives sufficient time to design a desirable future based on a heightened awareness of human values and social priorities. Also, in thirty years' time some of those who are now participating in the forecasts and the planning will be alive to see the results of their work and to ensure continuity of thought and action.

But there is a reason more cogent than any of these to choose the end of this century as the term for present forecasting and planning: the mounting crisis of the world cannot remain in a critical state much longer. Some time in the course of the next thirty years, the crisis will be over. It will either have been resolved by intelligence and energy according to a deliberate course of action or it will have been settled by the drift of present trends unchecked and uncontrolled because of unawareness and passivity. The solution will then be known. For better or for worse, it could even be final. By that time—not so far ahead—if human beings have not been able to design and to shape a desirable future, if they have allowed their future to go by default, it will have been shaped for them without reference to the priorities of culture and civilization, and they will have lost the chance to avert the condition that some already call their unavoidable fate.

There is something like a point of no return in most aspects of our world, but not in all. For physicists, who deal in matter, the point of no return is reached at every moment because of irreversibility of change and increasing entropy. For biologists, who deal in life, irreversibility is not absolute, especially in the relatively short term of life as compared to matter. For humanists and sociologists, who deal in human relations, the point of no return is always doubtful. There is in reality no irreversibility, except in the practical terms of assessing that the difficulties of reversing a trend or changing its direction are insuperable for the intelligence and energy of the individuals composing a society. But many sociologists and humanists, in the determinist fashion of our time, appear to have lost sight of this fundamental freedom, and to have surrendered to the difficulties that they name fate and necessity.

That the difficulties, the pressure of circumstances, may become insuperable is obvious; those essentially human qualities of will and energy do in fact have their limits. In particular, the time lost through passivity and unawareness can seldom be made good. But most men and women rightly believe that, if they will, they can shape their future by the use of intelligence and foresight. There would be no object at all to any sort of planning were it not possible by concerted action to bring about desirable social conditions which would otherwise not be realized, were it not feasible to avert undesirable conditions which would surely be realized if the trend of events were left to follow its drift. In its short-term form, planning is the ABC of government action. Governments and corporations are now turning to long-term planning, especially in fields where short-term action would be ineffective. Long-term planning is more complex, it requires better sources of information, more exact instruments of forecast, more effective means of execution. As experience is gained, planning increases in range and scope. Planning for the future has become a necessary safeguard of civilized society and the most important function of government.

For the human values and the social ends that derive from them, it is not so much a question of planning as of awareness and concern. Human values must be affirmed and social ends must be asserted not *by* planning but *in* planning. In terms of systems analysis and programme budgeting, this means that the human values, in so far as they are definitely or only possibly concerned, must always be (except unavoidably in time of war for survival) essential factors in the study of goals and means, the examination of objectives and costs; factors that cannot be eliminated and that, if found to be negative to the slightest degree, must invalidate the proposed plan or action regardless of whatever advantages may be expected to derive from it, such as financial economy, operational facility, increased efficiency, or the satisfaction of part of the people. No plan or action—however great or small be its scale, range or term—can be beneficial unless it gives absolute priority to the human values in its ends and in its means, in its means no less than in its ends. This is the basic principle, the conviction that all must share who have any part of thought or decision in political, administrative, economic and social affairs. It is strange to have to insist on such an elementary truth. Yet, because of the complexity and confusion brought about by the accelerated rate of population growth and technological advance, the principle is put in doubt and many of its consequences rejected or denied. The trend towards depreciation and rejection of human values is plainly discernible. The increasing contingency and confusion of social ends is no less discernible. The result of this double current, if left to drift unchecked, cannot be in doubt.

7

The Human Values

THESE PAGES are not written to take a stand and to make a statement of faith, but to propose a line of thought and suggest a course of action. I have kept away from religious doctrine and eschatological ideas, much as I am involved in them, much as I believe that the road to a desirable future can be lighted only by faith and vision, apart from the logic, the planning, and the technique required to make the vision come true. I have deliberately kept to a lower level. The human values, as here defined, are the perennial principles of civilization. They are the guidelines that may not be crossed, the parapet that prevents thought and action from falling into evil or absurdity. And they are also the positive and dynamic goals of society. They are basic more than any other notions related to the human condition, because all thought for improvement must account for them, the thought of visionary and philosopher and moralist, as well as that of economic and social planners. They are the framework within which visions for the future are delineated and they are the foundations upon which each age builds its economic system and its social organization. Systems and organizations must be in constant evolution, because the changing circumstances of demography and technique present ever-renewed challenges and demand ever-renewed responses; but, underlying this unceasing change, the principles based on the human values remain unchanged.

Nor, at the level at which we are placed, shall we turn to philosophy, which—lively and interesting as it may now be—is tainted with the decay and pessimism of the age. There is much in it that is new, but it is mostly influenced by the existentialist trend that has developed over the last hundred years as the specific contemporary contribution to philosophy. Not in the despairing relativism of French and German existentialists, or in Christian compromissions with that despair, can we find inspiration and guidance. We will not find them in depth psychology and the new god of Neumann, or in the objectivism of Ayn Rand and the positivism of others, or in down-to-earth English and American pragmatic attitudes, even less in the so-called realism that is the common man's flimsy refuge. All these theories or attitudes reflect the fading of human values by ignoring moral vision and normative action, or by rejecting charity and solidarity, or by picturing life as meaningless and absurd, or by resolving their contradictions in irredeemable relativism and ambiguity. Even though their accent may be on the individual, there is little in them to define human values and to provide a guide to a better future, little to help separate good from evil, mostly nothing but blind acceptance of present circumstances as the unalterable premises not only of action but of thought itself.

On a higher intellectual plane, Teilhard de Chardin made a bold attempt 'to build up a generalized theory or philosophy of evolutionary process which would take account of human history and human personality as well as of biology, and from which one could draw conclusions as to the future evolution of man on earth'.[52] He tried to define a conception of the universe rising towards ever greater complexity and organization and striving for ever higher and wider consciousness, in which mankind—as individuals and as a species—plays the main but not the only role. This is a great and a dynamic conception, though still hazy and uncertain, and it is too early to visualize its fruition. It does not help us now to define social policies, except in the most general terms, nor to answer the challenge of the present crisis in human affairs, except as a call to constructive optimism. Our argument here does not purport to study the genesis of the human race, whether it was born of chance interactions in primeval biotic matter or created by the will of a conscious God. Nor is it concerned to imagine the possible end of the human race in decline and catastrophe, or apocalypse and apotheosis. It is concerned only with defining the fundamental values that must determine individual and communal priorities in this time of rapid change, and to keep the ends of civilization well in view despite the current confusion of thought and disarray of action.

Is there support or guidance from other cultures? We can leave aside the Eastern cults that attract Americans, like latter-day Romans, from Zen to I-Ching, from yogis to would-be prophets: they may help lost individuals to regain some balance and composure, but not to recapture the sense of what is basic and fundamental. Regretfully, I must also leave aside the great Asian religions, of which I know too little; their notions of human values and their social priorities appear to be very different from those of the Western tradition. On the other hand, Islam shares a great part of the sources of this tradition, but since many centuries it has dropped out of the main current of Western development, to which it had earlier contributed so much. Now, it does not appear to be awake to the present critical juncture in human affairs nor are its thinkers concerned with the problems that are so urgent for the West and so important for the future of the human race. If China's traditional humanism is not entirely wiped out, it could one day contribute thinkers with beneficial influence on Western thought. The recent foundation of a Tibetan lamasery in Switzerland could be the start of something worth while.... But in reality, though much light (philosophical and scientific) came from the East and helped to enlighten the West, there is now little to hope or to fear from Eastern influence on the West. Western civilization is working out its own salvation or damnation and, with the one or the other, the future of the whole world.

Nor will it be required to dwell on the essence of the human person for which Western culture claims worth and dignity. This essence is now questioned and the autonomy of the person put in doubt by cybernators and others in the fashion. What is left of the person, they ask, now that machines can take over many of its muscular and mental operations, now that organs of the body can be replaced by artificially contrived parts, now that the mind can be conditioned to accept and even to like what it hated and refused? Very little is left, they say, that is irreducible to technique, so little that it hardly deserves the exalted importance with which man has endowed himself.[53] This line of reasoning is not new; though it is renewed by biological discovery and technological advance, it remains delusive. A grafted heart or kidney, a perfected artificial limb are different only in degree from false teeth or an old soldier's stump;

the action on the mind of complex drugs or electronic devices is not different in nature from that of the Assassins' hemp or the herbs of an African magician. Whatever means there are—ancient or modern —of aiding or subverting body and mind, the human person remains in essence and in substance autonomous and unique, and it continues to be the *only* factor that gives purpose and meaning to society.

Human values derive immediately from the autonomous quality of the human person, the unique character of each individual self. They constitute the fundamental rules that govern the relations of one person with another and, as such, they are the principles of society. All men have held and still hold that the dignity born of respect for oneself and for others, that regard for truth and the given word, that justice tempered by charity and solidarity, are essential for human relations. Civilization may be appraised by the degree to which social organization and operation respect these principles, by the extent to which a society recognizes the human values as its social ends.[54] These principles have the quality of permanence and universality. Political and economic systems, social and ethical theories, moral rules and commands, each and every one is of its time and place (even if the time is a long period and the place a vast part of the world). They change—as they must—because of changing circumstances, and none can provide principles of perennial relevance, but the fundamental values remain unchanged. The only stable beacons in the restless seas of history are the principles of freedom and justice, dignity and quality that derive from the autonomy and the worth of individual human beings. More than ever, in times of change and of stress such as ours, we need these guiding lights to avoid the shoals and to steer between the rocks that lie ahead.

These principles are not dependent upon any of the several understandings of natural law or natural order that have long been debated in theology as a basis for morality and ethical commands. Nature is a word with many meanings and the notion of natural law is vague and uncertain. In the course of history, it has been called upon to support contradictory views and to defend competing ideologies: individual and communal ownership, democracy and autocracy, feudalism and fascism and the open society, even slavery and war, have all in turn been justified on the grounds that they are founded on natural law. It gives no dependable criteria for good and evil as do the human values deriving from the autonomy and the individuality of each man and woman. These values may be called natural in that they are readily apprehended as good for human beings, but they are emphatically not natural in the sense that they could have been derived from the operation of nature, where there is no order for individuals other than the uneasy balance of eat or be eaten, beat or be beaten. The human values were gradually conceived and elaborated as a liberation from this balance of terror. For the West especially, they have been found good and durable and tested by experience, both in the positive achievements that followed their acceptance in some times and places, and in the failures that followed their denial in other times or other places.

But the balance of nature that is one of terror for individuals is the balance that ensures stability and fruitful diversity to the living world. Whatever pride men may justly take in their spiritual and social aspirations, in their awareness and in their powers, they cannot ignore nature and disturb ecological balance without endangering all life on Earth, and bringing their aspirations to naught. In the terminology of ecologists, the human race continues a sub-system which must exist in harmonious interaction with all the other sub-systems, the combination of which makes up the ecosphere in infinite and delicate complexity. Within their own sub-system, human beings try to replace the operation of natural controls by consciously regulating their societies according to the values and priorities of humane civilization. These natural controls are the more obvious ones of famine, disease and aggression, and the more subtle ones now being discovered in animal societies. Human beings have also abandoned brutal but effective controls accepted by earlier societies, such as destroying new-born girls as practised by the Greeks and the Arabs, and they have lost the sexual taboos devised by societies which we now call primitive.

All these controls preserve the species by preventing numbers from increasing to the point of overcrowding, thereby ensuring for all enough vital space and food supply; but they are inimical to the individual, which they subordinate to the group. The great and fruitful perception of humane civilization is the worth of an individual, a man or a woman or a child *per se*, and the elaboration of the fundamental values out of this perception. But in this attempt to replace natural or brutal controls by consciously regulating society according to these values, human beings can succeed only if they realize the human sub-system's place in the ecosphere, if they understand that—whatever degree of freedom from natural compulsions they may attain in their relations with each other—they will never be free from the compulsions of their ecological environment. Their intelligence and their will must be directed, with some humility, to better comprehension of natural processes and greater respect for their delicate complexity. Above all, they cannot let their numbers increase to the point of upsetting the balance of the ecosphere, so that not only they become incapable of regulating their societies according to their aspirations, but that their very survival becomes threatened. Thus human beings can continue to be guided by the fundamental values in their societies only if they use science and technology to preserve the ecological complexity and stability of the planet, not to destroy it as they are so industriously doing at present.

The fundamental values cannot lose their relevance, but the means for realizing them are not fixed for all time. Each age must define their content in its own style and affirm their application to the challenges it faces. That the challenges of this age are particularly grave and perilous does not modify the basic answers. The same truths and the same falsehoods are repeated from generation to generation, but they sound different because they are expressed in another style and they do not look alike because they are seen from changing perspectives. Old falsehoods appear attractive when they are dressed in the phrases of a new generation. The significance of old truths seems to be lessened when they are expressed in the words of an older generation. In a sense, the old truths—the human values—must be rediscovered by each generation. We need to recapture a feeling for continuity, that rapid change has made us lose. Even more, despite the disrepute in which it appears to have fallen, we need common sense. The founder of cybernetics wrote that 'any sensible man would consider the purposes of man as paramount in the relations between man and machine'.[55] We should add and be convinced that any sensible man would consider the individual human values as paramount in the relations between man and his social organization.

*   *   *

People feel strongly about human values, which they generally equate with their rights, but few are prepared to list them, much less to define their content. Most would no doubt include freedom and justice, which are indeed fundamental. Dignity and quality must also be considered fundamental. These are the four headings under which the human values may be examined and defined. They are complementary, for they all derive from the basic premise that human society can have no end but to satisfy the needs of the human person, its physical and its spiritual requirements. The notion of quality is particularly important. The human values are never absolutely respected or absolutely denied. In practice as well as in theory, there are different levels of freedom, of justice, of dignity for the individual in society, and quality may be taken as the measure of those levels. Naturally the higher levels must be the aim of civilization, and thus the concept of quality is part of the proper definition of human values and social ends. The following pages contain an attempt to define human values in terms consonant to present circumstances and to describe their practical content in the light of present problems.

I. FREEDOM

Of all the human values, freedom must be considered as the first because it bears the closest relation to the autonomy of the person. Without freedom, the other human values cannot be said to exist. It is the principle most widely supported in theory and most questioned in practice, most respected in word and denied in deed. Its scope is very wide. It is a general concept, which must be defined in relation to the needs of the individual and to the functions of society. In relation to the individual, freedom applies to movement, thought, expression, and action; in relation to society, it applies to central and local government, to administration and public services, to corporations and associations. Obviously, there is no such thing as absolute freedom. Freedom has its necessary limits for individuals and groups, and these limits are set by the freedom of other individuals and groups. Freedom requires a delicate balance between individual rights. The better the balance is kept, the greater measure of freedom there is for all. This balance is the first requisite of society, and it is the first important lesson that a child must learn in its slow progression to adult status.

When speaking of the advanced countries, it seems pointless to mention freedom of movement. People in Western Europe and North America take it so much for granted that they cannot imagine such an elementary right being taken away from them, nor can they readily picture the situation of other people to whom it is denied. They forget that freedom of movement was denied not so long ago under the dictators of Western Europe. They also forget that it is at present denied, in a greater or a lesser measure, to the majority of human kind. For the greater portion of humanity, administrative constraints prevent people from going from one country to another, from one town to another in the same country, even from one quarter to another in the same town, and so on according to the whims of authority. These constraints are enforced on whole populations or on certain groups for political, religious, or racial considerations. Apartheid, in its evil theory and its brutal practice, is an outstanding but by no means a unique example of such constraints.

Freedom for the body to move is indeed the most elementary right of the person. If it is not recognized and respected without condition (apart from proper legal and judicial process, which is reviewed under other headings) there is little purpose in further examining the content of freedom and other human values. Whatever the aim of authority in denying this essential freedom, it must be an unreasonable or an immoral aim because it rejects a basic premise of society. The often attempted justification that the rights of some are curtailed so that the rights of others may be better protected, that freedom is withheld today in order to build a better society where it will be upheld tomorrow, is a fallacy in theory and a deception in practice. If the means contradict the ends, the ends are lost. The most enlightened must be concerned to detect and to denounce any infringements of this most simple of human rights.

Next in logical sequence come freedom of thought and freedom of expression. They have been denied, and they still are denied in the greater part of the world for reasons of politics or religion. Christian churches denied the liberty to think differently from their doctrines and people were tortured and burnt at the stake for what could be proved or presumed of their thoughts. Heretics to communism are 'liquidated' in Russia and 'purged' in China. Many, very many lesser luminaries than Stalin and Mao Tse Tung do their best to follow their example. In the more rabid dictatorial states, persons whose thinking is suspected to be out of line with the current official doctrine are stripped of their dignity and despoiled of their livelihood, when they are not deprived of their lives. In the less rabid, freedom of expression only is denied and people are allowed to keep their thoughts in their heads. In the advanced countries of the North Atlantic, Australasia and Japan, liberty of thought and expression is still a reality.[56] But there the danger lies in that it is taken too much for granted.

Freedom of action has a wider and less precise content. It applies to action directed towards the government of society (political activity) and towards personal aims in society (economic, social, cultural). The limits of this freedom differ from country to country, and from one sphere of activity to another. Political action is more controlled here, while economic activity is less free there. In the democratic countries individual action and initiative are the most free, within the limits of laws more concerned to ensure that the freedom of each individual does not encroach on the freedom of the others, than to enforce the supremacy of the state. In many of the other countries, whether for political or economic reasons (and the two are not easily separable), individual action and initiative are confined within such narrow limits as to make the recognition of freedom a deliberate deception.

Political freedom does exist in the democratic system of government of the rich countries, with its corollaries of economic and cultural liberty. With the exception of India, it is curtailed or denied in the rest of the world, together with economic and cultural freedom. Independence movements are plentiful, and this is good, but they seldom bring freedom to the individual. Despite the current depreciation of key-words, due as much to loose thinking as to deliberate distortion, democracy still has meaning and content for people who think. Despite the fancy of totalitarian governments to call themselves democratic, democracy still means that each individual enjoys the right to express his free opinion on the policies of his country, to co-operate in appointing legislators and administrators at various levels, even to decry the form of government and to call for its change.[57]

Democracy still means all this, but overpopulation and advancing technique threaten to deprive it of its substance, which is freedom, and to restrict its scope in the future. In the poor countries, the widening gap between population and resources encourages the emergence of dictatorial governments to enforce the discipline of want and to attempt to hasten economic growth. In the rich countries, the confusion of social ends tends to empty the human values of content and to reduce the worth and the desirability of freedom. The following objections to freedom are often brought forward in the advanced countries, and they are more threatening than the actual denials of freedom in the countries under totalitarian rule or facing hunger and famine. For if democracy is weakened and freedom depreciated in the advanced countries, there will be no example left to follow. The others will have no hope, within any foreseeable future, of effectively affirming as social ends freedom and the other human values.

A. *Information.* Those who would run down freedom because it thwarts their deterministic views or because they have lost their faith in men, say that free will does not exist and that free choice is an illusion: 'Either a person is well informed, so that there is only one reasonable issue for him to choose, or he is badly informed, and he cannot make a meaningful choice.' The first half of the argument is false, for choices do not depend only on material factors, which may be determined by correct information, but also on moral or affective factors; these compete with the material factors to fix the priorities on which choices are based, so that more than one reasonable decision may be reached for any question. The second half of the argument, however, carries weight: the problems of society have become more complex and they are hard to grasp without sufficient information. Increasing technicality of public affairs (in economy, finance, administration, defence) and even private enterprise makes it difficult for insufficiently informed persons to form a considered opinion and to make a meaningful choice.

This is a serious difficulty. It must be overcome if real democracy is to be maintained, if public opinion is to share in shaping the future, if planning for the future is to respect the human values. This is the principal point at which increasing technicality touches democratic government, and at which human values must be asserted in shaping a desirable future. Permanent two-way channels of information must be maintained between specialists and technicians (including the administration) on one hand and public opinion (including the elected representatives of the nation) on the other hand. Public opinion must be brought to understand the problems to be solved, the means proposed for solving them, and the effect that these means may have on the human values. Specialists and technicians must be kept in close contact with public opinion at all levels, so that despite their particular concern with means, they will remain in line with the ends of society. This very important point will be further examined under another heading (see pp. 185–188).

B. *Social Pressure.* Another criticism of freedom as a quality of democratic society is that an individual cannot be free in his ideas because he is constantly subjected to a stream of carefully processed solicitations that influence his thoughts and colour his opinions. As to action, he is subjected to such pressure from his social groups that he cannot act freely. 'The limitation to thought and action is obvious in totalitarian countries, but it is also considerable in the democratic countries, where it is strong enough to amount to a denial of freedom. Thus there is not so much difference in the content of freedom between dictatorial and liberal countries, except that the citizens of the latter enjoy an illusion that is denied to the subjects of a dictatorial regime.' Such is the argument, and it is expounded in free societies in order to make people less attached to their freedom by depreciating its content in their minds. It is astonishing to see it often accepted in good faith by Europeans and Americans. People who get taken in by such a specious argument would do well to visit a totalitarian country: they would soon realize the difference.

Freedom is not to preserve the individual, strong or weak, from the influence and pressure of society, which would be nonsense. Freedom is to preserve the right to dissent for those who are willing to brave the displeasure of their social groups. The dissenter who has the courage to voice his opinion is ready to suffer the inconvenience or hardship ensuing from his action. He does this as an act of faith or in the hope of gathering around him a body of opinion. Those who do not approve do their best to discourage him by influence or social censure. This is not lack of freedom. It is the normal interplay of action and reaction of human beings in society. It is the mark of a free society. While in a totalitarian country there can be no dissent, because the would-be dissenter is forcibly prevented by the government from voicing his opinion. He is put into prison or killed in order to prevent him from trying to spread his ideas. He has no way to communicate his thoughts and, in the more perfected systems, he is prevented from keeping unauthorized thoughts in his own mind. He cannot even be a martyr as witness to his cause, because his would be an unknown sacrifice.

There is indeed no lack of freedom in a democratic society, such as that of the United States, but there exists a tendency for conformity in the individual and passivity in the social group, though not much more than in most other nations. This tendency is encouraged by some aspects of behavioural science and social engineering (and the mass media) to condition individuals to become well-adjusted units of the social machine. This is a dangerous trend (it is mentioned in several parts of this essay) but there is no common measure between it and the denial of freedom in a totalitarian system. In a democratic society you can still dissent at your risk, and the risk is not so great. Dissent in the United States against government policy in the Vietnam war is an outstanding instance of democratic freedom. However painful the division that it underlines, however perilous the lack of consensus, the expression of this dissent is a high example of a working democracy. Under a totalitarian regime you cannot dissent at all, unless you are a remarkably courageous and deeply motivated person. And as for the technicist society under construction, it tries to make all sides agree by conditioning off and rubbing away any desire to dissent!

c. *Education.* The formation of character and attitude by education is sometimes brought forward as proof that the idea of freedom is illusory: 'A human being is what his family and his school (or his lack of schooling) have made him. If he had been born in another social environment, if his parents had a different social position, if their religious or philosophical outlook had been otherwise, he would not be the same person, and the exercise of his so-called freedom would have led him to react in other ways to the events and problems of his life. Thus there can be no real freedom because everyone's character is shaped by environment and education (not to mention heredity)'. The mistake here is to draw unjustified conclusions from the fact that a person's character and outlook naturally have to be moulded by factors over which he or she had little or no control; to suggest that men and women, because they have to be educated to adulthood, become totally conditioned, so that they are unfree in their actions and incapable of changing their ideas or correcting their character through the exercise of awareness and will. On the contrary, it is only from education that men and women may acquire the independence of mind, the resilience of character and the self-reliance required for them to become responsible members of a free and open society, and the conclusion must be that more and especially better education is needed to ensure the survival and development of freedom together with the other fundamental values.

This subject is debated since men began to puzzle out the riddles they put to themselves, and it has become stale and over-argued. Suffice it here to add that to deny free-will because of education is to give denial to will itself, as there is no sense in a will that has no conscious choice, and there is no conscious choice without education. It is to repudiate a society based on the concerted wills of individual human beings. The very foundation of civilization would thus be inexistent. . . . However, it must be realized that this much-used argument takes on a new cogency with the present trend towards 'mass civilization'. This regrettable but fashionable contradiction in terms indicates a movement that could gain momentum. Ever in-creasing multitudes of human beings in an increasingly overcrowded, organized and technicized society do indeed threaten the content if not the principle of freedom, the substance if not the appearance of liberty. This threat is the great challenge to education of youth and information of public opinion in the coming years.

D. *Planning.* Another objection to the reality of freedom is the seeming contradiction between liberty of choice for the individual and planning for society. 'The more complex a society becomes, the more planning is needed for it to survive and improve. As this planning is directly compelling for every person's life, it reduces the scope of individual choice. Freedom to act becomes limited by the limitation of the options that are open. The individual is coerced to conform to the plan without which society cannot survive. The idea of freedom thus loses its meaning and the reality of freedom is no longer there.' In the sense of a theoretical or logical negation of freedom, this argument is futile. In a democratic society planning is a concerted effort based on values (priorities and choices) that are more or less consensual. To suggest that if men want to be really free they should avoid social planning, is to suggest that freedom belongs only to beasts that have no thought of the next hour. Neither anarchy nor haphazardness are freedom. The liberty lies in the planning, in making deliberate and explicit choices of ends and means, and in the revisal of plans and institutions according to changing circumstances. Planning is an expression of freedom, an affirmation of liberty against chaos and disorder as much as against necessity and determination. There is no contradiction involved in asking for better planning and more freedom at the same time. Planning for freedom[58] is not a vain expression: it is a proper and a practical design for democratic society.

But in the sense of a factual reduction of the content of freedom, it must be recognized that present political and economic trends all over the world give weight to this argument also. The reduction could be the result of four factors, separately or in combination, that are often touched upon in this book and may briefly be repeated here: (a) Poverty and the threat of famine in a great many countries call for more coercion in planning for equality in distribution, drastic birth control, and a balance between consumption and saving for investment. (b) The increasingly complex organization required to supply the material needs and to administer the social relations of crowded masses of human beings must reduce the scope of freedom for individuals. (c) Totalitarian rule imposes plans that are not the result of concerted choice, that are directed towards ends often far removed from the fundamental values and from the people's desires, and that are, moreover, detailed and coercive to a degree that is not required for planning in a democratic society. (d) In the advanced nations, the near abdication of humanists and politicians before the so-called imperatives of science and necessities of technique may insensibly take the essential choices out of the hands of the people, so that basic options for the future will be taken in specialized state organizations, with little reference to the public's opinion on what ends and means are desirable.

The contradictory promises and ambiguous position of the totalitarian approach to social planning were closely detailed and accurately exposed by F. A. Hayek in *The Road to Serfdom* (1944). This is still a relevant analysis of an always present threat to the human values. The road to serfdom is not a straight highway where the unwelcome end may be sighted from afar, but a winding and devious path with tempting halts on the way, so that the end of the journey is hidden from all but the most perceptive and the most aware of fundamentals. The majority realize that they have travelled the wrong road only when the last fork is behind them and it is too late to take another road. D. T. Bazelon in *The Paper Economy* published nearly twenty years later, defines the necessary role of a strong democratic government for preserving freedom. The main problem is that of ensuring a suitable measure of efficiency in organization without weakening the meaning and depleting the content of liberty. To combine freedom with planning and democracy with complex organization is not an impossible feat, as radicals of both left and right are wont to say, though it entails a balance that becomes harder to keep with overpopulation and overcrowding.

E. *Too Much Freedom?* The same radicals, progressive revolutionaries and diehard conservatives, think that freedom in the Western nations has not been entirely beneficial or, at least, that there has been too much of it. The radical left claims that too much freedom led to a take-over by the ruling classes and to alienation of the people as they are held in bondage by the Establishment. The radical right claims that too much freedom led to erosion of social discipline, spread of revolutionary disorder, and decadence of society. Though far apart in their premises and their aims, both extremes appear to agree on their means, which are violent and do not include the operation of democratic freedoms. For both, liberalism in any form has become a dirty word. The New Left is anxious to curtail freedom (of thought, of expression, of action) so as to set up their new order that they promise will make everyone happy in his or her appointed place; and the 'Old Right' is also anxious to curtail the same freedoms so as to revive their old order which they say made everyone happy by keeping them in their appointed places.

The fallacy of both contentions should be obvious. The disadvantages of the present structures in the advanced nations, the real threats for the future do not derive from too much freedom, but from a fading understanding of what freedom entails in rights and duties and a mounting denial of the fundamental values. With the resulting reduction in stature of the individual comes the alienation and the revolt that arouse the claims of radicals (the demands of revolutionaries and the counter-demands of conservatives) and their contestation of freedom as a fundamental principle of civilized society. The former are ready to sacrifice freedom in order to ensure equality and justice and their idea of human dignity, while the latter are disposed to make the same sacrifice in order to ensure the social discipline which they believe to be the main content of civilization. This is yet another instance of the confusion arising from dimmed awareness of fundamentals.

F. *Totalitarian Freedom.* Totalitarian regimes pervert the meaning of freedom in order to retain the emotional appeal of a hallowed word and use it for their aims. So they speak of freedom to follow one's destiny, of man's liberty to help the historical trend and live freely in it (or oppose it and perish). They say that 'freedom consists not in doing what one wants to do, but in doing what is right'. They explain that freedom of thought is only consciousness of necessity and reason, that social consciousness of necessity secures freedom of action, that consciousness of the communist (or fascist) path to liberty leads to an understanding of the 'positive' nature of freedom. They extol the individual's free choice to be absorbed into the collectivity, so that by relinquishing his freedom in its freedom he becomes more free. Freedom to do what one wants to do or to obtain what one desires is achieved through society, so the deeper we are incorporated in social organization the freer we become. The more advanced economic production becomes, the freer man will be of drudgery, therefore the more he is adjusted to technological requirements of production the more liberty he will have. . . .

There are endless ways of saying that freedom is not freedom, and that totalitarian oppression or technological conditioning are in reality freedom. The same sort of perversion is carried on for the concepts of justice and of dignity. It would be tedious to enumerate the preposterous variations that are made on these themes in order to pervert the simple and fundamental values of civilized society. They appear manifestly false to persons who have trained themselves to go for fundamentals, but they have great attraction for many people, even in the advanced countries. They have not lacked potent support, from French revolutionaries who were blinded by their passion for Reason, from German thinkers who were hypnotized by the simplicity of autocratic government, and even from Anglo-American pragmatists who sought to ensure efficient government with technological advance. Their arguments have had more influence than is generally supposed, especially among young people, and it must be the duty of political and cultural leadership in democratic countries to expose the superficial thinking that accepts such perversions.

G. *Statistical Prediction.* A mathematical objection to the reality of freedom is often thoughtlessly put forward, based on the high degree of exactness attained by statistical forecasts. Life insurance could not be operated if it could not depend on the accuracy of forecasts of births, deaths, accidents, incidence of disease and other vital statistics. Transport companies, restaurants and other caterers to the public must estimate the number of people that they are expected to serve at given hours, on given days. Gallup polls are sometimes accurate as forecasts of social trends and political decisions. 'There is, therefore, no freedom because the supposed liberty of individuals to choose does not destroy the accuracy of the forecast that a certain proportion of individuals will act in one way and another proportion in another way. You are thus pursuing a phantom, and human beings remain determined in their actions.' The answer is of course that statistical prediction never applies to an individual but only to a number of individuals: the greater that number, the greater the accuracy of the prediction, because the greater number leaves more room for variations of individual choice without invalidating the prediction. Statistically and mathematically, each individual remains unpredictable and undetermined.

H. *The Metaphysical Objection.* Finally there is the metaphysical difficulty of reconciling freedom with the foreknowledge of God: 'If every event and every act is known beforehand, where can liberty of choice and freedom of will find place?' This question, which worries many people, is related but not identical to that of predestination, which is determinism in the religious perspective. Without presuming to deal with this difficult problem which exceeds the frame of this discourse and which, moreover, has not been satisfactorily solved since men started meditating on its implications, it may be remarked that the spirit of fatalism latent in this argument cannot destroy the experience of liberty of choice and the reality of freedom of action. Philosophically, it can be shown that fore-known does not mean fore-ordained. And for those who are not adverse to extracting metaphysical arguments from physical science, the theme of relativity may help them to conceive the notion of god-like knowledge transcending the dimension of time as we experience it without weakening the meaning of freedom and the reality of free will.

*   *   *

Such are the answers to some of the main objections against the possibility or desirability of real freedom for human beings. But the threats to freedom (as well as to the other human values) arising out of overpopulation and overcrowding remain unanswered. These threats are real, and the content of freedom must inevitably be reduced if they are not averted. However free a society may be, the freedom of one is restricted by the freedom of others. If we are so densely packed that I cannot extend my arm without poking you in the eye, I have no right to extend my arm. The day could come when automobiles will be divided into odds and evens, and only allowed to take the road on alternate days; or when staggered hours will be imposed on the inhabitants of large cities to take their leisure in parks or streets. The subway at rush hours as a permanent way of life is one possible future. As an individual becomes more restricted in movement and action by the growing number of other individuals, his possibilities for self-expression must be reduced. The scope for initiative and self-reliance must be diminished. Man in society always had to strike a mean between solitude and gregariousness, because both are necessary for human beings. Now, gregariousness is practically obligated, and solitude (with its corollaries of privacy and quiet, aloneness not loneliness) may become impossible to obtain. However strongly and steadfastly a society is committed to uphold the human values, these must surely be reduced in content as the point of optimum population is passed and overcrowding becomes too great.

2. JUSTICE

Like freedom, justice is a general concept that must be defined in relation to the needs of the person and to the functions of society. In relation to the person, it means being treated according to one's rights and one's deserts; in relation to society, it is generally understood as equality in opportunity and treatment between its members. Justice is more of a relative value than freedom, but the feeling for justice is deeply ingrained in every human being, deeper perhaps than any other feeling. Nothing is more intolerable than an ill or a favour that is not shared by all; no insult is more galling than to be called unjust. If the human values are to be squeezed out by over-population or rejected by the technicist trend, justice will be the last to go. In these pages, we speak of social justice which—like freedom —is always respected in word but often denied in deed.

The foremost meaning of social justice is equality of opportunity and equality of treatment. Human beings are not born equal in their characters and their capacities, and it is not the role of society to make them equal, but to help each to develop to best advantage his or her mental capacities, to provide them with equal opportunities and equal treatment, and to let them go their ways according to their respective will, energy and intelligence. Equality of opportunity entails that each individual be given the same facilities for schooling, the same services for health, the same openings for livelihood. Equality of treatment implies that individuals rendering the same services be granted the same rewards, that there be no discrimination in benefits or punishment because of differences in race, sex, creed, or position. Collectivist theory has gone further than this, in an egalitarian urge that is one of the prime motives of totalitarian rule, but in no country and no age—or, at least, in no modern country—has a collectivist organization of society been successful as compared to democratic forms of government. The 'disastrous character of egalitarianism' and the necessity to 'eliminate egalitarian tendencies' were stressed in the remarkable document mentioned in Part I, the *Action Program* of the Czechoslovak Communist Party.

Equality of opportunity and treatment are the necessary basis but not the whole content of social justice. Solidarity between human beings is also a condition of justice, and society must ensure and regulate its operation. Individuals incapacitated by age, illness or accident cannot benefit from the opportunities provided for all. Children, old people and those who are diseased or deficient must be supported by family and society in the name of solidarity, if not of brotherhood and charity. Their material needs must be supplied and their dignity upheld. The scope of solidarity is wide and it can cover, by means of social security measures, practically every contingency of life. In the second third of this century, solidarity stepped over national boundaries and there is a start in social security on the international scale. Financial and technical assistance from some nations to other nations is an encouraging development and a real improvement in human relations. It is still rudimentary, and we shall see under another heading that it must now be considerably extended.

Finally, for social justice to be effective there is another condition to be realized: granted that we have equality and solidarity, but at what level? The notion of quality intervenes here. Equality and solidarity have little content if they are not set at a suitable level. If the level were irrelevant, famine for all and slavery for all could also be social justice. They would be a tragic parody of justice. Therefore, social justice also entails that a decent standard of living be assured and—above everything—that the other fundamental values be respected. At present, there is one factor which could make social justice impossible to achieve or to maintain: the growth of population to the point of intolerable density would make an adequate standard of living unattainable, and it would absolutely reduce the quality of life and the effective content of the human values. Equality in want will then be the justice of overpopulation, as equality in servitude is the justice of totalitarian rule. It is said that there will be more justice than freedom in a technicist society. That would be true if justice were equality and nothing more, but in truth there will be neither freedom nor justice.

3. DIGNITY

Dignity of the human person derives from its autonomy and uniqueness, and from the respect each person owes to others and demands from them. The sense of dignity has a wide range of application within the individual himself and in his relations with other individuals. Self-respect is the first condition of respect for other and from others; it entails many virtues that are required for improvement of body and mind, and many conditions that are required for civilized society. Here, we speak of dignity only in the relations of individuals with society. Political, administrative, and judicial institutions must recognize explicitly the fundamental dignity of every man and woman, regardless of race or creed, colour or culture. Without this recognition, in principle and in practice, savagery and barbarity come to stay however polished the procedure may be and well written the laws and regulations. 'A true society is sustained by the sense of human dignity. . . . A society holds together by the respect which man gives to man.'[59]

A human being, whatever his or her place in some social scale, however weak or defenceless, however morally or physically degraded, must not be made to suffer indignity of mind or body. The person may not be humiliated in a civilized society (but this does not mean that just punishment for evil doing must not be enforced). Neither mind nor body may be maimed or enslaved, whether it be by whips, drugs or electronics. Only the most brutish of men takes pleasure in humiliating another man, in exposing the weakness of his body or the infirmity of his mind. Among so many examples of disgrace and infamy in ancient and modern times, the excesses of brown-shirted, black-booted, or red-flagged militia must remain a distasteful but a salutary object of meditation for all who are concerned with human values. In what they did, they humiliated all mankind. Of all the values that totalitarian government rejects, it is most intolerant of human dignity. Any who presume to preserve some dignity, to show some independence in thought or act, are enemies of the state. They are made to grovel publicly, to deny and abase themselves under pain of death or worse for themselves and their families. Or else they may be proclaimed insane and interned in a madhouse, there to receive proper scientific treatment to cure their delusion of dignity by 'special psychiatry' and appropriate drugs.

In the advanced nations of the West, inside their own countries, dignity and integrity of the individual are respected, not completely to be sure, but more than at any other time or place. This must be recognized as the lesson and the principal virtue of the Western culture. But it must not be taken for granted, because it is a recent flowering. Rather must it be consciously defended, because it is now threatened by changes in attitude and perspective due to changing circumstances. Already, many among the best of those who think and act are on the way to denying the basic principle of the autonomy, the worth and the dignity of the human person. Already there is some reduction of the content, some debasement of the quality of this essential value, that is part of the foundation and the heritage of Western civilization.

Believers in karma or Nemesis may see this threat as retribution for the denials of human values that Europeans and Americans have so often inflicted on other nations. People of the West rarely conceded to others the dignity which they recognized between themselves. The slave markets of Liverpool and Saint Malo, of Savannah and New Orleans, the degradation of Africans and American Indians, the excesses of colonial rapacity, all these have left deep-seated scars. The best, the only reparation that the West can make is to recognize—in word and deed—the solidarity of all human beings based on their equal and essential dignity regardless of race or creed, power or weakness. By so doing, people of the advanced countries will be stronger to defend their own dignity. They will be more capable of preserving, in their own affluent communities, the respect for human values that is their only real claim to the respect of the rest of the world.

4. QUALITY

To strive for quality is human, and only human. The sense for quality is related to consciousness and creativeness, both of which are essentially human attributes. Only a conscious mind can imagine and compare, and then endeavour to achieve the best of thought or action; and without the notion of quality, creativeness would be a sterile urge. Quality gives tone and colour to every aspect of human activity, whether of the mind or of the body, whether in the in-dividual or the social sphere. Artisans and artists, writers and poets, athletes, scientists, politicians and administrators, all try to excel in their craft or art unless their manhood and their vitality have dried up within them. The reward of excellence is more in self-fulfilment than in material benefit. The satisfaction of achieving something of a difficult character or superior quality is perhaps the purest reward that a human being can claim and obtain. Unhappy are those who live in a society that gives them little opportunity to strive for such a reward in their respective fields of work.

As a value—more exactly, as a measure of value—quality becomes more desirable and more attainable as education is improved, culture refined and civilization enriched with a heritage of achievements. Primitive people have a strong sense for justice within the frame of their social order, as well as an ingrained sense of personal dignity; but the sense for quality develops only with maturity, and with it comes the desire for perfection, the effort to do one's best, to attain the utmost that one can reach and then, after that, to surpass oneself if possible. Civilizations differ by the levels of achievement that they reach in their social order, in arts and letters, in the place of human values in their individual and social attitude: quality is the measure of such levels.

Striving for quality means that each action one wills and each object one makes must be as near to perfection as conscious effort can achieve. The machine will do or make things very well indeed, but it will do or make them identically well, and it will never surpass itself. We are justifiably proud of our machines but, as soon as the accent is put on aesthetic or moral excellence, the handmade article and the unrepetitive act are at a premium. The object may not be more beautiful, it may be less perfect, but it has an individual character because it is individually made. Its value lies in this individual character as much as in any other of its features. It has an identity. A conscious effort has gone into it, and this the machine cannot do. The same remark naturally applies when services are rendered by machines or by machine-like organizations: they are less satisfactory because an individual human contact and an individual human effort are lacking. This is why most thoughtful and imaginative persons have a sense of unease, even of fear, when machines are not only used for quantity production (which is what they do best) but are promoted to co-operate in value estimates for systems designing and social engineering. Efficiency is the sole 'value' of the machine, and it is not a human value. The sense for quality is a human value, and it is alien to the machine. It could become alien to a technicized society, as it is alien in many ways to totalitarian society.

For this brief definition in the context of present problems, we are mainly interested to examine the idea of quality in relation to individuals in society and in relation to social ends. In this relation, quality can be considered as the *degree* or the *level* of freedom, of justice, of respect for human beings. The quality of life expresses something very real in material, in moral, in spiritual endeavour. It is the *measure* of the opportunities provided by society to fulfil its ends, the means by which it ensures the satisfaction of its individual members, the development of their physical, their intellectual, and their affective capacities.

5. THE FIELDS OF APPLICATION

Human values as social ends have been considered under the four appellations of freedom, justice, dignity, quality, and an attempt has been made to define their meaning and describe their content in the present juncture of human affairs. They could have been disposed otherwise, and other titles could perhaps have been included. The subject is vast, as it comprises no less than the whole compass of human activity, and analysis requires differentiation, but the view must remain whole. Roots and branches may usefully be considered separately, but it is the tree that is important. The human values are complementary, and it is a frequent and a dangerous fallacy to suppose that some can exist without the others; that justice can abide without freedom, or freedom without justice; that independence of the nation can make up for enslavement of the citizen; that the honour of the state can compensate the individual for his loss of dignity; that quality is only a condiment, and not a necessary ingredient without which the broth has no nourishment.

There may come a time—quite soon if there is no reaction against present trends—when it will be blasphemy to assert human values and personal worth; when it will be a crime reproved by society and punished by law to speak of individual rights and dignity as things apart and sometimes opposed to the 'rights' and the 'dignity' of a community. It is already a crime in many countries, and human rights are now denied to a large portion of the human race. Even in the democratic nations, it begins to be considered as 'reactionary' to oppose measures proposed for public interest or common good if the argument invoked is that they violate individual rights. It would not now need very much, only more unawareness and unconcern in the advanced countries, for the fundamental values to be further depreciated, to the point where Western civilization in all but technological pride will have ceased to be. After all, World War II could have ended otherwise, with dire results for humanity. What it was fortunately not able to accomplish, the present intellectual, moral and social trends may yet achieve more surely.

Readers will ask, 'But how can Freedom and Justice, Dignity and Quality—the human or fundamental values as you call them—be forgotten or ignored or denied when they are on everybody's lips, invoked by all people in all countries?' Yes indeed, they are on everybody's lips, but they do not inspire everybody's minds and hearts. The link between principle and application is weakened; what is invoked in word is often denied in deed. Governments ignore these principles, in the name of sovereignty or for reasons of state. Corporations and individuals compromise with them for expediency or efficiency or any one of the bad reasons that go under the name of necessity. Most of us, in private life or public office, have connived at some exception to these rules, some debasement of these values, because we believed that our ends—which were good—justified our means. Through compromise and weakness, unclear thought and unthought action, there is a reduction of content of fundamental principles and it is not easy to recharge them with the power that will strike a spark in our minds when they are invoked. We find it hard to realize that these apparently overfamiliar ideas are still the foundation of civilization, upon which everything stands and without which everything falls.

Others will say, 'Granted that men seldom live up to their principles, what's new in this and when was it otherwise?' What is new is that at no time in the history of Western civilization have the principles elaborated over three thousand years of pain and effort been subjected to such assaults as since the start of the present century. The assaults come from three fronts, and they were reviewed in Part One. Philosophical constructions that deny freedom in the name of determinism, and justice in the name of necessity; political theories that deny individual values by putting state or race above individuals; technological progress that forms an outlook divorced from the human values; these varied influences are squeezing the fundamental values—which are exclusively spiritual and moral concepts—out of the advanced societies. This is why compromises and exceptions are more dangerous now, in the advanced countries, than they were in previous times when there were the actions of autocratic rulers but, at least, no political and technological systems to impugn the absolute character of the human values.

What is the defence against the pressures of the present crisis? How can the human values become really respected in political and administrative organization, in education and social services, in scientific research and technological application? Human values and social ends are not always taken into consideration in studies slanted towards the future on historical, political, economic, social, educational and other subjects, *and they are seldom the focus of attention.* Present trends have had a deeper influence on thinkers and writers than is commonly realized, and the time has come for a vigorous reaction.[60] The need is now for thought more independent of present trends and imagination less confined by present pressures. Whatever the evolution of Western culture and Western civilization may be, whatever the form that European and American societies will take before the end of this century, let it be with open eyes. If human values are to be depreciated, perhaps lost, let it not be because they went by default, because the required concern was not aroused. If human values are to be affirmed against the present drift, this will be achieved only through the consensus that it is possible to reach in a democratic society. Nothing less than complete consciousness and general awareness is worthy of an advanced and still free society.

*   *   *

The following headings contain an attempt to answer the challenges exposed in Part One. They come within the fields of application of the human values and they comprise some of the fundamental problems that must be the concern of all those who can influence society by thought or action.

8

Change and Technology

MEN ADVANCE in science and machines advance in efficiency, population increases in numbers and society increases in complexity, and all this is called progress. It is indeed progress according to the original sense of the word: to move forward, to advance along a path, to proceed in some direction. But progress has also come to signify improvement and betterment, maybe because it would be unbearable to think that the effort required to keep moving will not improve one's condition. And as progress necessarily entails change, so change has come to signify improvement. Change in itself, the bare fact of change is now taken as an improvement, irrespective of what is changing and of the direction in which it is changing. The lack of change thereby becomes regression and retrogradation, irrespective of what it is that remains unchanged, and of whether it is good or bad. This is partly the reason for the cult of the new and the rejection of the old, because change (therefore improvement) is expressed in what is new, and the lack of change (therefore regression) is evidenced in what is old.

And, to follow the immature argument a little further, what is new is therefore good because it is new, and what is old is presumed to be bad because it is old. By a natural transition, this is transposed from the field of material objects (where it is often justified) to that of social institutions and traditions (where it is sometimes justified) and even to the fundamental values (for which it is never justified). These values must also have decayed and gone bad because they too are old. They have become obsolete together with last year's model and unfashionable like last year's hem-line. So, say uncultured revolutionaries and superficial radicals in their presumptuous ignorance, well meaning as they may be, let us change it all, make a clean sweep of everything and pull down all institutions and traditions, destroying far and deep so that we may begin again at zero and start at scratch, building anew on empty ground and clean foundations.[61] Small wonder, then, that their new buildings are rickety and unsafe and unlovely! This siren call of the new is primarily that of technological progress permeating all elements of personal and social life. It is a potent factor for rejection of fundamental values and the consequent confusion of ends and means.

What led to the notion that progress and change must automatically bring improvement? How did such confusion take hold of social thinking? What are the results of change and newness being taken as good in themselves? These questions touch the mainspring of Western culture. They concern the rupture of continuity, the cleavage of old and new that threatens to discard the heritage of social tradition and to break-up the moral and intellectual legacy of civilization. Clear thinking on these questions would help to recreate consciousness and awareness, to recapture the essential importance of the human values, and to reaffirm their necessity, relevance, and validity as the sole ends of civilized society.

I. PROGRESS OR IMPROVEMENT

The idea of progress in the accepted modern sense is not an old element of Western culture. It was born during the European Renaissance, from the marriage of laicization with science. By re-discovering the rationalistic outlook of Graeco-Roman culture, thinkers became independent of the purely religious outlook. With the laicization of intellectual activity came the possibility to think of this world not only as a vale of tears and a place of trial, but also as a field of endeavour where life may be lived in a rewarding manner apart from the claims of an after-life. The world is therefore not determined by recurring cycles or by a universal fate; it can be improved, and life can attain a fuller content and a more satisfying taste. This intellectual liberation excited a rational curiosity that promoted scientific research and speeded up technological advance. The increasingly successful technological applications of scientific discovery associated the visible forms of change with the tangible benefits of material production and accumulating wealth. The notion of continuously beneficial change was thus formed and the modern idea of progress took hold.

The idea of progress, as an evolution necessarily linked with material achievements and tangible gains, was further elaborated during the 17th and 18th centuries and it became a cardinal dogma of Western culture. It remained supreme all through the 19th century and up to World War I, and it inspired the philosophy of action that spurred Europeans and Americans to change the face of Earth. The principle of dynamic society (i.e. progressive society as opposed to the static or regressive) was understood to warrant that movement and change would naturally and automatically be directed to amelioration of the human condition. This optimistic faith began to weaken in the second third of the 20th century when, despite acceleration of change by scientific and technological advance, improvement of the human condition—especially in its spiritual and affective elements—was obviously not forthcoming. The idea of progress loses its sacred character. It becomes dimmed and uncertain. And the philosophy of action that helped Western civilization to reach the fruits of affluence now threatens to sour the expected sweetness and to debase the anticipated rewards.

There is a deep reversal of orientation from confidence to anxiety. This reversal is manifest in social studies as well as in novels and science fiction. The following illustration is taken from the books of a distinguished observer of the human scene. In *Technics and Civilization*, published in 1934, Lewis Mumford wrote: 'As social life becomes mature, the social unemployment of machines will become as marked as the present technological unemployment of men. . . . Any appreciable improvement in education and culture will reduce the amount of machinery devoted to multiplying the spurious mechanical substitutes for knowledge and experience. . . . The passive dependence on the machine which has characterized such large sections of the Western World in the past was in reality an abdication of life. Once we cultivate the arts of life directly, the proportion occupied by mechanical routine and by mechanical instruments will again diminish' (p. 426). In *The Transformations of Man*, published in 1956, he writes: 'Considering these conditions, one may doubt if any factors now known will be capable of bringing about the needed transformation of man in time to avoid the self-destruction of the human race—either by swift thermonuclear annihilation, by slow atomic pollution of air, soil and water, or by the insidious conditioning of man to post-historic compulsion. . . . A more benign alternative would call for something like a miracle. Therefore let us consider miracles. . . .' Only twenty-two years for such a reversal of outlook.

From the start the idea of progress was limited by the circumstances in which it was born. It held that improvement of the human condition would follow material advance without need for ethical purpose and restraint. The moral and spiritual qualities of society would be progressively improved by the spread of material wealth and rational education. In a very important sense, this was a determinist faith. Such high hopes appeared to be fulfilled while the driving force of the philosophy of action left little time to pause and assess the overall benefits of material affluence. But now people are realizing—as the realization is forced on them—that improvement is not inherent to change, that amelioration of the human condition does not necessarily follow material advance, that the human values are in danger of denial and rejection by progressive society, that the most brutal aggressions against human rights have been committed in the century of the greatest scientific and technological progress. The idea of progress is plainly not adapted to the present juncture. There is something wrong with it, and the time has come to redefine it in the light of past experience, present needs, and a vision of a more desirable future.

People have varied reactions to the miscarriage of the idea of progress. Some do not recognize its failure: they are willing to deny society's need for ethical aims and moral ends in order to vindicate their faith in the ultimate and absolute good of technique and material progress. Others are discouraged by the failure: they deplore the fixation on technique and material progress, and the trend to reject human values, but—whether led by romantic defeatism or Christian despair or liberal impotence—they see no way out because of their deterministic or fatalistic orientation. The majority realize failure less clearly, but they are disturbed and insecure: they need to become aware of the issues at stake. The feeling of insecurity is not due to movement and rapid change, but to the lack of conscious ends, which can only be human ends. When it is in the direction of an aim of which men are aware, change gives a sense of achievement and security, but change without aim induces helplessness and despair. To misquote another well-known saying, if we are on the way without knowing where we are heading, every turn of the road is a fearsome adventure or an unsettling change; but if we know where we are going—because that is where we want to go—the way may be arduous, but each turn marks a stage nearer to the desired end.

The anxiety that unnerves the bold and weakens the strong is due less to danger or to change than to not knowing the goal of one's activity (save the obvious and immediate necessity of providing for daily life), to living only in the present and for the present, with no vision of things to come, no desirable image of the future. It is due to being ignorant of the ends of society, of 'our own age, which often seems to be rolling over us towards goals of which we are unaware'.[62] In stress and danger, anxiety is often absent. In battle the aim is known and participants, despite the danger, often have spiritual quiet and even security in the consciousness of pursuing a known aim, which may be lacking in them at less perilous times of their lives. It is not resistance to change that makes people feel insecure, but the sense of drifting towards an unspecified and undefined country, of being carried away in a torrent of velocity without direction, of falling 'into the ugly sea of action without aim'.[63] We must be clear in our minds about the future and the sort of progress we want:

A. Progress is naturally to improve the human condition, that is, to ensure—for an ever greater proportion of men and women in ever widening and deepening scope—satisfaction and fulfilment of their physical, intellectual, and emotional capacities. Material progress (increased affluence, advanced technology) is a factor of the desired improvement, but there are other factors more deeply related to human aspirations. We now see very clearly that material progress alone, when human values are not explicitly recognized as the ends of society, tends to destroy the other factors required for improving the human condition by a balanced and harmonious development of human beings.

B. Real progress is possible. There is no determination for human beings and the societies they form. They are free to shape their future by concerted and energetic action. There is no necessity compelling them to develop in one way and not in another, no fate to direct their steps where they do not want to go. The only fate is the one men make for themselves by remaining passive and unaware.[64] To say that human beings make their own unhappy fate is another way of saying that they are the masters of their destiny on Earth because they can shape it as they will, by joining in concerted action to face the challenge of the present crisis and to come out safely from the present drift.[65]

C. Progress is not fore-ordained nor does it happen by chance. There is no assurance of progress, either in a particular case or as a general tendency, unless the proper action is taken to carry it out. Whether preference lies in movement and change or stillness and conservatism, neither the one nor the other attitude is pregnant of improvement or deterioration. Progression and regression both happen in human affairs, and nature is equally indifferent to both. One thing alone brings progress, in the sense of attaining or drawing near to desirable ends, and it is to start by knowing those ends.[66] *What do we want?* When the members of a society have the answer, things follow more easily than we think.

2. THE ATTITUDE TO TECHNIQUE

There are two main attitudes to technique and they are both unreasonable because they both proceed from an incomplete view. Both have been analysed in some detail under previous headings, but it will be useful briefly to recall them here. The first is to consider technological achievements as the sum of progress for mankind and to think that science and technology can provide all the requirements of human beings. Thus the developments of technology must all be beneficial and all other considerations must be submitted to its necessities. This attitude was prevalent but it is on the way out, because the disadvantages of unbridled technological advance have become too manifest to be ignored. The second attitude, that bids to become prevalent in its stead, is to recognize the disadvantages but to consider them as unavoidable because the progress of science and technique cannot be checked, so that it carries everything before it and crushes what it does not push out and leave on the way. From this follows that society must be adjusted to the progress of technique, not technique to society, and that human beings must be conditioned to become contented particles of the mass moved by technique.

Many observers believe that this newer attitude is setting the pattern of the future for the advanced societies. The emphasis is now on the 'system' in Western Europe no less than in America (as it is by definition under all totalitarian and collectivist regimes). This is advertised as the social principle of the future, the grand promise of the technocrats, and they can make it come true. In the view of many perceptive persons, it is starting to come true. Naturally the price is steep, but the new-style soft-spoken white-collar technocratic revolutionaries assert that the system is worth it. Old social stocks will have to be liquidated of course, not at reduced price but just written off. People afflicted with bourgeois individualism, or with a retrograde sense of their freedom and dignity, must be scrapped (gently to be sure but none the less completely) as a preparation to writing off the individual and the traditional human values in the totally organized social system of overcrowded societies. Fifty years ago the Russians plunged with inhuman violence into a liquidation of this sort, and the Chinese appear to have been engaged in a similar liquidation on a tremendous scale, with a fury and a passion that left the onlooker breathless. The same liquidation may come to be effected in the advanced countries—gradually and without violence admittedly, but with greater efficiency—by the deliberately restricted thinking of an active minority and because of supine unawareness in the majority.

Indeed, Mao's China could well become the model for all humanity in an overpopulated future. No drugs, no disorders, no sexual promiscuity, but also no variety, no independence of spirit, no creativeness of mind, no place for those who cannot be adjusted to regulation of every activity for every hour of the day. Total organization, relentless conditioning and extreme regimentation, but a fair sufficiency of food and clothing, housing and medical care, may turn out to be the very best that tomorrow can provide if no remedy is found for mounting population and aimless technology. As for less than the best that tomorrow may hold in store, it could simply be a foundering of the advanced societies, with the less advanced helplessly in tow, a breakdown of which there is warning and foretaste enough to damp the most unthinking optimism. Unless wisdom and courage come to guide our policies, the only alternative appears to be painful and degrading disintegration or no less painful but perhaps less degrading Chinese-style integration.

Now is the time for people in the advanced societies to ask themselves if they want to follow the social engineer who promises to make them happy if they submit to his conditioning; if they agree to be so well adjusted to his design for society that they will feel no stress or anxiety, nor longing for another design in which the human person and its values could have remained as the foundation of society. This question must be taken seriously, for the tempter can make good his promise; he can design society to make an inhuman use of human beings and he can condition human beings to become the inhuman units of his social machinery. Thoughtful persons want none of this design and their hope for a more desirable future is fortified by the knowledge that it is still shared by most people, and by many of the younger generation. At the present stage of population growth and technological advance, the majority of people can still—given the occasion and the information—think rationally and feel deeply about what they want their life to be and how society can make their wish come true. If I appear here to be breaking down a still open door, it is because I perceive as do many others the pressures mounting behind the door to push it shut.

There is a third attitude that proceeds from a more mature view: to look forward to continued technological progress not as an uncontrollable movement, nor—above all—as an end in itself, but as a means of improving the human condition; to plan for technique to be subordinate to the requirements of more freedom, greater justice, a better sense of human dignity, a keener regard for quality in social organization, and real concern for ecological balance and variety.

This is the reasonable and the practical attitude to maintain. We are *not* faced with the alternative of progressing towards an automated society with pre-taped human units or of reverting to barbarous primitiveness amid the ruins of a nuclear holocaust. We can on the contrary look ahead to real improvement of the human condition if the present crisis is solved by using all the resources of technology to promote the human values. The alternative before us is to make the effort to assert the human values as the ends of all social activity or to go on supine and nerveless to face the temptations of technology divorced from human values. The technicist society is not the unavoidable fate or the foregone conclusion that some would have us believe. It is to despair too soon and to put human beings too low, to picture them as necessarily conditioned by their mechanical and their electrical inventions. Only by carelessness and lack of energy do we turn our mindless slaves into unheeding masters.[67] We make of technique an idol when we accept to make the unnecessary sacrifice of our human tradition.

3. THE WAY AHEAD

We should be proud of man's progress in science and technique and we can confidently expect continued advance in this immense field of human endeavour as long as nature has secrets to give up and resources to offer. But we should be more proud of the less spectacular, less successful, and infinitely more difficult advance towards human improvement. Technological progress and scientific discovery are a series of ascending steps, while human improvement is a succession of ups and downs with a very slow general upward trend. The level of science and technology is equalized all over the world in a relatively short time, but not the gains in human values. The progress and rewards of freedom in the Western countries have coincided with the spread of totalitarian systems in other countries; humane concern for suffering, as exemplified in Red Cross development, grows together with the destructiveness of war; as human rights are generalized in principle, they are more brutally trodden down in various parts of the world; improvement in social aid and security comes at the same time as the threat of a mechanized organization of society. 'We live in an age that is witnessing new heights of social justice and new depths of social degradation.'[68] But slow as it has been and threatened as it is now, the improvement in human values remains the basic factor of human progress. What is important in the present juncture is not so much that an equal concern for the human values be distributed at the same level all over the world, as that there remain some nations (mainly in the smaller countries of Western Europe) where this level is the highest ever reached.

But an adverse tide is rising. Its forms are varied but they all tend to submerge the individual, to deny his absolute worth and dignity because of demographic, economic, technological and ideological pressures. Demographically, it becomes difficult to distinguish the individual in overcrowded masses and costly to give him individual care. Economically, force is considered necessary in the poor countries to ensure justice in want and equality in poverty, and to impose the hard work, the discipline and the sacrifices required for development. Technologically, individual values tend to be set aside in the systematic and quantitative operation of mechanical and electronic so-called extensions of man. And ideological totalitarianism receives strong support for overpopulation, general poverty, and technological progress. The tide is flowing strong and the islands of democracy and freedom are surrounded by the rising waters. Both from the inside and the outside, the pressures are mounting; much care and forethought are required to withstand them. As long as these islands do not subside into the waters, as long as the nations concerned do not fall from their level, they stand as witness to what society can achieve.

The free and open societies are the holders of a priceless tradition, the inheritors of the Mediterranean cultures, of Egypt, Greece, Palestine, Rome and Europe. The values of Western civilization are the culmination of a long process of development, religious and philosophical, political and legal, economic and technical. But it is a recent culmination. The human values have but lately attained fullness and generality. The glory of Greece must be dimmed by the exposure or burial alive of new-born daughters, by acceptance of slavery as a natural institution of society, by relegation of women— of one-half of humanity—to an inferior status. Torture as a legal and

F   161

judicial procedure for establishing guilt or innocence, truth or false-hood, was applied in Europe until near the end of the 18th century. Witch burning flourished in the New World as late as in the Old, and it is not much over one hundred years since slavery was finally abolished. Colonialism has not yet been entirely swept away. Religious fanaticism and race prejudice are still very much alive. Equality of opportunity for all is a general rule but not yet a general fact. Rank poverty for sizeable minorities still mars the image of some affluent nations. The social, legal, and political handicaps of women were lifted as late as the 20th century. Only in the course of the last few generations have the perennial values of freedom and justice, dignity and quality been established in principle as absolutely good and right for all human beings without distinction of race or sex, strength or weakness, wealth or poverty.

Thus the roots of Western culture go deep, but its present stage is a recent flowering, brought out of brutal and bloody contests for religious, political and economic power, which took a toll of death and suffering perhaps unequalled in any other culture. Now, in the sense of human rights and social principles, Western civilization—despite its shortcomings and tragic weaknesses—is the highest form of social organization in mankind's career, but it is still fragile and easy to distort. The human values have hardly attained their full content, in principle if not in practice, and they are already threatened with denial and rejection. Nothing can be taken for granted and assured, least of all social institutions, which are vulnerable as life itself. Maybe the expression of a flowering, often used in these pages, is well chosen. The human values have to be tended and protected, or they will grow dry and wither away. If they do, they will not flower again until the factors of aimless technology and mounting population are eliminated or superseded. The gardeners are the present leaders of thought and action. Should they neglect their trust, should they become confused by the problems of an increasingly unstable society, there will be none to take their place.

The human race may still be, as some think, at the very start of a career that will eventually take it to hitherto undreamed of heights of physical control and mental power; or, as pessimistic observers are wont to say, it could be under the shadow of death or a return

to primitive beginnings. Nobody has the answer to such specula-
tion, but what is certain is that human beings are now in a crisis
compounded of many crises (spiritual and intellectual, social and
political, demographic and ecological) the outcome of which may
well decide which of the two conjectures will be realized. Whether
the crisis is resolved in some acceptable solution or whether its
problems will prove too hard for human intelligence and will, it
must in any case involve some extremely difficult choices along the
road to salvation or to perdition. It will also involve measures that
will appear unbearably harsh. Only constant awareness of the
human values and their implications, only real understanding of the
fundamental priorities based upon those values, will enable us wisely
to make the difficult choices that lie ahead and bravely to find the
determination to see them through.

In the first part of this book it was stated that the challenge
facing humanity is probably greater today than at any time past, and
the fifth reason given was that the penalty for failure to resolve the
present crisis will be more intolerable than for any previous failure,
while the reward of success will be more precious than it has ever
been. With the advance of science and technology, everything becomes possible, continued ascent or a catastrophic fall.[69] The
Western nations now stand higher in human achievement than any
other people and they set the pace for all others, but they are as on
a narrow ledge on the side of a precipitous mountain, and continued
advance depends on keeping the balance between human values and
technique, between the human species and the rest of the ecosphere.
It is now that the balance is most threatened. With the resolution to
uphold the human values as the only ends of society and to subordinate technology to those ends, real improvement of the human
condition can be won. Without this resolution, the new fatalism must
hold sway over the future, and the forecasts of discouraged humanists and determinist technocrats must come true for all people on
this planet.

*　　*　　*

Revolution is on everybody's lips and everything is supposed to be
in revolution. Here we have the technological revolution and there

the social, without omitting the sex revolution, the green revolution, and the Jesus revolution. In the inflated parlance of these days, every change is a revolution. In fact, there is a real revolutionary situation, but misuse of the word revolution encourages two attitudes both of which are destructive, that of violence (nothing can be usefully changed without coercion and destruction) and that of extremism (reforms are no good and radical re-structuring of society is needed). The danger is in the accent that is thus put on revolution *per se* with little or no thought for the principles and priorities that must guide the revolution; no care for the material and moral losses brought about by violence and destruction; no concern for the material insufficiencies which unless remedied will prevent any improvement; no regard for the new social structure that is to replace the present one.

At the Exploratory Conference on Technology, Faith and the Future of Man, held by the World Council of Churches at Geneva in 1970, the need for 'a second ethical revolution' was discussed.[70] The necessary revisal of ethics may be called a revolution if it is wished to stress the urgency, the depth and the scope of the problems to be solved; but this cannot entail that the basic premises should also be revised in order to substantiate the idea of a revolution. Rather should it be made clear that the aim of a second ethical revolution is to solve the new problems arising from rapid technological and demographic change by a *return* to awareness and understanding of the fundamental priorities; not a new morality, but a restoration of morality. At the same conference, the question 'what are human ends in a technological era?' was asked. The answer is that they are, as always, the ends based on the human values, but that they must be realized by means adapted to changed and changing circumstances. This is the proper perspective in which to examine the problems of change and technology in their social and economic, ethical and political contexts, and to define the answers with some hope of reaching agreement on the attitudes and the measures that are required.

A philosophy slanted on action rather than thought is blind: it is to have means without ends. A philosophy slanted on thought more than action is impotent: it is to have ends without means. Thought and action must be combined in a philosophy of life that is based on fundamentals. Abandoning the idea of progress for a deterministic or fatalistic attitude is to retrograde to a more primitive stage of civilization. Keeping the idea of progress attached to technological advance is to court the disaster that is visibly approaching. To be supine and helpless, and distracted by the excitement of constant change, is unworthy of a civilized people. The philosophy of thought and action defines progress by first defining social purpose and social ends. It will be found that they cannot be defined as other than based on the human values. And when social ends are made clear, they are half-way towards their achievement. But already 'the hour is very late, and the choice of good and evil knocks at our door.'[71]

9
Policy and Administration

ECONOMIC PROGRESS and political freedom appear to be linked. The relation cannot be fortuitous and it may be causal, but to consider which is the cause and which the effect may be less important than to realize the fact that advance and democracy now go hand in hand. Advance is naturally understood as the sum of achievements conducive to a better life for human beings, by raising their standard of living and improving the quality of their moral and intellectual environment; it is not understood as mastery in the race for outer space or the competition for perfecting weapons of destruction. Unless we return to the discarded theory of inequality of human races in their capacity for progress, we must accept the conclusion that the societies that most respect the human values become the most advanced. But people in the democratic countries are drifting into a lessened awareness of the values that are linked with their success and a weaker attachment to the social order that is based upon those values.

Applying the fashionable touchstone of efficiency to 20th-century political systems, it is manifest that some systems produce better results than others. Compared to democracies, totalitarian systems are wasteful and inefficient. The suffering and sacrifices inflicted by the Stalinist regime upon a generation of its hapless subjects should have ensured for the succeeding generation more benefits than those now enjoyed by the Japanese who, with so much less of natural resources, have not paid the same price in human pain. But the rate of progress achieved in Japan in the last fifty years is greater than the rate achieved in Russia. Moreover, the Japanese made their greatest economic advance after World War II, in conjunction with the progress of freedom and democracy. Short of accepting the notion of racial inequality, it must be inferred that the Japanese used a political system better contrived and more efficient than the Russians. 'The Communists . . . inherited an economy that had taken off; and one which had developed a substantial export surplus in agriculture. . . . The drive to maturity in Russia occurred with something over 10 million of the working force regularly in forced labour. . . . In housing the Soviet Union lived substantially off the Czarist capital stock down to recent years, minimizing housing outlays, letting space per family shrink; in agriculture it invested heavily, but within a framework of collectivization that kept productivity pathologically low.'[72] Despite this apparent advantage of reduced labour and social costs, the rate of industrial growth in Russia (which had been roughly equivalent to the United States' rate up to World War I) became considerably slower after the October revolution. It may be deduced from these facts that the achievements, undeniable even if too loudly acclaimed, in half a century of Soviet rule have been made in spite of and not thanks to Communist organization; having been made under the handicap of an ill-conceived system, they must be considered as an honourable, even a remarkable accomplishment that testifies to the patience and the resilience of the Russian people.

The industrial revolution led to particularly harsh exploitation of workers (men, women, and children) in a system from which they could not escape, but the notable achievement of Western Europe is to have eliminated the greater part of this exploitation by the operation of free and democratic governments, or at least governments that were led by public opinion. A measure of social justice was established in conjunction with an accelerated rate of economic advance, thus disproving the predictions of Marx and his successors. It showed that the hard road taken by the Soviets towards the goals of economic and social progress was badly designed. Their's was ruthless exploitation and total organization in a 'monolithic' state, and the return was not commensurate with the expenditure in time, effort and suffering.

However, the fact that satisfactory solutions have been found for exploitation of men by other men, or by an economic system, does not mean that these solutions have been applied everywhere in the Western world or that social justice has so far progressed in the world that there is no longer exploitation of men. The poor minorities in the rich countries, the majorities that live in misery in the poor countries, are witness that social justice remains an unrealized dream for the greater part of humanity. For them violent revolution will be the only way to take if wise and timely evolution is not ensured by the classes and the states that hold wealth and power. But it does mean that the methods successfully evolved and applied in some parts of the Western World to prevent exploitation and ensure social justice could now, with sufficient energy and goodwill, be applied to the rest of the world. It also means that the Marxist dream of social justice in prosperous equality is impossible to realize with the means that Marxist theory has devised and Marxist practice has applied.

Liberal democracy, so often charged with disorder and inefficiency, proves more practical, more efficient, more economical than state socialism and total organization. Political totalitarianism, whether of the 'right' as under Hitler and his imitators or of the 'left' as under communist rule, just does not work well enough. It is too slow, too cumbersome, too wasteful of moral and material resources. Neither will technological totalitarianism work well enough if it is allowed to take hold. The technological and organizational drift towards a new totalitarian system should convince present-day sophists and pragmatists, determinists and fatalists, not to lose sight of the social purpose deriving from the fundamental human values and make them more attentive to preserve the political system under which that purpose may be achieved.

*   *   *

Organization is not order. Order implies a sense of the hierarchy of things, a response to good and evil. Orderly progress is an end of society and organization is a means to that end. A basic distinction must be maintained between the order of society, its priorities on the scale of human values, and the organization required to implement that order. An organization may be run by strict rules, rigid discipline, efficient operation and yet be nothing but organized disorder. Buchenwald and Dachau were near perfect organizations, but they were the essence of confusion and derangement. Many less malefic organizations nowadays increase disorder because they tend to be an end in themselves and not a means to a goal which can be derived only from the purpose of society. Once they are set up, they have a tendency to remain and to proliferate as self-perpetuating disorder.[73] Organization (the comparison has already been mentioned) must be equated to the machine and it must be given an end. Political and administrative organization must promote social ends based on the human values. The problems that properly come under this heading are numerous and complex, and a choice must be made. Some of the most important are considered here.

I. FEDERALISM

Despite mighty forces at work to bring ever wider tracts of land and ever greater multitudes of men under unified political authority, despite that large states still absorb smaller states by force in this 20th century (such as Russia in Lithuania, Latvia and Esthonia or China in Tibet), there is a revival of a sort of parochialism or regionalism, expressed in the efforts of relatively small ethnic or national groups to assert their distinctive characteristics against engulfment by larger political or cultural entities. There is a sharpening of group awareness despite or perhaps because of the increasingly strong forces arrayed against the continued existence of separate groups. This is a general phenomenon, which may be observed alike in the advanced and the less developed countries. It comprises many gradations, all the way from civil war to set up a separate state (such as the Ibos of Biafra in Nigeria, the Dinkas and Nuers of South Sudan, the Bengalis of East Pakistan, the Kurds in Irak, Turkey and neighbouring states) through conflict and rebellion to achieve a measure of autonomy within a state (such as the Basques of Spain and France, the Jurassians of Bern canton in Switzerland) to resistance for preservation of cultural, linguistic, religious and other characters (such as exists in practically every country all over the world).

This sharpening is not unhealthy. The aspiration to distinctness and separateness should not provoke the violent reaction that it nearly always encounters. Of course there is the natural zeal of every government to retain as large as possible a territorial and numerical basis for its power; and there is the more legitimate concern for economic planning to be made on the widest feasible scale in order to be more effective; but the fears that derive from the one and the other concern are often exaggerated. Even the disadvantages of separation—as an extreme measure—are obviously less than the ravages of civil war to preserve the integrity of a state. After all, as remarked by an African leader, 'integrity is about human beings'. It is hard to see what concern could be worth the death or the suffering of thousands or millions of human beings. It should be generally accepted that a group wishing to separate, or to obtain a degree of autonomy, or to resist assimilation be allowed to do so if certain conditions are present: that its resolve is based on tradition as well as cultural and geographical fact, that it is not fostered by political intrigue or enemy interest, and that it is shared by a considerable majority of the people in that group. These conditions are not difficult to examine and to ascertain by means of an independent agency, and in effect they are often met.

The ideal of political philosophy is not to build a world state, but to ensure the orderly co-operation of all governments in a world community for the benefit of humanity. The goal is not to end up with a totalitarian world under a super-government, but a democratic world in which governmental relations between nations would be akin to the relations between individuals in a free and orderly society. In the light of such a goal, what is the best size for a state, that of India or Japan, Sweden or Costa Rica, or Luxemburg? What is the right number for a nation, five hundred million or more, ten million or less? What is the proper number of states for the world, one, ten, one hundred, two hundred? There is but one answer to such questions: size and numbers are irrelevant, except for power politics, and the only significant factors are those that ensure the internal peace and stability of a state, great or small. The urge towards smaller groupings, inasmuch as it derives from real desires and is based on authentic distinctness, is a beneficial trend because it enriches the variety of human creativity and it gives more scope to human values as social ends, thereby encouraging peace and stability.

The best union is one that preserves individuality while it ensures solidarity and co-operation. The best political organizations are those that allow for the existence of smaller groups in an atmosphere of democracy and freedom. The United States of America and Switzerland are examples of such an achievement, the former a very large state, the latter a small one with only 0.5 per cent of the area and 3 per cent of the population of U.S.A. (size and numbers are indeed irrelevant in this context). Though both have problems with minority groups, there are no separatist movements because co-existence and co-operation of different groups may be obtained by the effective guarantee of equal rights, or by a degree of autonomy within the state, or by some form of federation. But if a group is prepared to fight in order to separate, elementary political sense would concede the claim—if it is properly based—without a civil war. It is absurd so bitterly to resist a political break-up or loosening of large and semi-large states, when midget statelets, micro-states such as Mauritius and Saint Helena are on the way to reach in-dependence and to enter as full-fledged members into the association of sovereign states.

It follows that the principle of absolute state sovereignty, which the democratic and the totalitarian states alike inherited from the monarchical system, must now be considered as obsolete. Separat-ism need no longer mean balkanization. This will have beneficial results for peace, by avoiding much of the friction generated by the idea of national dignity (so often invoked by governments for reasons far removed from the nation's interest) and by making it easier to compromise by mutual give and take rather than to solve disputes by trial of power. Economic co-operation will thereby become less hard to achieve; and to save even part of the resources consumed in preparing and waging war would by itself be a major contribution to improvement of the human condition. The nation-state remains a viable basis for political grouping in the world of tomorrow (es-pecially for the developing nations), a good framework for the con-sensual policies and the concerted efforts required to make a group progress in co-operation with other groups, but it must become a more pliable concept, a more elastic frame. The boundaries of the nation-states cannot remain as the sacred limits of all social organization; they must now allow for the federalism and regional co-operation that will help economic integration while preserving political and cultural distinctness.[74]

However, absolute sovereignty of the state remains well entrenched, mainly because of the ever-present option of war, but also because of the desire for power that motivates many of those who speak in the name of the state. In developing countries absolute sovereignty of the state is a notion that is precious for people who only recently acceded to political independence, and it is exacerbated by the hardy remnants of overt or hidden colonialism, especially in Africa. The foolish and retarded colonialist policy of the Portuguese, the South African Government's cynical refusal to give up the mandate on Namibia, are stumbling-blocks in the path of African progress, mainly because they divert so much of African Governments' limited care and energy away from implementation of regional co-operation and practical economic solidarity. The same may be remarked for the regimes of South Africa and Rhodesia, whether they are termed colonialist or racist. They will have to change sooner or later, either by disappearing, or by giving up racial discrimination, or by breaking up into smaller geographical units divided between the contending races. The question, important for Africa and for the world, is whether the required change will come in violent upheaval or with a measure of smoothness and control. In Latin American countries also, nationalistic ideology is embittered by a too visible economic hold of the United States together with disappointment at the meagre results of the aid promised by or expected from their powerful northern neighbour. In international relations and particularly in the relations between the rich and the poor countries, an understanding of the ends and means of solidarity between nations is long overdue.

The primary factor of world politics is now the co-operation needed to put to best use the limited resources of overcrowded Earth. The best use means the most beneficial to human beings and the most conserving of resources for the future. Economic co-operation in production and distribution, up to a final stage of world integration, must include all political entities, large and small, but it does not require that political liberty and cultural freedom be sacrificed in the process. Rather does it mean the contrary, that is, that for economic integration to solve the problems of overpopulation, peaceful co-existence is required. Peaceful coexistence entails, not a uniform conditioning of the human races, but the variety and differentiation of groups and individuals. What is important is that there should be balance and stability inside each state, giant or midget, so that economic development and co-operation shall not be impeded by strife and conflict. Preservation of smaller national and cultural groups will remove many causes of friction and make international co-operation more fruitful. Only in this way can economic. integration—as the final and inevitable goal—preserve the human values in the ends and the means of society.

The efforts made in this century for bringing states to co-operate in regional organizations show that economic goals are a more fruitful influence than the aims of political supremacy or concerted defence. The European Economic Community achieves a considerable measure of success by a vigorous approach to economic co-operation coupled with a cautious and tactful handling of political issues. Groupings which have been comparatively less successful, such as the Arab League or the Organization of African Unity, have been handicapped by an approach that had to be practically focused on political considerations. The Central American Common Market has had some success because of its economic approach. Recent regional groupings in Africa aimed at economic co-operation could be the answer to some of the difficulties faced by developing countries. The policy for furthering international or interstate co-operation is to encourage the maintenance of political distinctness and cultural diversity, and to concentrate on economic co-operation, the conditions of which are more amenable to factual considerations and practical give and take.

Thus movements for asserting distinctness do not endanger the still infant trend towards world co-operation to improve the human condition through economic development. The two trends here outlined, political and cultural distinctness on one hand and economic integration on the other hand, are complementary. State sovereignty, in a new understanding of international solidarity, will become less absolute; economic autarchy is a thing of the past, to be replaced by general co-operation; military confrontation must hopefully be superseded by the reduction of the causes of friction; but local liberties and cultural freedom for groups and individuals must increase in order that respect for the human values be maintained with the economic integration which is required to keep the human race alive at an acceptable level of prosperity and civilization.

2. RESPONSIBILITY OF POWER

Much of the Third World's dislike and distrust of the advanced countries naturally stems from envy of their wealth and fear of their power. This applies more to the United States than to Western Europe, even though their history counts few colonial excesses abroad to embitter their relations with the developing countries. Wealth and power are not light to carry and American policy often seems unsatisfactory in spending the one and wielding the other. Aid is not easy to give with tact and power never begets love. Envy and fear are natural reactions and Americans do well to discount them. But there is a deeper reaction against Americans, which is not born of envy and fear, and which cannot be safely discounted. It is a sense of disappointment with the United States because of lack of principles and a bent for expediency and opportunism.

Much was expected of the American people in the sense of being a model for other nations, an example of holding firm to policies based on right and wrong, of preserving an attitude governed by value judgments and moral principles. Seldom did European nations preserve such an attitude, though they were always prone to proclaim high principles, but the United States held out better promise. The opportunist policy of the unprincipled may befit the weak and the poor, who are obliged to compromise their values and principles because they lack the capacity to withstand the pressure of greater than they. This is true for governments as it is true for individuals. In international as well as in national policies, to be consistent with their principles and values (and with their solemn international commitments on human rights) may be a luxury in which few governments can indulge, but for the richest and most powerful nation in the world it is a necessity that it can well afford. That Americans' professions of faith and declarations of principle should so often be belied by their policies and their actions inside their own country and towards their own people is resented by public opinion all over the world. That American policy and action in the international field appears to move exclusively on the level of power politics and ugly compromise (when it is not just fast deals and subversive intrigue) induces in the weak and poor nations a sense of disappointment and defeated hope.

At least, at the very least, the United States government could faithfully implement the decisions of the Security Council and the General Assembly of the United Nations in the battle for human rights, but even the small material sacrifice that this would entail appears too hard to bear. So the president, his advisers and his ministers, decide that chrome must be imported from Southern Rhodesia, that arms must be sold to the South African apartheidists or given to the Portuguese colonialists. That the French government should want to further lucrative arms sales to South Africa or that the British government should be reluctant to press decisions against its rebellious white Rhodesian subjects, is understandable for countries that can no longer hope to maintain a world picture because they no longer have the power to do so; but this sort of situation ethics is absolutely wrong—as a matter of principle and as a matter of practical policy—for the government of a major power. In the governing body of the U.S.A., such cynical disregard for principles and plain moral duty, especially in these days when nothing is hidden from public opinion even in the most retarded countries, can only stem from incomprehension of where the priorities really lie, and misunderstanding of the meaning of world responsibility.

'Responsibility of Power' is one of America's headaches. It is an expression much misused by empire builders and it means something better than European colonialist governments appeared to think. It means that when a nation has power, when it is big and strong, nothing should prevent the government of that nation from being honest in every occasion, from acting consistently according to the principles of a humane civilization. *This is the responsibility of power.* America is not powerful enough to police the world or even part of it (even if its policies and tactics were sound, and the Vietnam war should finally have removed any illusions on that score). It is powerful enough, however, to stick to principles in its international policy. That it seldom does so is the real cause of dislike and distrust of the United States. They are competing in the wrong arena, the arena of power, when—precisely because of their power—they could set a standard of real progress and civilization for their own people and for the rest of the world.

Besides the outright use of power, American policy in the quarter century since World War II is replete with Machiavellian intrigue, downright dishonesty, and plain irresponsibility. Publications like *The Invisible Government*, *The Game of Nations*,[75] and others that purport to be factual reports reveal incredibly thoughtless interventions in other countries' affairs, with little knowledge of their people and their problems. Superficial thinking and presumption appear to be the weakness of many self-styled specialists as they are called upon to excercise their talents on weaker countries. Underdevelopment is not only economic, and underdeveloped mentalities are as common in the governing bodies of the advanced countries as in the others. The redeeming feature (apart from, sometimes, good intentions) is that Americans speak frankly and write freely on subjects that are not mentioned in other countries because of public security or national pride. It compensates for some of the glaring faults of American policy, for so long as this freedom lasts, criticism remains possible and it holds out the hope of correction and improvement.

However, this does not change the fact that such cheap intrigues and cloak-and-dagger ventures have most often been unsuccessful, sometimes producing results contrary to those for which they were planned. They have made the American image hated in many parts of the world. They have increased people's suffering and compounded difficulties for the countries concerned. To take one instance, the Russian advance in the Middle East is mainly a direct result of American policy, carried out by public and secret intervention, and designed to prevent a communist take-over. The same sort of failure may be observed in Cuba and some other Latin American countries. Elaborate war or policy games, that are supposed to help policymaking, could be entertaining intellectual exercises if they were not in earnest and if they did not often lead to tragically unexpected results. Even played by experts, they are dangerous unless checked by the common sense, the ordinary wisdom, and the minimum of psychological empathy that appear to be cast aside by the enthusiastic proponents of such new thinking aids and policy-making machinery. Irresponsible interventions by various federal departments, when backed by American power, irresistibly call to mind the antics of the proverbial bull in the china shop or elephant in the vegetable garden.

This is the field for bold and creative ideas. For instance, if American policy were based on honesty and equity, if it only supported or befriended governments that respect the human values, if it withheld military aid to murderous rulers, if it refused to support totalitarian regimes regardless of possible disadvantage in military strategy or diplomatic tactics, it would command widespread respect. It would induce in other nations a feeling of solidarity with Americans, of sympathy for American difficulties (considered as set-backs by which all are harmed) and satisfaction for American successes (considered as goals for all to aim at). It would greatly enhance the position of the United States government, increase its influence and its capacity for action. Above all, it would help Americans to clarify their dimming vision of a democratic and humane society, so that they become more aware of the human values as the purpose of social activity and no longer risk alienation from the institutions of their own society. Only a strong nation could give the lead for such a policy.

Leadership of quality and vision would thus command the respect and evoke the sympathy of other nations. It would set a goal, a pattern, an example of real civilization in these difficult and alarming times. This would be a realistic and an intelligent policy for the government of a powerful country, of a 'super-power'. As it is, the picture of America is spoilt for people in all countries and for many of its own people too. This would not be so bad for the world if the required example could be given by another country, but the capacity to do so appears to be even more lacking in the two other major states. Neither the Russians nor the Chinese, having successfully raped and quartered the Baltic and the Tibetan peoples, can provide the moral leadership that many countries disappointed with

America vainly expect from them. From Russia and China come declamations without end against imperialism and colonialism and racialism, but they are as guilty as any other state of these perversions that plague humanity. No totalitarian society can give an example of humane policies. Western Europe is another matter. Its nations could bring out of renunciation of their colonial past a real understanding of humane civilization. If united, they would be a greater power, in every sense, than any other and they would exert immense and perhaps beneficial influence on world affairs. Some Europeans have this vision.[76] Possibly it will be realized one day before it is too late. The enlargement of the European Community by the accession of Great Britain and some other countries to the European Common Market certainly improves the chances for this realization. Meanwhile there is America alone on which to pin hope for a brave change of direction in the policies that affect the future of humanity.

Such hope may not be out of place. America is setting the pace and blazing the trail that all others follow, some close behind and some far back. Where the trail will eventually lead to is hard to say. Where it is now heading should be clear, and only the fundamental values can give it the right direction. The spirit of constructive change cannot come from countries that are economically or politically retarded. If it is to reach to essentials, it can appear only where freedom and affluence allow human beings to attend to matters other than survival of mind and body. Americans are experiencing revulsion against the attitude and behaviour of their government. Recent forms of contestation by students and minorities started in America. And never before have sizeable groups in a nation at the height of wealth and power violently denounced the policies that are usually supposed to ensure wealth and power. Maybe out of the torment and tragedy of the Vietnam war, the ferment and turmoil of the Negro confrontation, Americans will emerge with a new sense of purpose, a fresh understanding of responsibility, a renewed assertion of fundamental values and priorities. That individuals with stature will be elected to catch the spirit of the time and to provide bold and imaginative leadership is a question for chance or Providence. But much may be expected from a consensual definition of socials ends by those whose greater responsibility derives from deeper understanding and keener awareness.

3. PERSONAL AND SOCIAL RIGHTS

Human rights in the Western world have been solemnly affirmed in political documents. After the earliest assertions of political rights in England (Magna Carta 1215, Oxford Provisions 1258, Declaration of Rights 1689) the first comprehensive declaration, in scope if not in detail, was the preamble of the American Declaration of Independence in 1776. The Constitution of the United States of America was adopted in 1787 and, excepting British constitutional practice, it is the oldest in force in any country. Amendments I to X (1791) make up what is called the Bill of Rights. Human rights as expressed in these documents have on the whole been respected by the nation for which they were affirmed, due allowance being made for the intellectual outlook and the moral limitations of each successive age. They retain political significance and they are still present-day concerns of the American people. They are developed and refined by legislative and judicial action related to the problems of each generation, the principal of which are today those of equal civil rights and economic opportunities for Negro citizens and other minority groups.

The American declaration had a direct influence on the similar but more detailed Déclaration des Droits de l'Homme et du Citoyen made in France in 1789. The French revolution proclaimed a new age for mankind. In effect, it was the first totalitarian dictatorship exercised in the name of the people. It respected neither liberty nor equality nor fraternity, nor indeed any of its articles of faith, but its declaration became the most celebrated document of its kind. It won extraordinary favour and it exerted great influence all over Europe and in other parts of the world where Western political ideas were accepted. Since then the constitution of every newly formed state— the result of revolution in an already independent country or of accession to independence from a subject or colonial status—has included an affirmation of fundamental human rights. These are now principles that cannot be denied in word, even though they are so often ignored or cynically travestied in the operation of state and society. The rulers of every country, however opposed they may be to the principles and the practices of democracy, are careful to proclaim their concern for human rights in practically identical terms.

The present century witnessed a new affirmation of human rights in a wider sphere. The United Nations Organization sponsored a declaration to which nearly every state in the world has officially adhered. The Universal Declaration of Human Rights was formally adopted by the General Assembly in 1948 and was proclaimed 'a common standard of achievement for all peoples and all nations'. It is a concise but comprehensive document in which social ends based on the human values are explicitly affirmed. Close interdependence, on the national and the international plane, is thus asserted between the social order and the rights of man. Were rights ensured because they are proclaimed, were they respected by all the states that have subscribed to them, this would be a happy world. We can at least recognize that it is for the time being a remarkable accomplishment that human rights should be unanimously asserted all over the world.

The Universal Declaration of Human Rights is now supplemented by two International Covenants, on Economic, Social and Cultural Rights, and on Civil and Political Rights. After pending nearly twenty years before the General Assembly of United Nations, the two Covenants were unanimously approved in the 21st session held in 1966. They constitute a detailed assertion of human rights in their respective fields. They are clear and uncompromising to a degree that would put in doubt the understanding of many governments by which they were approved, were it not for the words 'law' and 'lawful' in almost every article. The meaning of law is so twisted and the content of lawfulness so depleted in many countries that their governments can subscribe to such covenants without fear that their denial of the human rights which they undertake to respect will ever be brought to account. When the law gives the Minister of Interior or equivalent executive the authority to sequestrate, dispossess, arrest and imprison any persons by administrative decision for 'the superior interest of the state', the arbitrary acts thus sanctioned become lawful under the terms of the Covenants. We should not, however, regret these escape clauses, for without their inclusion the Covenants would not have been voted, and an affirmation of principle even if it is not translated into action is better than no affirmation at all. A Protocol to the Covenant on Civil and Political Rights was approved by two-thirds of the member nations. It allows individuals to bring violations of their rights to the notice of a Committee established by the Covenant, but it empowers the Committee only to examine the complaint and to bring it to the notice of the state concerned. Despite this limitation, there is progress in the fact that so many states have accepted this small measure of interference with their sovereign powers.

More noteworthy is the European Convention for the Protection of Human Rights and Fundamental Freedoms signed in Rome in 1950. It repeats many of the articles of the Universal Declaration, but it also institutes a European Commission of Civil Rights and a European Court of Human Rights, both of which have been established. This is the really new step in the recognition of individual human rights. For the first time in history there exists a judicial court not subject to any state, before which individuals can bring actions against a sovereign state, even their own, on any violation of the rights affirmed by the Convention. This court is in function and actions are regularly brought before it. That the number of governments which undertake to submit to the judgments of this court is still small, that the first effective protection of individual rights is— not unnaturally—established in countries where those rights are least in danger, does not detract from the importance of this step. This humane conception of state sovereignty redounds to the honour of Western civilization. We tremble to think that it could be a last flowering of the human values at a time when nuclear bombs proliferate like a plague, and when the spread of totalitarian regimes lessens the chances for effective protection of human rights in most parts of the world.

Already the government of one country, barely twenty years after the Rome treaty, has revoked its adhesion to the European Convention for the Protection of Human Rights and Fundamental Freedoms. The decision taken by the Greek government in December 1969, to forestall a humiliating vote in the Council of Europe, is portentuously significant. Whatever the reasons of that government for its internal policy, whether or not it is thereby avoiding a greater evil as some believe, the fact remains that the exercise and the protection of human rights become increasingly difficult. It is not fortuitous that a peripheral member, in the geographical sense, should be the first to drop out, despite that it is traditionally a birthplace of democracy. The pressure on democratic institutions in the few remaining democratic countries is increasing. Whatever encouragement may be derived from the protection of individual rights in the few Western democracies, the fact must be faced that they are being gradually depreciated in other parts of the world, following the reduction in stature of the individual in overpopulated and underdeveloped countries.

In relations between states the sovereignty of each is limited by that of the others, with due consideration for their respective size and power, but in the relations of most states with their subjects there is no brake and no curb. The appellation of subject is only too apt. Most people continue to feel that it is natural that a government (not their own to be sure) should enjoy total power over its subjects, and they are little concerned about what happens to individuals in other countries when it does not touch their real or their supposed interests. The larger portion of mankind is under dictatorships that prevent recourse or redress for violations of human rights. It is said that people have the government that they deserve, but this can no longer be true, because of the prepotent means of coercion that a government can now bring to bear on the people living within its territorial limits.

Besides, there is a tendency to interpet the maxim of 'the greatest good of the greatest number' as sanction to deny the rights of the smaller number. The immoral political arithmetic already referred to derives from the decrease in worth of the individual human being. His worth and his rights are not the basic fact of society and so it becomes permissible to sacrifice one for the good (as defined by authority) of ten, one million for ten million. If individual rights were regarded as essential (within the limits of the rights of others) and social benefits (real or imagined) as secondary, this sort of computation would be inacceptable. It is just and proper that a long line of loaded trucks and automobiles filled with people in a hurry should be held up while an old man feebly crosses the street. It is just and proper that no person be deprived of his or her basic rights, even if this should deprive a large number of certain benefits. Basic human rights have an absolute value, that is not dependent on the number of people who claim those rights or on the number of people who want or need to deny them. The rule of the majority must not mean the crushing of the minority.

Some thoughtful observers think that totalitarian ideology reinforced by technological organization is gradually eliminating liberal democracy, which will thus soon have been a brief and brilliant historical interlude for some Western nations. Such a conclusion may come to pass, through negligence of determinists without hope and blindness of realists without vision. This is the place again to say that if fundamental values are depreciated and social purpose obscured in the advanced nations, they will be lost for humanity. They will not be lost if those nations remain conscious of their cultural heritage and the principles that they are committed to uphold by their solemn national and international undertakings.

4. REPRESENTATIVE RULE

The goal of democracy is effective participation in the government of a nation by the members of that nation. This is achieved when the people freely elect their representatives to fill offices of power and responsibility, and when the institutions and bureaucracy of the state are guided by the people's opinions and desires. The organization of democracy still corresponds to this goal in the advanced nations, but serious new problems have appeared, and they must be solved if democracy is to survive. Mainly they derive from the difficulty of maintaining political (democratic) control over long-range policy and providing the information required for making meaningful choices. Increasing complexity of public affairs makes it hard for elected representatives to be adequately informed. They still control legislation and restrain government action, but the basic options tend to escape their supervision and even their attention. This trend is strengthened by an enormous development of the bureaucracy required for regulating increasingly complex social organization. This bureaucracy is run by specialized technocrats, men of intelligence and ability who like to think that they know what is good for the people better than the people themselves or their representatives, and who try to avoid public discussion and to short-circuit parliamentary control.

Another difficulty is that parliament is no longer the sole political forum, since the communications media have made it possible to reach the people immediately and to avoid parliamentary control by appealing directly to their feelings and sympathies. A sort of Caesarism may thus be established, whereby the leader who obtains the votes of the masses need not be hampered in his policies or hindered in his action by supervision or control. This is not democracy any more. The fact that the leader has been mandated or plebiscited by the people is not enough. Only effective participation in government can be termed democratic, not abdication of the people in the hands of their leader. With these trends, the operation of democracy insensibly becomes an illusion, because the real lines of policy-making gradually by-pass the public who thereby tends to lose interest in democratic institutions and becomes less aware of the necessity to preserve them. The United States congress is reacting against these trends and it is answering the challenge without weakening the reality and efficacity of its functions.[77] Parliaments in Western Europe are not resisting so vigorously the pressures of television and increasing complexity of public affairs. They seldom contribute new elements to policy discussions. They most often approve or reject government initiatives without proposing major legislative innovations or policy programmes.

There is the start of a decline in parliamentary institutions. An aspect of this decline is the spread of totalitarian regimes in the second half of this century. In Eastern Europe flourishing democratic institutions born of World War I were destroyed in World War II. In Africa and the Near East numerous states recently emerged from colonial status appear unable to develop healthy representative rule. But the more threatening aspect is the challenge to old and well-established parliaments in Western Europe, by reason of the difficulties outlined above. The threat is greater because if the higher forms of representative institutions degenerate, there will remain no living models for the less developed democracies to emulate, and the spread of totalitarian regimes will be further encouraged. A democratic parliament (again the redundant adjective is required because of the pretension of totalitarian regimes to have their parliaments) is the fundamental institution of an open society where individual freedom and personal rights are principles of the social order. Much study and research are devoted to this important problem and there is no need here to consider it in further detail.

5. CIVIC RESPONSIBILITY

Declining trends of truly representative rule in Western Europe are reflected in people's tendency to take their political rights for granted together with their increased affluence. Except where the direct interest of individuals or groups is concerned, they are less solicitous about the operation of democratic government, mainly because they are losing sight of the direct connection between their prosperity and their fundamental values. The sense of individual responsibility for society as a whole, regardless of direct interest, is weakening. Even in the oldest democracy there is some fading of civic sense, as evidenced by the falling proportion of active voters in the Swiss federal and cantonal elections and referendums. Young people in particular appear to set little value on the principles of democracy and to be attracted either by a vague anarchism or by power-snatching techniques in totalitarian style. All the factors deriving from technological advance and increasing population and building up the present critical juncture in human affairs (growing multitudes of human beings and declining stature of individuals, increasing organization and complexity of society, concentration of power in economic or technocratic oligarchies) tend to weaken civic responsibility provided that a comfortable standard of living can be maintained.

And yet it is wrong to say (with dictators and technocrats) that people naturally shy away from responsibility. Rather would they welcome it in order to have a sense of being of service and to give meaning to their existence. But if they have little opportunity to exercise responsibility by effective participation and if, moreover, they have the necessities of life and some of its superfluities at their disposal, they will feel little concern for the welfare of their national or local communities. But the concern that may be lacking in the wider sphere of a nation's politics is often present in the smaller spheres of benevolent service. If social priorities based on the fundamental human values were recognized, a better and more balanced social order could prevail and society could be organized to provide individuals of all types and characters with opportunities effectively to participate in public affairs.

Human beings are neither stupid nor heartless and, if they are informed fairly, they understand with their minds and with their hearts. On an average, they choose wisely. If they are not fairly and adequately informed, because of the lack of truthful information and honest authority, they cannot estimate the import of problems and events and they cannot choose wisely. They take the wrong decisions (often those that dishonest interests want them to take) or they resort to unreasonable violence and anti-social attitudes. Information has become the leading political issue of this age.[78] Survival of democracy depends on the scope and quality of information available to the public. Even with a free press as a basic condition of a working democracy, the information available may be insufficient. There is urgent need to improve the sources of information and the methods by which it is collected and disseminated. The administration has its statistical centres, technical agencies and planning offices, without which it could not operate. If the information on which it bases its proposals and its decisions is not also available to public opinion, in an objective, impartial and understandable form, there can be no democratic control of public affairs and no effective participation in government.

There is much exaggeration in current statements about the incommunicability of scientific concepts, technical mechanisms, and economic problems. This paves the way for a technocracy where specialists may retreat behind a would-be impossibility of explaining their reasons to those who are not conversant with their specialities and therefore cannot understand their ideas and their language. New words were no doubt required for the physical sciences to express notions for which no words existed and for which paraphrases would be inconvenient, but the gibberish of many specialists is quite unpardonable. With a little effort the same meanings could be expressed more simply and more intelligibly by an ordinary use of language. Any person of average education and intelligence can discuss significantly with specialists, though he is naturally incapable of doing their work. He may also be incapable of doing the work of the cook. He can usefully examine any action proposed by the nuclear or chemical engineer, the expert in strategy and foreign affairs, the banker or the financial genius. There is perhaps a residue of relative incommunicability, but it is restricted to some mathematical concepts. There is no difficulty for understanding the biological discoveries that will demand the most serious value judgments and policy decisions from legislators and public opinion. As for sociology and economics, everything in them is easy to communicate except the extraordinary language affected by some of their exponents.

The treatment of specialized disciplines as arcana intelligible only to initiates does not correspond to reality. The esoteric attitude to science and technique puts the 'common man'[79] and even the humanist at an unfounded disadvantage in their relations with scientists and technicians. It is an attitude unsuited to a democratic society but quite natural for dictatorial regimes. In reality, the need is for the really able generalist and he is seldom found. The call is out for more scientists and better technicians, but the need for those who are not specialists goes unheeded. With increasing division and partitioning of knowledge comes the requirement for persons whose minds are not restricted by specialization, who possess enough of culture and general knowledge, besides some wisdom and character, to hold the balance in decision and in action between the specialists. In effect, political men of sufficient stature and appropriate calibre are required. Such as these, if they are to be found, will be the uncommon men of the future, not the specialists as scientists and technicians like to think.

More difficult than to ensure the scope and availability of information will be to guarantee its objectivity and impartiality. This cannot be expected from government departments, even with the best intentions. Independence and integrity could be ensured only by autonomous bodies, staffed by advanced scientists and specialists in all disciplines, directed by persons of great culture and unimpeachable moral standing, with free and easy channels of communication at all levels with the general public, government departments and the elected representatives of the people. The function of such institutions will be to collect and to disseminate information, and they will be established with the legal powers and practical means to carry out this double assignment. Statistical data would be one of many sources of information, which would include political, sociological, economic and scientific papers and reports, books and articles. Part of the information would be in the form of indexes and bibliographies for easy reference to published material. The most up-to-date methods of data storage and retrieval would be used. Important sections would deal with providing information on specific problems as requested by any person, group or administration. In each country the 'Institute of Public Information' would be permanently funded from the central government's budget. It would be affiliated to an international organization of same nature which would co-ordinate the collection of information and help to ensure its free dissemination. In this way one of the main conditions for the operation of democratic government in this age would be realized and one of the main threats to survival of democracy and freedom averted.[80]

6. SOCIAL SERVICES

There is great variety in the scope of services rendered by a community to its disadvantaged members, in the name of social solidarity, through its state and local authorities. These services may apply to every stage and every accident of life, or they may be less inclusive. Following economic and social progress in each country, a gradually increasing proportion of inhabitants enjoys a gradually widening scope of services. But social services are basically the same everywhere in one important aspect, namely that they are services rendered to the individual. Whatever difference of opinion there may be about the purpose of society or the relation of a state with its subjects, there can be no two opinions on social security, public assistance, medical care and other services: they are established to serve human beings and if they do not serve them in a humane way they do not achieve their purpose. If they do not treat the individual as a person worthy of respect and attention, they are inefficient however fast and accurate they may be. This is a domain where a qualitative concern must predominate, and where the quantitative outlook destroys the purpose for which the services are established.

A French politician recently remarked on the inhumanity of social services in his country. The remark also applies to many countries and many sorts of services. It is hard to avoid impersonality, especially when dealing in large numbers of human beings. The poor, the sick, the aged are not pleasant company. It is difficult for social workers (even if they are well trained and highly motivated, which is not often the case) to provide a sufficient supply of the human warmth and the personal attention that each individual needs. And yet this is the field where, more than in any other, the human values should be given full regard, where human beings are most in need of being treated with dignity and respect. It is likely that whatever the level of affluence and the degree of justice in a society, there will always be a proportion of poor and sick and aged for whom the community will have to care. Social services will always be in demand in the rich countries, and naturally in the poor countries. One measure of the improvement of society will always be the provision of complete, efficient and, above all, humane social services. It is already a measure of real progress in this age that the services deriving from the principle of social solidarity are considered as essential duties for every national community whatever its political regime.

Communist achievements in the social services must be noted. Socialist promises of comfort and plenty for all, so conspicuously unfulfilled, have at least been carried out in generalized instruction and health care. In the Third World, lack of resources and the rising flood of population make the development of social services an arduous and a heartbreaking task. Yet, considering the poor countries' heavy handicaps, some are not doing as badly as could be expected from the simple comparison of their revenue with that of the rich countries. The smaller European nations, particularly the Scandinavians, are well ahead in the scope and quality of their services. The richest country, with the highest *per capita* revenue in the world, lags well behind Western Europe (as well as Japan,

Australia and New Zealand) in the social field. Americans themselves, in their present fit of self-accusation, speak of the breakdown and collapse of their social services. Many other nations complain that their social services are insufficient. Added to these difficulties, care for the aged will demand a rising share of the community's resources as average age of the population rises and life expectancy is prolonged. Much more will also have to be spent on care for the mentally deranged, if their numbers continue to increase as expected with the stresses of modern living. Provision of adequate social services promises to remain as a major policy problem for all governments.

*　　*　　*

The six headings in this chapter are examples of the problems of according state policy and public administration with the fundamental human values. To review all such problems, or even a considerable part of them, would far exceed the scope of this book. In particular, economic and social problems related to equitable distribution of the tax burden and of social benefits have not been touched upon, as they are so often studied and discussed, and as the opposing contentions of interested groups are always energetically defended. While the overall interest of society in the seemingly theoretical problems of applying the fundamental human values to general policies that do not directly affect personal or group interests is not enough studied and discussed, and seldom defended. It is therefore required to attempt to bring out the very positive connection between such 'high-level abstractions' and the practical choices for policy and action that can be made from among the options that remain open for the future in the political and administrative operation of society.

10

Population Policy

ENOUGH HAS BEEN SAID in Part One concerning the perils of population increase for rich and poor nations alike. More surely than the risks of war and nuclear catastrophe, accelerating overpopulation imperils the future of humanity, both in the short-term result of hunger and famine, and in its long-term bearing on the human values. The highest national and international authorities have pointed out the danger. Conferences of specialists in demography and agriculture have time after time exposed the approach of 'mass famine' and 'unlimited disaster', each year with words more pressing and figures more portentous. It should now be clear that overpopulation is in the present juncture the greatest threat to the human condition, as it is either the primary cause or the aggravating agent of all the other perils that appear to be more present in people's minds, such as war and totalitarianism and overbearing technology. Yet the practical response is strangely weak and positive action remains unaccountably slow.

In terms of immediate urgency, birth control and increased food production are equally necessary to prevent widespread hunger and famine, and their attendant evils of suffering and social disruption. In terms of long-range planning, food production cannot be indefinitely increased, and birth control will remain the principal condition for preserving a liveable environment for human beings. Yet family planning has become official policy in very few countries and the advocates of natural or divine prohibition of birth control have only recently begun to arise from their torpid incomprehension. Even nations that are fortunate enough to have a low or a declining birth rate cannot leave well alone: Romania which recently embarked on an energetic policy to encourage population growth (at this time!) is an instance of the ancient subjection to the spell of numbers combined with the new magic of quantity rather than quality. As for the increase of food production, it still appears as secondary to manufacturing industry (and of course defence) in most development plans and foreign aid programmes.

Population problems should become the primary concern of the whole world, no less than the questions of war and peace. Immense amounts of wealth and ingenuity are expended on space exploration while the most pressing issue of life and death remains far behind in the scale of priorities. Expenditure of efforts and resources without delay, on a sufficient scale and under an overall plan, *may* avert disaster; it *will* reduce its extent and it will surely reduce the need for immensely greater expenditure of funds and energy later on. Population policy should be planned and supervised by an existing international organ or by a new supra-national institution established for the purpose. With proper information, it should be possible to enlist the co-operation of all countries in an enterprise that deeply affects the future of mankind, the rich and the poor alike. The programme would be in three parts:

I. BIRTH CONTROL

Family planning must at least be recognized as a normal element of government policy and private conduct. The delay in realizing that birth control is the necessary corollary of disease control, that family planning is the logical counterpart of health planning and an integral component of social security, is having catastrophic consequences for humanity. Besides, birth control is not only needed to avoid demographic disaster but also to improve the standard of health, as proper spacing of children ensures the well-being of the family. Those who still maintain that birth control is harmful or sinful bear heavy responsibility. They are not more consistent with morality or sympathetic to human need than those who said over a hundred years ago that chloroform (then recently discovered) should not be used in childbirth because it is written 'in sorrow thou shalt bring forth children'.[81]

From whatever angle one considers the Vatican ruling of July 1968 against personal and social freedom in family planning, the inescapable conclusion must be that it is an ill-advised decision. It condemns humanity to increased difficulty and suffering and it creates yet another problem for the world's most important religious institution. It does this at a time when it comes to be generally realized that the population explosion constitutes a grave threat to civilization, when the Christian faith is exposed to the growing strength of materialist philosophies, when Christianity is faced with problems more pressing than birth control and more relevant to the essential doctrine of salvation through faith and charity. This was not the issue on which to make a stand and, in so far as the ruling will be ignored or defied, Christianity will lose more ground to materialism and atheism. One cannot doubt that the encyclical *Humanae Vitae* is a fateful event that should and could have been avoided for the peace and hope of the world.

It will increase the difficulties of the poor nations and it is understandable that in some parts of the Third World it should have been stated quite seriously that the encyclical was in line with the rich countries' plot to keep the poor nations in a dependent position! Although its influence will naturally be felt more in Latin America than in other parts of the world, it will deprive the whole birth control movement of the additional support it could have enjoyed following approval by the Catholic church. It will prevent family planning from helping many of those who need it most among the poor and uneducated, and it will slow effective development of birth control in countries where the government may not wish to defy the Vatican decision. An opportunity has been lost and some hope dimmed, but the birth control movement will continue to develop with the momentum imparted to it by the pressures of overcrowding and the logic of poverty and famine.

The success of birth control in slowing population growth depends on three main factors. First, the availability of safe and easy to use contraceptives; a six-months pill or similar achievement would immediately solve three-fourths of the problem. Secondly, a well-designed and energetically operated organization, in order that information and supplies be regularly distributed to all parts of a country. Thirdly, that the arguments for family planning be adapted to people's mentality and knowledge. People may be simple but they are not stupid. Neither are they insane. They do not *like* poverty and disease, but they reasonably base their judgments on the knowledge they have and they must be spoken to in terms that they understand. Underpaid and insufficiently trained social workers are sent to sell birth control to tens of thousands of villages and they naturally achieve little. Then it is said that the poor peasant or worker does not understand, that he is too wedded to his ways, that his values are different: a lot of theoretical stuff that does not stand up to investigation. The vaunted publicity technique of Madison Avenue would be used to better advantage in this field than in pushing the sale of unwanted goods or beautifying the public picture of this or that dictatorial government.

In Japan, with the education and discipline of its people, birth control is successfully established, though it may be regretted that its success should be due to abortion as much as to contraception. In India, family planning has been part of official policy since the first five-year plan, but progress has been slow. In Pakistan, a bold plan for slowing population increase has been initiated. In Egypt, birth control as public policy (though much delayed through unforgivable shortsightedness) promises to be an interesting experiment in administration and information. The governments of South Korea, Turkey, Chile and several others have also adopted programmes for birth control, but there are still too many countries where badly needed family planning facilities are inexistent. The government of China, which is responsible for one in every five human beings, is at last committed to an energetic policy for birth control. Meanwhile humanity is increasing at the rate of some two hundred thousand additional individuals *every day* (the amount by which births exceed deaths) with an average rate of growth of 1.9 per cent yearly. The average for Europe is only 0.8 per cent, while it is 2.0 in Asia, 2.5 in Africa, 2.9 in Latin America.

Abortion may soon have to be legalized and even subsidized in many regions, despite grave moral and medical objections to this practice. A measure of the seriousness with which the situation is rightly viewed is the recent decision by the Indian parliament to legalize abortion, despite the fact that Hinduism is as opposed to it as Christianity and Islam. In India also, besides monetary and fiscal inducements to sterilization, a decision was recently taken to offer condemned men a reduction of penalty if they accepted to be sterilized. This morally questionable but practically sound action is a first and timid example of the sort of regulations that will be forced on governments by unbearable demographic pressures. Far better to push forward with family planning with first priority in national and international policies. Whatever is spent in effort and money on avoiding the conception of a child destined to destitution and famine will be much less than the amount of effort and money that will have to be spent in order to keep him alive in misery and suffering as a reduced human being.

However, much progress has been made and the birth control movement may now be expected to gain momentum. Donald J. Bogue points out some encouraging facts in this connection, with which my own experience puts me in complete agreement: basic approval of the principle of birth control all over the world, acceptance of birth control aims and methods (properly explained) even by the most simple rural populations, poverty and privation as motivating forces for fertility control, advance in research and technique in contraceptives and educative information.[82] But I disagree with the impression he gives that the population crisis is thus resolved and that the next thirty years can now be viewed with optimism. The effects of a decreasing birth rate come slowly and however much the development of birth control may be speeded, the results will not come in time during this period to reduce in a substantial measure the fast widening gap between population and resources. The last third of this century is the critical period, during which a great and sustained effort will be needed, and after which— as already remarked—a solution will have intervened for better or for worse. It is the responsibility of this generation to make sure that the solution preserve the principles of civilization.

One principle especially must be clear: there should be no constraint to enforce birth control, either by police methods or by genetic manipulation. Besides the fact that constraint, in this field especially, would be contrary to the freedom and dignity of human beings, it is obvious that it would lead to serious social unrest. It would also be self-defeating unless overwhelming force were used, and this entails the establishment of a totalitarian regime. Experience invariably endorses that the only effective method of persuasion is to speak to people as the intelligent adults that they are, to explain where lies their interest and their duty to their family, to use arguments suited to their often limited knowledge, and to provide them with the material means for applying the advice they are given. The spread of birth control, which needs little communal consciousness and organization, is easier to achieve than other aspects of social advancement which require a greater measure of community development. There is practically no risk of failure for a birth control programme if the required means are used, and these means are now well known.

The achievements of the birth control and family planning movement are impressive in terms of human will and individual initiative, no less than in terms of the cause that it serves so well. They are an outstanding example of what can be accomplished by the concerted effort of a few dedicated individuals. These persons put into motion a movement that now holds out some hope for the future of the human race in its present predicament. Their efforts counteracted trends so general and so strong that it seemed nothing could oppose them. They did this without government help, against the opposition of established institutions, despite contempt and sarcasm from the public. They bear witness to the influence of individual thought and creativeness, of individual initiative and driving force, in matters that affect the whole of human kind.[83] Their success is the promise of a civilized solution to the population problem by voluntary discipline in bearing children. In this success the small elite who is aware that civilization will survive only if the human values are asserted as the only ends of society may find inspiration and encouragement. In it they may find the assurance that their voices, if they are not ashamed to raise them loud and clear, will be heard and that their efforts, if they are not too tired and dispirited to combine them, will be successful in counteracting present trends and in opposing the pressures at work to deny individual worth and dignity.

But the good fight for population discipline has only recently started in earnest. The success to date of the fertility control movement must not lead us to underestimate the danger and the long road ahead. Development of this movement has come late. Even if it should now be pushed forward with all the force of public opinion and all the resources of governments, it cannot prevent a culmination of the crisis. And if it fails to generalize in time civilized solutions, the logic of the ensuing situation will dictate other solutions which could be incompatible with the preservation of human values in the ends and means of social policy. Force will have to be used to impose the measures required by a situation that was not prevented in time, and these measures must inevitably deny individual freedom and personal dignity. Unless people accept generalized self-discipline to control population growth, the discipline that must be imposed upon them in the name of survival will be harsh and monstrous. It will mean direct state interference, first in the underdeveloped countries and then in the others (by police methods and genetic manipulation) in each person's most intimate physical and moral concerns, in each family's most private affairs. Mass contraception through water supply systems, electronic suggestion or control of people's minds are among the practical possibilities that are already being actively explored. Such intrusions will put in question the basic principles of Western culture. These considerations, which may be impatiently brushed aside as Cassandra cries or science fiction fantasies, are possible futures terribly near to the present generation. Every intelligent person should give them close and honest attention.

2. FOOD PRODUCTION

Human food comes primarily from the land and subsidiarily from the seas, lakes and rivers. Land is overloaded with people in many parts of the world. Its total area cannot be extended nor can the arable area be increased above certain quickly reached limits. Irrigation of deserts by nuclear power may come one day, but not in time to help in the present crisis. Synthetic foods are being developed from the chemical elements of air and earth, but it is not clear when they will be practically available on a large scale. In the most thickly populated regions agricultural land is actually being reduced by the need for more space (space to move and to work, space to live and to be buried). In many of the poor countries people are eating less than a generation ago. The fantastic numbers of human beings predicted by statisticians would soon reach the stage where they would have no food to eat and no place to move.

A survey of agricultural development areas on a world-wide scale will show the feasible increase in food resources, the comparative ease or difficulty of development, and the expenditure of time, money and effort required for each area. Before the limit of agricultural development possibilities is reached, factors of relative time and effort will help to decide whether to concentrate on increase of yield or extension of cultivation in each region. The information for a survey of this magnitude already exists. There is already a start in overall agricultural planning with the World Indicative Plan for Agricultural Development. Perhaps this enterprise could obtain the co-operation of all governments in West and East even in the present state of international relations.

A programme based on the possibilities of food production and the increased food requirements according to demographic forecasts can then be drawn up to plan and describe the agricultural development projects.[84] Implementation would be entrusted to an international organization, such as the World Bank; probably better than any other existing institution, it could centralize the funds required and supervise expenditure, be flexible enough to direct operations according to each country's conditions, and enjoy enough authority for its advice and its control to be accepted by the governments concerned. There will be three categories of countries or regions: those that will contribute funds and personnel, those on the territory of which agricultural development will be undertaken, and those whose people need the food produced; several countries will be included in more than one of these categories. Some of the political and financial implications of such an enterprise are touched upon in the next chapter.

3. OPTIMUM POPULATION

Finally, it is not enough to make every possible effort to spread birth control and increase food production without knowing where we are heading and what we want to reach. Population growth even if basic food requirements are met entails many other conditions, such as increase of housing and consumption goods, expansion of public services and utilities, including administration, education, social services and medical care. It is not possible to shape a desirable future without introducing the notion of optimum population. It is self-defeating to go blindly and breathlessly ahead enlarging towns, increasing production, expanding public services, depleting natural resources, without having the least idea of where it would be best to stop. Planning for the future of a nation without any estimate of the best numbers for that nation is no planning at all. It can be called a race or a wager, but not a policy. No long-term planning can be expected to have beneficial results if it is not based on the term or limit of an optimum number of the population for whom the planning is required.

Since it is the fashion to speak of human problems in terms relevant to material questions, it may be remarked that the 'social productivity' of society does not increase indefinitely: it starts to fall after certain combinations of size, density and complexity are reached. Human beings are fully themselves in a community which gives them material and moral security, and provides the frame wherein each individual can improve himself and help to improve others. Primitive bands slowly evolved into larger groups, growing in size and complexity, until the modern nation-states came into being. Size and complexity are required to provide the members of a community with the benefits of material affluence, physical defence, intellectual interest, and moral security. Below a certain number, that in modern societies may be estimated in millions of individuals, a community cannot provide these benefits.

But it now becomes clear that increases in size and complexity above a certain level do not increase the 'productivity' of a community. The benefits for the individual are actually reduced or they are negatived by detrimental factors that appear to be inseparable from a high density of population and impossible to overcome. Too much society appears to be as bad as too little: both provoke suffering and neuroses. With multitudinous communities and urban overcrowding, whatever the degree of affluence, come three symptoms of disease: (a) Uniformity becomes the rule and diversity (or individuality) the exception. When people were fewer and less crowded together, diversity was greater and individuality better preserved and expressed. (b) Solitude of the individual comes with increase of the crowd. Loneliness of spirit grows with density of the herd. (c) Instead of enriching the life of individuals, an overcrowded, over-complex and over-numerous society impoverishes it.[85] As remarked in Part One, this social disease is compounded by the deterioration of physical environment that results from overcrowding, as disposal of sewage and waste becomes difficult and costly, and as natural sites are overrun by the works of men, their cities, roads, factories, markets, cinemas and cemeteries.

Thus there must be an optimum size and density that varies with the geographic conditions and the economic factors of each nation. A curve may be drawn for each national community, showing the point at which social return starts to drop after reaching a peak. The return falls because benefits are offset by new disadvantages following increase in size, density and complexity above an optimum level. Only in classical geometry can figures be indefinitely enlarged and keep their features unchanged. In social organization, as in biological evolution, size is closely linked with character. Increases in numbers bring about changes in quality. There is an optimum number for each nation or country, which ensures the greatest benefit to individuals, and above which society becomes impoverished in quality.

Optimum population is naturally a difficult notion to define and to apply. It depends in the first place on material elements, principally resources (including space) in relation to population. It also depends on the economic stage reached by a community, national or regional, and its expected rate of economic progress. Finally, it depends on the priorities of a community and the environment that it means to have or is prepared to accept. In effect, population policy can be designed only in the light of *a reasonable standard of living*, which includes moral as well as material elements. This standard must have a range wide enough to allow for necessary differences between national or regional communities. The lower limit of this range would be understood as the level below which a society declines in quality and the human values are depleted of content. The higher limit would be the level above which social return starts to fall, either because of a predominance of material over moral factors or because of exaggerated complexity and specialization, besides using a too great proportion of the planet's resources which should be fairly (but not necessarily equally) distributed to ensure that one day all humanity will be in the range of the reasonable standard of living.

The best way to apprehend this notion of a reasonable standard is to consider one of the material elements of living: the diet or food intake of individuals. A reasonable diet is now an accepted and well-defined notion, with a lower limit below which food intake is too little and an upper limit above which it is too much, and a sufficiently wide range between the two limits to allow for regional, professional and individual differences in the required food intake. Within this range, optimum diet is defined as being sufficient and well balanced. The measures of sufficiency (calories) and balance (the combination of carbohydrates, proteins and fats) are established. The parameters of a reasonable diet have been worked out and are now accepted by all. So must the measures, the parameters of a reasonable standard of living be elaborated until they too become accepted. Though more complex, this is a problem of the same nature as that of defining a reasonable diet.

A quick look at the world makes us feel that the majority of the human race is living below a reasonable standard and that a minority of affluent communities has probably reached the upper limit of a reasonable standard of consumption in the material elements of living. We feel this mainly by intuition, springing from a collection of more or less reasoned or conscious factors, such as the content of human values, a sense of possibilities for humanity as a whole, past progress and expected scientific and technological developments, and observation of the present. This intuition should now be proved or disproved by a combination of factual information and logical consideration. The question that should be answered is: 'Up to what level of consumption should the people of North America and Western Europe aspire to rise? Must it be indefinitely on the increase or should a ceiling be suggested—the same sort of ceiling as is practically attained for the diet and food intake of the affluent nations—above which it would be useless and even harmful for it to rise?' The notion of a reasonable standard of living, as a necessary factor in designing population policies, must now be elaborated and defined.

At present, there are no population policies because there are no population targets. In most countries of the world, except perhaps Australia and Canada, optimum number of population has been reached and probably exceeded, and should therefore be stabilized as far as possible. For very many countries, optimum population has certainly long been exceeded and there is little hope of returning to it, but even in such conditions a target must be fixed. Now, without targets, we just repeat that world population will be doubled by the end of the 20th century (imagination boggles at what it will be after that), that this is creating disastrous situations, that everything must be done to avert the disasters that can be averted, but there is little serious research on what population growth means in terms of human values in rich societies, in terms of famine and despair in the already overpopulated countries, in terms of perhaps insuperable difficulties for the world as a whole. Research on optimum population must be a primary concern of future-orientated institutions. It will include human values and social priorities with physical and material factors in order to reach balanced conclusions. Instead of going blindly ahead and hoping for the best, which is what every government without exception is doing now, long-term goals will be clearly defined. Information and action will be directed and concentrated towards those goals.

A favourable development in this connection is growing understanding in the advanced countries that money cost and return in every field of human endeavour, even purely economic, is only part of the total cost and return. Social profit and loss is receiving increasing attention as an essential factor for an overall and balanced view of a nation's position and progress. The idea of estimating the benefits, the social return that human beings obtain from social organization and operation, is thus gaining ground. The start of a *National Social Report* in U.S.A., as the necessary complement to the established *Economic Report*, is an important turning-point. The few men, sociologists, economists and administrators responsible for this initiative render great service to future generations, not only for America but also for all the other countries that must follow this lead.[86] Much research and experimentation are needed fully to develop the social indicators required for evaluating social trends and estimating social quality. These indicators (aimed at showing changes in the level or degree of positive factors such as culture, learning, family cohesion, public morality, democratic practice and negative factors such as crime, disease, alienation, pollution and plain ugliness of surroundings) can be elaborated only in the light of the fundamental human values and the social and individual priorities that derive from them. On the solid foundation of such research, optimum population can be defined, population targets determined and social policies designed for long-term goals.

II

World Community

EARTH WAS IMMENSE when men were few. The groups they formed were separated by much space. They ignored one another or they fought when they were too near. National communities evolved out of the growth and the coming together of these groups, and the process generally entailed coercion and violence. Within each national community a social conscience emerged, whereby individuals came to recognize their solidarity with each other as something natural. Now, with the human race spreading in multitudinous masses, Earth has shrunk and nations are in very close touch. They are still ready to fight and technology has armed them with weapons enough to obliterate them all. The juncture in human affairs is critical and it is slowly forcing the emergence of an ecumenical conscience that is not only religious, but also social and to some extent economic and political. It brings the gradual realization that mankind must become solidary on a world scale if it is to survive the present crisis and, with survival, retain hope and capacity for future progress. But time is short. Unless nations come without delay into a world community that will carry into effect the solidarity of all mankind, the crisis will be resolved in death and suffering and destruction. However, if world community cannot be born without coercion and violence, it can as well stay unborn, for violence at this stage will only bring the death and suffering and destruction that world community aims to avoid. The alternative is now world solidarity, quickly, or ruin of civilization. There is no third term.

I. THE WIDENING GAP

The national communities into which the human race is divided are at very different stages of cultural and economic development. The differences related to political and social institutions, philosophical and artistic achievements are not readily comparable, by numerical parameters or even by value estimates. The more comparable are those of economic development and technological advance, medical and social care, literacy and education. In most of these fields, the gap between the advanced nations and the others is very slowly narrowing. The exception is economic production and accumulated wealth where the rift is widening fast. The rich nations become richer; some poor nations become less poor, while others are stagnant or actually becoming more poor as development lags behind population growth and *per capita* income falls. All are falling further back in relation to the advanced nations. The reasons for the differences in present levels of development may be briefly reviewed as follows.

1. Progress alternates with stagnation, and sometimes regression, in national and regional histories and the periods do not coincide. This is the principal cause of the unbalance which has always existed between nations and which has in our time reached an absolutely critical stage. In Western history the Greeks, the Romans, the Arabs were in turn the pioneers of progress for several centuries. The nations of Western Europe took over with the Renaissance and since then their progress has been uninterrupted. With their natural offspring (North America and Australasia) and their relations by choice (Japan in particular) they are now the vanguard of civilization. The others dropped back. Nations that were civilized when Europe was inhabited by unknown savages have become poor and retarded. Nothing induces more comprehension of the solidarity of the human race than the realization that all of its ethnic divisions have at one time brought their contribution, great or small, to the human heritage. The sympathy of the advanced nations of this age must be aroused by the present distress of the others (especially considering that they are responsible for a good part of it) and by the recognition of the earlier breakthroughs in philosophy and art, in agriculture and technique, that laid the foundations for the European advance.

2. That, apart from the unique example of Japan, the effort to catch up with the advanced nations appears to be unavailing is due in part to another factor that aggravates the effect of the time-lag.

This is the accumulation of wealth in the rich countries, which makes for accelerated progress in technological skills and production capacity. The legendary inventor of chess is said to have claimed for his reward one grain of wheat on the first square of his board, two on the second, four on the third and so on. The poor nations are as at the beginning of such a sequence, while the rich nations have moved on from the sixty-fourth square. Even without arithmetical progression and compound interest, the regular percentage of revenue is large when the previous accumulation is very great. In the last seven years (1965 to 1971) the yearly increase of the gross national product of the United States of America was roughly equivalent to the total gross national product of all the African countries together (including South and North Africa) for each of the years concerned.

3. With scientific progress came the control of disease by prevention and cure. The Western countries helped the others with their health techniques and mortality rates fell rapidly. But birth rates remained high because the poor countries could not provide for their people the better education and living conditions that gradually led to a fall of the birth rate in the rich countries. Thus the phenomenal population increase in the poor countries is not covered by economic advance and social progress. Many of the poor nations become more poor as the greater part of their meagre resources is used to keep them at subsistence level (and sometimes not even that) without possibility of saving enough to invest in a significant increase of production capacity. This vicious circle is well known and there is no need here again to labour the point.

4. In some ways, social change in rich countries tends to inhibit development in poor countries. For instance, one result of technological progress and economic advance is more pay for less work. Workers in retarded nations are quick to claim this benefit without realizing the hard work of previous generations in the advanced nations (hard work that often involved the inhuman exploitation of slavery and sweat-shops) to build up the accumulation of wealth that allows for accelerated progress. Claims for social and economic benefits that do not correspond to their level of development tend to slow down progress in retarded nations, the people of which do not

understand the amount of work that must somehow be done *before* they can aspire to the first fruits of development. Naturally the underdeveloped nations are not required to submit to the same phases of exploitation that the presently advanced nations underwent or inflicted in the 19th century (though the Soviets did make a determined but unsuccessful effort in this century to exploit slave labour in detention camps) and in this they may be considered as privileged. But, on the other hand, agricultural and industrial workers in the retarded nations, besides the masses of unemployed and underemployed, cannot hope to obtain before several generations (if ever) the remuneration and the benefits now enjoyed by their counterparts in the advanced nations.

5. There are also the rising expectations in general of people in the poor countries, due as much to the promises of optimistic or demagogic governments as to the spread of literacy and information and the irresistible attraction of the expensive toys and gadgets of the affluent society. How can the poor countries provide the necessities for an exploding population, satisfy the demands of rising expectations, and retain the savings needed for productive investment? The answer is simply that they cannot fulfil the three requirements. To fulfil only the first unaided is already a well-nigh impossible task for many of these countries. The poor nations of the present time have no hope at all of reaching or approaching in the foreseeable future the standard of the presently rich nations. The projections in Herman Kahn and Anthony Wiener's *The Year 2000* are one more illustration of this unpalatable fact.

6. In addition to the resources required to provide necessities, satisfy demand and generate savings, funds are also required for armaments and war. Despite sanctimonious denials, there is sharp competition between the governments of arms exporting countries to market their costly and remunerative products (and incidentally to try out their latest weapons in contests between small nations). There are also the efforts of arms merchants to liven up the market for their goods, though such intrigues appear now to be taken up by government agencies. And there is the natural but scarcely rational desire of poor country rulers to possess the most and best of these traditional attributes of power. But besides these potent induce-

ments to purchase armaments, there is real necessity for many small and poor countries to have some power of defence and attack in order to subsist in the present violent and disorderly state of the world. Armament expenses contribute substantially to slow down economic development. It is obviously more serious for a poor nation to use part of its scanty resources for armaments than for a rich nation to spend a much greater proportion of its ample revenues for the same purpose. And armament purchases by poor countries do not even have the specious excuse of furthering technical progress and promoting industrial expansion in those countries such as are brought forward in the rich countries where armaments are manufactured. They are strictly waste of grievously needed resources which, materially and figuratively, go up in smoke.

7. Finally, there is exploitation of poor nations by the rich nations. In the past this was deliberate policy to benefit colonial powers by keeping their colonies in a state of dependency. Not only were the conditions for development neglected (save for production of raw materials and the basic equipment in ports, roads and railways required for delivering them at preferential rates to the so-called mother country) but even established industries where they existed were discouraged and destroyed.[87] Throttling of balanced development was a general policy under colonial rule, the only apparent exception being colonies where a pleasant climate and good prospects attracted European settlement with consequent displacement of the native population. Colonialism in this form is now out of date, though its baleful effects are still manifest in many of the difficulties that beset developing countries. The new exploitation arises more out of the nature of relations between rich and poor nations than out of deliberate intent. In the main, exploitation of the economically retarded by the economically advanced nations derives from the overwhelming disparity between them. This process may be observed from three angles:

(i) Exportable goods of the poor countries (generally the products of primary industry, agriculture and mining) are exchanged at increasingly disadvantageous rates against the goods of the rich countries (generally the products of complex secondary industry) which are needed by the poor countries for their economic development. This trend is due to the rising cost of the skills embodied in technologically advanced products and to the falling importance of many agricultural raw materials owing to the development of synthetic substitutes. As for the mining products required for advanced industry (a great part of which comes from the poor countries) their price is kept relatively low by the rich countries' control on the market, and to some extent by their control over the extraction of these products.[88] The growing disparity is exemplified in the increasing quantities of oil-seeds or coffee or hides that are required for the purchase of a standard machine, such as a jeep or a tractor. For more advanced machines, the disparity grows even faster. Economic development of the poor nations is thus slowed down by depreciation of their exportable resources, upon which they are expected to build up their economy.

(ii) In addition to the weighted rate of exchange between the products of the retarded nations and those of the advanced nations, there is also a draining away from the poor countries of capital return that could be better employed, in part at least, for the benefit of their economies. Notwithstanding the low price of mining products compared to their relative scarcity and to their importance for the advanced countries, profits from mining investments of the rich countries in the poor countries are often higher than profits from their manufacturing investments in retarded and advanced countries alike. Despite recent increase of the formerly scandalously small direct return (royalties or concession dues) to the country of origin on some mining products, notably oil, there is still room for improvement before some underdeveloped countries receive fair payment for the depletion of their non-recurrent natural resources, which constitute the mainstay of their development programmes. The United States in particular, since World Wars I and II practically wiped out European investments in Latin America, obtain from their mining and agricultural investments in Latin American republics profits exceeding what they pay to those countries in aid, part of which covers payment of profits as well as repayment of interest and principal on previous aid. Because of their financial weakness and inferior economic position, poor countries are helping to finance rich countries. The relation between them helps the rich countries to grow richer, while it does little to help the poor countries to grow less poor.

(iii) Then there is the brain drain. The flow is first towards the U.S.A. from the rest of the world, both developed and under-developed, and second towards Western Europe and Canada from the underdeveloped countries. Japan is practically not in this double circuit. Many thousands of qualified specialists (in medicine, biology, engineering, chemistry, electronics, law, etc.) go to work in U.S.A. every year, and their numbers are expected to grow in coming years. About a third of these graduates come from the poorer countries, who also compensate Western Europe for its own brain drain across the Atlantic.[89] Such emigrants from the under-developed countries are among their best human assets, in energy and initiative, in mental and physical health, in educational qualifi-cations. The social loss is considerable. The financial loss must also be noted, as the poor countries are not refunded for the expense of raising and educating these emigrants. Even if educational aid is taken into account (some British, French, German and Italian schools in underdeveloped countries, a few American universities abroad, scholarships for study in Europe and America) it does not compensate the poor nations for the loss of some of their most valuable members, who go to further the rich countries' develop-ment. Granted that graduates often emigrate because they cannot find in their country work to suit their capacities; granted also that the individuals concerned are glad to be able to escape to an ad-vanced country where they may find better material reward and an atmosphere more congenial to research or advancement; the fact remains that, because of the disparity between the rich and the poor nations, this is one more way for the former to be enriched by the latter.

* * *

This sombre picture must become darker and more ominous in the coming years. The rift between the advanced nations and the others is widening fast, and this growing unbalance is a mortal threat to peace and a grave challenge to the future of humanity. Judging from the quick succession of contemporary events and changes, the present crisis will be over by the end of this century, either by exploding into total disaster or by gradually subsiding through intelligent planning, generous effort and a basic concern with human values. The world is now really one and mankind is one community, because of the speed and volume of communication that makes every nation react to what happens in other nations; because of the complex interdependence of all countries, so that no country may remain isolated however powerful and self-contained it is; because of the considerable sacrifices that must be borne by all, the rich and the poor, in order to avert the dangers that threaten all alike; because the future such as it will be must eventually be shared by all alike, so that all in the long-term view have an equal stake in the march towards progress and hopefully towards real improvement of the human condition.

2. INTERNATIONAL SOLIDARITY

As private and voluntary benefaction often preceded, in the social evolution of a nation, public assistance through imposed contributions, so must the voluntary assistance afforded by the rich to the poor nations now be superseded by an imposed or rather a formally accepted charge on the ones in favour of the others. Private benevolence helped to establish the principle of social solidarity in a national community and social services gradually became the responsibility of the community, to be rendered by its constituted authorities. Likewise, the assistance granted by prosperous nations to other nations temporarily or permanently impoverished helped to spread the wider concept of an international community, to extend the principle of solidarity to all mankind, and to pave the way for an international authority to render assistance where it is needed. The total volume of assistance from the richer to the poorer members of a national community was greatly increased after contributions became determined and imposed by taxation; so must the total volume of aid from the rich countries to the others now be greatly increased by an international agreement to fix the amount and nature of this aid.

The idea of international human solidarity is thus slowly ripening and left to itself could eventually, unless disaster intervenes in the meantime, materialize in practical and generalized implementation. But the present juncture is urgently perilous, and every effort must be made to hasten the process. Within a very short time arrangements should be completed for a world organization of contributions from nations who can afford them to nations who need them. Primarily, it is a question of informing public opinion. Why should we submit to more taxes for foreign aid? Why should we give up part of what we could enjoy in order to help people whom we do not know and who will not be grateful? Do these people have votes to help our parties and support our establishments? Have we not our own poor to help and our own problems to solve before we help other people? Why should we make sacrifices to aid other nations, less estimable perhaps or less deserving than we? These are questions constantly asked or implied. They are similar to questions debated at an earlier stage of social evolution, when solidarity was not yet an undisputed principle of national societies.

The answers are simple, but they must be explained and illustrated by speakers and writers, statesmen and pressmen, by all advisers of public opinion. The parallelism of social interdependence in the national and international fields, the logical and ethical basis for extending the principle of solidarity to humanity as a whole, the recognition that all must live or sink together on this shrinking and overcrowded world, the argument of self-interest in co-operating to avoid the common danger, the understanding that human values can be respected only if they are respected for all—these are the main themes in support of a practical and general implementation of international solidarity. Considering the generosity of people in many of the affluent countries and their liberal contributions to foreign aid through non-government institutions, religious and others, it may be observed that in this as in so many other aspects of social progress, individual recognition and private action preceded political and administrative institutionalization.

There is a price to pay, as there is for every act of forethought and wisdom. It is the same kind of price as was paid when the notion of solidarity between the members of a nation grew to be an uncontested principle: the sacrifice of short-term benefits for long-term interests. The investment then made in human solidarity was repaid a thousand-fold in improvement of social relations, increased cohesion and stability of society, and the consequent development of human activity and invention in fields more productive than social strife or violent revolution. There is still a long way ahead before the notion of solidarity on a world scale becomes as ingrained in every human being as national solidarity has become in every citizen of a modern state. Too many interests, political and financial, still conspire to keep aid to poor nations dependent on the short-term benefit (in terms of immediate profit or saving) to influential groups in the contributing nations, rather than the long-term benefits (in terms of peace and consequent progress and development) to their nations and to humanity as a whole. But there is no other way to go. . . .

*   *   *

In 1967 the total output or GNP of the industrial nations was esti-mated at $1½ trillion and they allocated $7½ billion in new funds to developing countries. About $2½ billion were returned in interest and instalments on principal of previous loans, leaving a net flow of $5 billion, about 0.33 per cent (one-third of 1 per cent) of the industrial nations' GNP. The same year, military expenses were near to $100 billion for the West and probably half that amount for Russia and the communist camp. The poor nations are getting deeper into debt: in the ten years from 1955 to 1964 their indebtedness rose from an average of 6 to 18 per cent of their GNP, while repayments on past loans increased from 8 to 30 per cent of aid received. In the circumstances, it is disastrous that the flow of aid should be growing so slowly, especially as the cost of equipment, commodities and experts to be financed by international assistance is constantly rising.

American aid is naturally the highest in amount and it still ac-counts for roughly half of the total flow of aid from the industrial Western nations, but it is no longer the highest in relation to revenue. That distinction is now with some Western European countries, especially France whose foreign aid keeps close to 1 per cent of GNP. The United States government pioneered most of the now well-established forms of international aid. American economic aid reached a peak in 1951, when it was $7,836 million, over 13 per cent of total federal expenditure and over 2 per cent of GNP. Most of this assistance served to rebuild Western Europe. Since then it declined, not only in proportion to the fast-rising GNP, but in absolute amount. It was $4,175 million in 1966, just over 3 per cent of federal expenditure and 0.6 per cent of GNP. In 1967 it was $3,386 million, 0.37 per cent of GNP. For 1968, the amount of $3,126 million budgeted by the administration was reduced by congress to $2,300 million, 0.25 per cent of GNP, one-quarter of 1 per cent. In 1969, American aid rose slightly to 0.43 per cent of GNP. In 1970, it fell again to 0.38 per cent. These approximate figures do not include military aid.

The relative stagnation of aid from the rich to the poor countries since 1965 may be ascribed in part to disappointment with the apparently meagre economic and political results of the money and effort expended, as well as to irritation at the dubious response of some of the receiving governments and the small amount of goodwill generated in the recipient nations. Four causes may be suggested for the defects and inefficiency of foreign aid: (1) It seldom corresponds to the real priorities of the recipient countries, because of competition and lack of co-ordination between donor countries. (2) Co-ordination is also lacking in aid programmes to neighbouring countries, which would often require regional or sub-regional planning in order to be more effective. (3) It is impossible to organize aid to underdeveloped countries on the basis of long-term plans because funds are not available on a long-term recurrent basis. (4) In any case, the amount of aid is insufficient in money and in the provision of technical know-how and skills.

These causes appear to be related to some forms of aid more than to others. The term of aid is loosely used for a variety of international transactions, some of which should not be considered as aid: (1) outright donation of money, equipment or foodstuffs, (2) technical assistance free of charge, (3) very long-term loans at nominal interest, (4) long-term loans at reduced interest for purchases of raw materials or foodstuffs from the giving country, (5) long-term loans at current market interest without condition, (6) long-term loans at current market interest with condition of using them to purchase goods or services from the giving country, and (7) capital investment in economic enterprises. Categories 1, 2 and 3 are properly aid, in the sense of assistance given without financial counterpart. Categories 4 and 5 are also aid, but with some financial counterpart. Categories 6 and 7 are not aid, as they are simply credits opened by the giving country for purchase of its goods by the receiving country or investments in the receiving country which are expected to bring an adequate return in dividends for the giving country. Such operations are normal commercial and financial practice, useful to both parties but hardly deserving to be treated as beneficence, and they should not be included as part of the total aid given or received by a country. In effect, a good part of foreign aid as it is now defined is little more than a form of subsidy for the exports of the rich countries.

Bilateral aid, involving only one giving and one receiving country, is the most frequent and it provides for the greater portion of foreign aid in the world. It may take the form of any of the transactions that are usually considered as aid. Bilateral aid tends to be geared to the giving country's political and economic interest. The political strings are well known. Each of the advanced powers has its own political conditions for giving or withholding aid. Economic strings are neither so frequent nor so apparent. They generally entail that development of production that could compete with that of the giving country is discouraged, even if it is in line with the receiving country's best interest, while useless or uneconomic projects are sometimes fostered on receiving countries in order to serve some interest in the giving country. Aid from or through an international authority (a world organization) is not influenced by special political and economic interests as it has no special interests to serve. Some forms of multilateral aid, such as aid from the European Economic Community to groups of African countries, partake of some characteristics of bilateral aid (in that it is not independent of the political and economic interests of the giving group) and of aid by a world organization (in that it can be guided by a wider and more coordinated perspective).

Aid from private enterprise is often mentioned in the context of international assistance, and its scope and character must be made clear. First, it should not be considered properly as aid because it is limited to transactions involving current rates of interest or normal return on investment. Also, it is practically limited to agricultural and industrial enterprises with a marketable production. It cannot provide funds for basic equipment of developing countries in transport, communications, irrigation and power supply, as well as general and technical education. Finally, it requires from the host country normal legal, fiscal and administrative security, together with some incentive from its country of origin, such as guarantees against loss of capital or fiscal facilities. Within these limits, private enterprise has a vital role to play in the Third World by collaborating with local capital and executives to establish and operate agricultural and manufacturing concerns that cannot properly be in the field of public aid. Such collaboration, when implemented in a spirit of fairness and equity for the interest of the host country as much as that of the foreign investors and managers, gives a healthy impetus to economic development and usefully improves the supply of local skills and know-how. But government to government aid, preferably through an international authority, remains the basic source of assistance to developing countries.

While the defects of international aid to the poor nations are painfully manifest, its beneficial results are apt to be passed over. It could not indeed arrest the widening gap between rich and poor countries but, insufficient, provisional and unco-ordinated as it has been, the situation of the poor countries would now be very much worse had this aid not been given. It has averted widespread famine many times and reduced the incidence of natural catastrophes such as floods and earthquakes. It has provided a considerable part of the basic equipment of underdeveloped countries. It has helped (certainly not enough and perhaps not always wisely) to provide general education and technical instruction. It has also made a great contribution towards raising the level of public health, both for prevention of endemic and epidemic diseases (malaria, bilharzia, sleeping sickness and others) and cure (hospitals and clinics). It has established pilot plants and rural development projects.[90] In short, it has helped the poor nations to reach their present level of development which, low as it is compared to the advanced nations, would now be lower had international aid not been forthcoming. Despite its defects, it has laid the foundation and provided the experience for establishing real international solidarity.

The Marshall Plan was outstandingly successful because it combined all the conditions required to avoid the usual defects of international aid: (a) it was understood that it would be continued as long as needed, (b) there was a measure of co-ordination between the receiving countries and (c) the amount of aid was relatively much greater than the present loans or donations of the rich to the poor countries. To be sure, these conditions cannot be met to the same extent in aid to the underdeveloped nations, who are at a technical and social level lower than the nations of Western Europe and who, moreover, do not enjoy the same basic unity of history and culture. But the Marshall Plan remains the best model for international aid, and organization of the urgently needed help from the rich to the poor nations should be inspired by its conception and its implementation. There is no alternative to a co-ordinated flow of aid to the underdeveloped countries. The flow must be directed and controlled by an international institution enjoying adequate assurance of integrity, independence, and expert knowledge. The World Bank, with its divisions of IBRD, IDA and IFC and such other divisions as may be required to expand its operation, appears to be the best nucleus for this institution.

Assistance—economic and financial, educational and technical— must be organized on a world-wide basis, in order to carry out an overall plan of development independent of diverging political aims, thus ensuring full co-ordination and avoiding duplication or contradiction in the allocation of funds. The overall approach will also stress development planning on the basis of regional rather than strictly national needs and resources. At the start it may not be possible to include communist countries as givers or receivers in the organization, but once it is established it should not be long before most countries of the world decide to join. The receiving countries will be obtaining assistance from the international or rather supra-national institution, and only indirectly from the contributing governments. The source of assistance should no longer be a particular country, but the whole group of contributing countries. The same anonymity of relation between contributors and recipients should prevail in the operation of international solidarity as now exists in the funding and operation of national social services.

Contributions of the giving countries should henceforth be in equal proportion and on a permanent basis, in order to ensure a fair distribution of charges and a continuous supply of funds, thus allowing the international organization to promote and co-ordinate long-term planning. At present the World Bank is expanding its operations in the poor countries after having devoted the greater portion of its funds and efforts to reconstruction of advanced countries devastated by World War II. But despite the relatively small volume of its operations, it cannot be certain of its future possibilities and it has to borrow part of its funds from the money market. Thus it cannot make long-term plans for regional development and its action, beneficial as it is, remains of limited use compared to the magnitude and urgency of present need. With regular and sufficient contributions coming to feed a constantly growing fund for assistance to recipient countries, it will be able to expand its operations and promote agricultural and industrial development on a scale commensurate with the gravity of the situation.

The basis of contribution should be a fixed percentage of the GNP of the giving countries. The undertaking to make this contribution should be embodied in an international agreement, binding for at least twenty years with possibility of revisal from time to time according to well-defined rules. Foreign aid, in the sense of an accepted 'tax', will thus become a fixed post in the national budget of each contributing country, to be computed every year by the same method in relation to national revenue. Thus foreign aid will not be subject to yearly budgetary discussion by parliaments and policy-making bodies. The total aid to needy nations given by the fifteen richest nations of the Western world is now less than one-half of 1 per cent (on an average) of their total output or GNP, and part of this aid is nullified by the increasingly disadvantageous rate of exchange between raw materials and technologically advanced products. From the standpoint of the needs of overpopulated and underdeveloped countries and the extreme gravity of the present unbalance and disparity between nations, this aid cannot bring effective remedy and it holds out little hope for a civilized solution to the present crisis in human affairs. A contribution of 2 per cent of GNP would now be a reasonable basis for discussion.[91]

Though some believe that this target of 2 per cent of GNP is far too low[92] and others that it is too high,[93] it appears to be both adequate and feasible as the overall goal for implementation of human solidarity between all nations. It is adequate as it would ensure that sufficient material equipment and technical know-how are transferred from the rich to the poor countries, so that the standard of living of the poor nations may be expected to improve despite population increase, i.e. that the rate of development will be higher than the rate of population growth. It is feasible because there is a precedent, when Americans generously gave over 2 per cent of their GNP over a period of time when Europe was in dire need. A realization of the need of the underdeveloped countries and of the danger of the present unbalance for rich and poor alike should elicit a similar response from public opinion in America and the other advanced countries. Also there is hope—there must be hope unless catastrophe is inevitable—that defence expenses will be reduced and that funds will thereby be released to fight poverty abroad as well as domestic poverty. Besides, a four-fold increase in the present flow of international aid will certainly bring complex administrative problems which will have to be solved in the most practical and efficient manner. A greater flow than the one proposed would appear to present insuperable practical difficulties, at least until more experience has been gained in international assistance.

While there is obvious need to augment the flow of multilateral aid, which presently accounts for about one-tenth of the net receipts of financial resources by developing countries, it cannot be expected entirely to supplant bilateral aid. Besides military assistance, there will always be a field for bilateral aid, both as an instrument of competition between states and as special consideration to nations with particular cultural appeal or political importance for the donor country. However, as the advantages of multilateral aid become more manifest (better use of assistance through co-ordination and overall planning, avoidance of the stresses that often derive from direct donor-recipient relations) it will channel a growing part of international assistance. Further, as the World Aid Organization becomes better able to cope with overall planning, up to the final goal of a world plan for development, its directives will influence bilateral aid transactions, which will tend to fall in line with the overall plan and thus avoid some of their present defects. The World Aid Organization will act as the centralizing and co-ordinating agency for international assistance rather than as the sole channel for the total flow of aid. A useful start is being made in this connection with the meetings of groups of representatives of donor countries which are convened from time to time by the World Bank in order to co-ordinate the flow of aid to a given country or region, and to obtain a clearer picture of the views and the needs of the recipient country in discussion with its representatives.

If the poor nations' urgent need may thus become in the name of human solidarity the basis for a moral and contractual right to aid from the rich nations, this right will entail as a necessary counterpart duties that must also be recognized. Tentatively, such duties could be defined along the following lines and they should be the object of explicit undertakings by the governments concerned: (a) effectively to respect in law and in practice the human rights as listed in international declarations and covenants in their dealings with their subjects and the subjects of other governments; (b) to refrain from diverting resources and revenues for unproductive use, such as political propaganda or subversion in other countries, or war unless for strictly defensive purposes; (c) to implement an effective programme of family planning and birth control as an integral part of public policy; (d) to carry out, with the speed and to the extent compatible with each nation's circumstances, the legal, administrative and financial reforms required to open the way to economic growth; (e) to ensure social justice as far as compatible with the requirements of development, to fight corruption, and to abolish anti-social and anti-economic privilege; and (f) fully to co-operate with the international development organization in all social and economic aspects of national and regional planning. The difficulties of defining such duties and supervising their execution are obvious. It will not be easy for such changes in government behaviour to be effected. The noxious idea of absolute state sovereignty will long remain a stumbling-block for real international co-operation and solidarity. But a code of duties will have to be accepted or the effective solidarity so desperately needed by humanity will not materialize.

The international development institution will have, within closely defined limits, a right of supervision and control in the assisted nations. This control can be carried out by a joint office or commission in each country, composed of responsible officials of that country and of the international institution, whose role will be to approve projects in line with national and regional development plans, and to supervise their execution. The fact that the control will be effected at high level, by members of the government in collaboration with foreign officials independent of any other government, will allow it to be smooth and effective. Governments of assisted countries will accept from such a commission the advice and the control which they now reject—with much justification—when they come from the representatives of other governments, even those that are directly providing much needed aid. This is not a veiled return to a sort of neo-colonialism, but the establishment of human solidarity on a world scale; not a doctrine of limited sovereignty enunciated by the strong against the weak, but a sacrifice of some part of sovereignty by strong and weak alike in order to ensure real international co-operation.

Direct aid must be supplemented by measures to improve the terms of trade between the advanced and the developing countries. The latter's share in international trade is falling (31.2 per cent in 1950 and 17.6 per cent in 1970, twenty years after) and it consists mainly of raw materials (40 per cent of world exports) and very little of manufactured goods (only 6 per cent of world exports). Improvement may be achieved by encouraging exports of finished and semi-finished products from the developing to the advanced countries. Preferential treatment, such as duty-free importation for these products, will stimulate industrial development in the poor countries and, at the same time, help to raise their frighteningly low level of economic employment. Many products of technologically non-advanced industries can just as well be produced in the developing countries, with contributions of capital and know-how from the advanced countries. Naturally, such a policy will discourage the further growth or even the continuation of such industries in the advanced countries, and this will entail sacrifices which it is only fair to recognize. The European Economic Community, with much foresight and some courage, has made a start in this direction. It may be expected that this lead will be followed by other industrially advanced countries, especially U.S.A. and Japan, and that the preferential treatment accorded to manufactured and semi-manufactured goods from the developing countries will be expanded in scope and value.

To recognize that massive aid is required for the poor nations does not mean to say that they will have less need for self reliance, but rather that without more self-reliance they cannot benefit from increased aid. The maximum transfers of capital and know-how will not ensure economic advance of the underdeveloped nations without their own self-reliant efforts. But, conversely, the utmost effort and self-reliant austerity by the poor nations will not promote their economic development at a rate commensurate with the magnitude and urgency of their need unless sufficient aid is forthcoming from the advanced nations.[94] The balance between internal effort (savings, initiative and hard work) and external assistance (in capital, knowledge and experience) should not be hard to maintain for proper coordination and efficient execution. Important adjustments yet have to be made in the application of financial resources and technical know-how to the problems of developing nations. This will entail some short cuts and some new methods, as it will not do just to continue retracing the steps of the advanced nations. Also, present trends of the advanced nations in most things besides their material progress are not so attractive that their image of the future cannot be bettered. Above all, regional co-operation between the developing countries themselves in Asia, Africa and Latin America is absolutely essential in the fields of industrial development, education and technical research.

*   *   *

Nothing less than arrangements of the breadth and scope outlined in the preceding pages can be expected to avert the threats and the dangers of the present juncture in human affairs. The more they are delayed, the less chances there will be to resolve an explosive situation by civilized means. The second United Nations Conference on Trade and Development (UNCTAD) held at New Delhi early 1968 was a bitter disappointment. One is left with a sense of wonder at the short-sightedness and lack of statesmanship shown there by the governments of rich and poor countries alike. For the world to continue with declining aid and deteriorating ratios between the rich and the poor nations, with the former unable to realize their responsibilty and the effort that is required of them and the latter unwilling to accept the supra-national planning and control that this effort entails, is to plunge towards inevitable catastrophe. As the secretary-general of UNCTAD stated after the New Delhi meeting, 'there is a great opportunity for world leadership. . . . Now the whole world is at stake. There is tremendous opportunity for bold initiative. . . .' Indeed, it depends on a few men in key positions that bold initiative be exercised and farsighted leadership be forthcoming.

But it must be stressed again that, if war continues to be a normal contingency, there is little hope that the growing unbalance between nations will be corrected and that the extreme gravity of the present crisis will be reduced. Even the United States (which with 6 per cent of world population provide nearly one-third of its industrial production) cannot wage a war—even a limited one—and at the same time make a significant advance in its internal fight against poverty and an adequate contribution to foreign aid. Ardent believers in the cure-all power of technology count on its accelerating progress to solve the problems of overpopulation and underdevelopment, but they have to admit that the solution will be impossible to realize if wars continue and if war industries cannot be converted to pacific uses. The policy to be boldly, imaginatively and perseveringly pursued is to achieve co-operation between U.S.A. and U.S.S.R. By this co-operation peace may be maintained and military expenditure reduced, so that humanity may live through the next thirty years without disaster, after which—with population control established and balanced economic progress on the way—the worst of the crisis should be over. The prospects for such an outcome are hardly favourable at present. . . .

12

Education and Instruction

EDUCATION AND INSTRUCTION refer to complementary aspects of bringing human beings to maturity and adulthood. The first is the process of developing the person, of bringing out its intellectual and emotive qualities, its powers of self-expression, its capacity for service to itself and to others; while the second must be considered primarily as the process of imparting the information required for understanding the world and keeping alive therein. The distinction should always be maintained. Education is directed towards the harmonious maturing of the person, by keeping the difficult balance between the claims of the individual and those of society. Instruction aims to impart a framework of facts and skills, and keeping the not less difficult balance between general and specialized knowledge. The two notions unfortunately tend to be confused and the two words are indiscriminately used as interchangeable terms.

In practice the two obviously go hand in hand. They are carried out in the same periods (childhood, adolescence and on into maturity), by the same organs (family, school, college, university, social relations) and sometimes with the same subject matter (for example, a high-school text-book on sociology has both an educational aim and an instructional content). There should be no conflict between education and instruction, but such a conflict now exists. It derives from the growing complexity of society and the accelerated progress of science and technology. It is expressed in the opposition between general education and specialization, humanities and science, moral order and conditioned behaviour. Because of this opposition, the ever-renewed task of raising the young to adulthood becomes increasingly hard. Never has the perennial problem of bridging the generation gap been so difficult. Each generation must in turn instil into the young the accumulated heritage of human achievement.

This entails keeping yet a third difficult balance between a grounding in tradition, without which there can be no civilization and culture, and a capacity for change, without which there is also no civilization or enduring culture. No less is involved than the whole conception of education and instruction in modern society.

Logically, the process of bringing up the young may be divided into four parts or stages. The first is to learn the physical accomplishments of eating, walking, speaking and keeping clean. The second is to be trained in the basic rules of social discipline. The third concerns the tradition of thought and culture, while the fourth concerns the knowledge and skills required for earning a livelihood and being of service. Except for the first, which requires no elucidation, the others are here examined under successive headings, but only for the purpose of analysis. In reality, the process is continuous and indivisible. Many of the shortcomings of education and instruction, so visibly manifested in contestation and alienation and inadaptation, derive from discontinuity and division, both in theory and in practice. Some would say that the shortcomings are with society itself, and maybe this is so, as education and instruction are so closely woven into the fabric of society. Closer examination of this very complex problem may help to discover some pointers for present and future.

I. SOCIAL DISCIPLINE

Social discipline derives from the basic requirements for relations between human beings: respect of self and others, respect of the given word, not to kill or hurt or insult, not to lie, not to steal. These rules and prohibitions are applications of the fundamental human values. They have generally been unchallenged in theory, though they have been denied in the past and are still sometimes denied in the name of race or state or party. This is not a reference to war, when all rules and prohibitions are lifted for the enemy, but to sacralization of the state under totalitarian rule. 'Honour neither thy father nor thy mother, but denounce them and condemn them to death if they work against Me.'[95] In such reminiscent form may be paraphrased the precepts of totalitarian society, that are inculcated into its youth formations (Hitler Jugend, Komsomols, Red Guards and varied brown, black, green and other hued shirts) in order to weaken their allegiance to personal and social morality and to condition them as servants of the state. People in the democratic nations are still repulsed by such ideas, because they are not yet conditioned by a mechanistic conception of society, by the creeping ambivalence of morality, by the insidious submission of the good to the useful, of the right to the workable.

Educators, who work on constantly renewed material, can take nothing for granted, least of all the basic values and the rules of a free and decent society, which are often regarded as so elementary and self-evident that they are not in need of definition and affirmation. If these rules are not presented as inherently good and right, but only as useful to behave in society and to get on in life, there may come a time in an individual's career or a nation's history when they do not look so useful: it will be easy then to deny them, because usefulness was the only reason for holding to them. 'Honesty is the best policy' is an immoral saying, for it implies that there could be another policy which would be indicated in other circumstances. Honesty is not a policy at all, but an essential condition for human society. This sounds like moralizing, and so it is. How can a civilization be preserved and transmitted and improved without moral ideas and ethical priorities? The fundamental human values, and the basic rules of social discipline that derive from them, are the essential heritage of civilization. They must be passed on to each generation. They must be instilled into boys and girls, even if men and women will later suffer because society denies or ignores the principles that they were taught in their formative years. Without these values, the individual becomes one of a herd, ready to follow the opinions of others because he has none of his own and to copy group behaviour because he has no personal code of conduct.

This is a point of friction between an inherited order and present-day pragmatism. With the erosion of the morality based on the human values, caused as much by immobilism and stagnation as by materialist and determinist trends, comes a breakdown of intellectual and social discipline. The technicist society is now in formation, guided by the pragmatic determinism of technique. Those who abide by its rules and its logic constitute an extreme branch of opinion. On the other side are those who suffer from the rejection of moral order, because they are more sensitive or more imaginative. In their recoil from the shallow logic of determinism and the inhuman reason of technique, they plunge into the depths of a new nihilism, that excludes neither curiosity nor activity, but recognizes no order and no restraints (social, moral, intellectual, and even aesthetic).[96] They constitute the other extreme. Between the two, the majority vegetates with tranquillizers and constant distraction, while a minority preserve their human poise and anxiously observe the trends of the new society. Both extremes are irrational, though logically consistent; both are alienated from society; with neither can civilization be safe. This is an urgent problem that confronts educators in the widest sense of the term, all those who take a part in instructing the young and edifying the not so young.

What should be taught for the future, a set of values that corresponds to the worth and dignity of a human being, or a system of behaviour that is adapted to present trends? Freedom of mind and body, self-discipline and self-reliance, initiative and imagination, courage and acceptance of risk, the character not to be one of the herd, fearlessness in the expression of charity and the defence of what is right, none will deny that these are the qualities which make a civilized human being, and which are the spring of energy and the inspiration for achievement in a nation. But many people wonder if they are still the qualities that should be encouraged in the boys and girls of today, if they will not be a handicap for them in the overcrowded and technicized society of tomorrow, as they are in fact already a handicap under regimes that deny individual liberty or distort the idea of freedom into some totalitarian monstrosity. Should young people now be taught the lesser qualities of acquiescence, of conformism, of compliance and unthinking obedience to the social system? The answer is no, a thousand times no, unless a debasement of civilization is to be accepted. There are signs that young people all over the world, but more forcefully in the advanced countries, are groping in their violent and muddled way towards the same refusal and trying to resolve for their generation the discord between the human values and present social trends.

The young generations are socially conscious and they are not con-

tent with lip service. In the poor nations, the weakening of traditional social structures and the increase of education and information
makes for rising awareness in young people of what is wrong with
their society. In the rich nations, the relatively high average level of
prosperity helps to liberate and to focus the need for an ideal, which
otherwise might not have emerged out of the general obligation of
labour. It is a mark of the inherent kindness of human beings that,
when they do not have to worry about bread and roof, many start to
worry about less material aims for their activity and that this change
of perspective often leads to a concern for the well-being of others.
Young people cannot find an ideal in the materialist outlook of
modern society or, for the greater part, in the rituals of the established churches. They have not been taught the fundamental values
of their heritage, neither in family nor in school, neither by precept
nor by example, or else they have heard them presented in a per-
functory manner and then observed how little they are respected by
their elders. In a sense, they try to discover the human values, to
think them out for themselves. Their feelings are strong but often
confused. Generous impulse alone seldom leads to right action.
Some dissociate themselves from society with groups and communities that try to realize the timeless dream of human brotherhood.
Others escape into drug addiction from the reality they refuse. Many
are motivated, more maturely, by charity and brotherly understanding which often find expression in service to others. And some
adopt violence as an outlet for their feelings and their energy, but
they are still a minority.

There is movement and fermentation everywhere, perhaps more
visible and more varied in America than elsewhere. In the present
crisis of human affairs, young people appear to be taking up the
challenge and trying to find an answer. Whether the right answer
will be discovered, whether it will rally a consensus of opinion, and
whether it can be translated into action, these are the important
questions for the near future. Meanwhile, it is a pity that the social
establishment is generally hostile to young people's ideal of justice
and charity, unmarred by the prejudices of older generations. What
some of the new generation are trying to prove by contesting war and
poverty and discrimination is often worth while. If they prove it

badly, with little sense of measure, only their lack of years and insufficiency of education are to blame. When they are attracted to violent nihilist or leftist subversion, the ones to blame are their elders who did not prevent the opposition between fundamental values and the structure and operation of social relations. Young people need an ideal to look up to and to work for. Voluntary service organizations[97] provide some answer to this need. The best answer would be a society where the fundamental values alone set the priorities and the goals. Education in social discipline based on the human values would help to channel young people's energy into ways, peaceful but forceful, that would be more conducive to building such a society.

2. CONTENT OF CULTURE

One feature or power in men's minds sets them apart from everything else in the universe as we know it. It is not intelligence in general, which is shared in some degree by the higher mammals. It is not the capacity to suffer, though man has it in an infinitely greater measure. It is not even the power of reasoning, which may be observed and developed in some animals. Stretching a point, it can be said that bees are intelligent, that dolphins can speak, dogs can reason and some animals can love. Only reflective consciousness makes human beings absolutely different and puts them on a higher plane: the faculty to know and judge oneself; the capacity to suffer and to see oneself suffer, to be joyful and aware of joy; the power to think and to realize the range and limit of one's thought, to know that one is alive and to know that one will die. A human being would be near to an animal if, despite his power of reasoning, he were unaware of his deeper self and unperceptive of the selves of others. A man is not a man because he can reason, but because he is conscious and aware, and it is to make him less of a man to develop his reason and at the same time to deaden his conscience, distract his awareness and narrow his perceptions.

'We are still a long way from understanding what it signifies that nothing has any existence until some small—and oh, so transitory—consciousness has become aware of it.' Nothing can be said to exist if there is no conscious mind aware of its existence, through the senses or by logical inference. The really inspiring prospect of space travel is one day to encounter thinking beings that are not of Earth, but until this stupendous event may come to pass, man remains the only conscious entity in the universe (apart from a first cause, a transcendental creator, God on the nature of Whom human beings are not agreed). Man 'alone has given to the world its objective existence—without which ... it would have gone on in the profoundest night of non-being down to its unknown end'. Culture and creativity, civilization and social order can be conceived only in terms of the human person. Thought kindles 'a light in the darkness of non-being' and this is accomplished primarily by consciousness of self, which leads to awareness of others and awareness of the world around and all it contains. 'Attainment of conscience is culture in its broadest sense.'[98]

In its objective meaning, culture is the complex of ideas and priorities, arts and techniques that form the character and the distinctive features of a civilization. In its subjective meaning, it is the portion of these several elements that finds place in the minds of individual persons. Objectively, there are primitive cultures and advanced cultures. Subjectively, people are more or less cultured. The more cultured person is the more conscious: he holds in his mind a greater portion of the elements (moral and intellectual, technical and artistic) that make up the culture to which he belongs; he is more aware of fundamental values and this gives him a perceptive understanding of other cultures. A less cultured person is less aware: he possesses a lesser portion of these elements; he has less understanding of other cultures because he is less well grounded in his own. Proceeding in a descending scale through broadening sections, the elements of culture become less varied and less defined as the number of people who share them grows greater. The base of the pyramid is mass culture in its proper sense. In a balanced society the higher and lower levels of culture are complementary and there is fruitful interaction between them. The *quality* of a civilization depends mainly on the higher levels, the outstanding individuals, the exceptional minds, the leaders of thought and action, those who are most cultured because they are most aware. While the *vitality* of a civilization rests on its common cultural denominator: the higher this denominator is—that is, the more elements of culture, the more feeling for human values, the more understanding of right and wrong are shared by all members of a society—the greater will be the cohesion and the resilience of that society.

With this definition in mind, we can ask: 'what are the traditions, the philosophical and moral rules, the social and political principles that must be consciously upheld and transmitted to each generation?' The question should not be hard to answer. In the first place, there is the substratum of fundamental values that are essential to any civilization. If they have become more linked to Western civilization, it is because Western thinkers have thought more about them and Western people have had more experience with them. They are part of the heritage of mankind, but they are part of Western culture more than of any other culture. In education, they must be the basic content of the culture that is transmitted from generation to generation. In this study, an effort has been made to show that the best quality of Western civilization has been to recognize individual human values as the ends of the social order, and individual rights and duties as the foundation of social organization; that its achievements derive from this recognition more than from talents and abilities inherent to the nations that belong to it; that its faults and its failures came out of its denials of human values and human rights to its own people and to people of other cultures; that the danger which now besets it—and with it the rest of the world —is that these values may be squeezed out by demographic and technological pressures.

In the second place, the content of culture is the theoretical and practical superstructure of principles and priorities and institutions that each nation or group of nations has built on the substratum, and which constitute the features that distinguish one civilization from another. Thoughtful historians and gifted writers have been concerned to make the inheritors of Western civilization better acquainted with its roots and its flowering, more conscious of its virtues and its defects, more aware of the challenge with which it is faced. But, to come down to practicalities, for the family sphere, for school curricula, for TV programmes, what is the understanding of average Europeans and Americans regarding the things they hold good and the things they hold bad, the philosophical and moral heritage that they would want to pass on to their children? All would no doubt think of peace and social justice, public welfare and a measure of material affluence, but there would be little else. Now that value judgments are shunned, that reason must be divorced from emotion, that the issues of right and wrong, good and evil tend to be replaced by considerations of what is practical or unpractical, workable or unworkable, few would think of a moral and philosophical heritage. There would be pride in scientific, technical and economic achievements (a minority would add artistic acccomplishments) but little awareness of the values and priorities that made these achievements possible and without which they will not prosper. For the great mass, the content of Western civilization is distressingly poor. The highest common denominator is too low. 'A civilization whose grandeur is appreciated only by a vanishingly small fraction of the population is not a very safe one.'[99]

The problem is more complex—and no less important—for the Third World, where there is much ferment over national identification, together with the difficulty of adapting traditional society to the requirements of social and economic development. Besides these two questions, which are common to all the poorer or less advanced nations, the position is different for those who boast a long history and those who do not. For the latter group (which includes some African countries) the problem is often to find the elements of national identity in a frequently meagre cultural and historical heritage. For the former, it is more likely to be the problem of combining the elements of a rich and varied heritage into general awareness of a well-defined social and political identity. A case in point could be Egypt, where consciousness of national identity—albeit vigorous—has not yet fully combined the pharaonic, the Christian and the Islamic legacies into a harmonious whole; the difficulty is compounded by the vital but somewhat undefined character of Arabism, which all Arab-speaking countries share to a larger or smaller extent. Such complex cultural questions, with their delicate political implications, are much studied and discussed. The same sort of questions are posed in Latin American countries, in varying degrees according to the proportion of autochthonous races still living in each country; Mexico is no doubt the first in which conflict between the Indian and the European elements has been resolved in a real national identity and a rich cultural harmony.

Interesting as it could be, there is no place here to review questions of cultural heritage and national identity in the Third World, and to compare the position of some of its countries in this respect with that of European countries, in which national identity was achieved generations and even centuries earlier. These questions are of utmost importance for some of the developing nations for, until a consciousness of national identity is generalized and spread over each nation, it remains a combination that is not stable enough to provide the backing for sustained internal development and real international co-operation. A cultural identity appears to be the indispensable first step for integration of a group, large or small, into the World Community that must be the aim of all nations. But exaggerated claims to cultural eminence, such as some leaders make to fire their people with pride, towards greater cohesion and effort, are useless and sometimes dangerous. Far better to give honest education, whereby an understanding of humanism and the fundamental values may be reached through the cultural elements proper to each nation; and if certain cultural and historical elements appear to be lacking in the heritage proper to certain nations, they may be supplemented by the fact of belonging to regional or continental groupings and organizations, and thereby sharing part of a richer heritage without losing their own identity.

Totalitarian states have their way of looking at this problem. They encourage archaeology which uncovers cultures and events too old to have any connection with their political preoccupations, but the name of history is dishonoured by that which is taught in their schools. Distortion of history is by no means confined to them (colonial wars are still glossed over for European children as useful steps for the spread of civilization or, at worst, as worthy feats of courage and endurance) but only dictatorial government holds that historical fact must be manipulated to suit its directives. Text-books on national and contemporary history are constantly modified to follow the policy of the day. Much mental agility is thus gained by

233

students who have to learn and to unlearn the shifting tale, but little grounding in tradition, little attachment to fundamental values, little understanding of a cultural heritage, of the future as linked with the past. It is not unexpected to observe a similar opposition to tradition and culture, a like indifference to fundamental values in people who naïvely believe that science and technology are creating an environment so new and so different to anything yet known, that no inherited wisdom, no previous experience can serve to grasp its nature and its implications. Tradition and history become unimportant for those who think that neither inspiration attuned to present problems nor precepts relevant to their political aims can be derived from the past. These are the new barbarians. And as they disown the past, they cannot imagine the future that proceeds from it. They stay chained to their passing days, existentially content to give up the added dignity derived by man from projecting his awareness out of the present, the additional dimension he gains from prolonging his short life by linking it with both past and future.

The democratic nations are fortunately still free from totalitarian manipulation, but the problem of the content of culture to be transmitted to the new generations is not thereby made more easy to solve. Practical solutions, such as better text-books and TV programmes, are not possible before there is a change of mind and a change of heart to reverse present trends in the advanced nations. Without this change, their freedom will not avail them in making the proper social choices, because they must first be aware of the values and the priorities upon which the choices may be based. As it appears now, the future is going by default because of a deadening of the awareness that is the spring of culture. Many pertinent essays and deeply meditated studies are published on this subject. They help to clarify ideas, to point out the danger, to define what attitude and policy may avert a deterioration of culture and civilization. More than that they cannot do. It would not be the first time in history that perceptive men understood the signs of the time, but that their voices were not strong enough to stem the tide. . . . This problem is closely related to the problem of general and specialized instruction, which must now be considered.

3. KNOWLEDGE AND SKILLS

The fourth part or stage is mainly instructional. It has to do with science and technology, the human and the social sciences, as well as the literary and the plastic arts—in fact, the accumulated knowledge and techniques that must be handed over to each new generation. It is concerned with culture, as all knowledge is part of culture, but less as education in values and priorities and more as instruction in facts and skills. The time when a man could aspire to learn all there was to know is long past. Now, many lifetimes would not suffice to absorb the enormous amount of available information. A choice must be made by each person and this leads to some specialization. Furthermore, as techniques and skills are developed and refined, there is increasing professional specialization. Pushed to an absurd extreme, this would bring complete division, and people would not understand each other any more. In practice, the capacity (time, expense, IQ) for learning is shared between specialized professional knowledge and general knowledge, which must include something of the physical and the human sciences as well as of the liberal arts, in short a grounding in the elements of the whole circle of knowledge.

But as far the greater part of the accumulation of knowledge has been in science and technology, there is considerable pressure to reduce the share of the liberal arts, the human and social sciences. The pressure is strengthened by the increasingly technicist character of modern society, which naturally puts a premium on scientific and technical studies, and tends to discount the humanities and the social sciences. And the pressure is intensified, to the detriment of general education, because of the increasingly complex scientific and technical knowledge required for graduation. It would be wrong, however, to deduce from these trends that exaggerated specialization is only found in the scientific and technological camp. Many people think that a graduate in one of the human sciences or liberal arts (literature, law, anthropology, etc.) has of necessity more all-round knowledge than a graduate in one of the physical sciences. This is not the case. Graduates in human sciences are often as narrowly specialized (and therefore as ignorant of the physical sciences, and even other human sciences) as graduates in physical sciences may be narrowly specialized (and therefore ignorant of the human sciences). Specialization, which is partly an unavoidable trend and partly a current fashion, is a general phenomenon that is not restricted to one field of knowledge.

Basically, it is a matter of priorities, of relative value. It appears to have become an immutable premise or a foregone conclusion that specialization in science and technology must obtain the lion's share of time, funds and staff, and of course jobs. The humanities, the study of history and religion, of moral priorities and ethical values, of philosophy and sociology, are a sort of left-over from earlier times, having little to do with contemporary life based on scientific and technological advance, a sort of luxury which society can afford to subsidize together with the plastic and the literary arts, but which must not be allowed to interfere with the serious business of scientific and technical instruction. Like Indian reserves and national parks in America or wild life preservation in Africa and Europe, some care and money must be devoted to such survivals, but they come low in the scale of priorities. Only sociology and its allied branches have improved their status in recent years by adjusting their aim to 'useful' research, such as motivational analysis and depth psychology for advertising or propaganda or intelligence, and thereby increasing their share of research and development allocations.[100] This attitude is representative of the new technicist mentality. It bids fair to become the general attitude of society.

An unhealthy opposition has arisen between humanist and scientist. There was no such opposition in earlier Western tradition, at times when thought was most daring and imagination most creative, as in classical Greece and during the Renaissance. Then science, i.e. knowledge, was one and it included all that is now divided between science and the humanities. The wise men—those who knew—were complete men, generalists to whom nothing was alien of though and human endeavour. Now, by a social and semantic evolution that it would be too long here to retrace, the scientist is he who deals in matter while the humanist is he who is concerned with human relations and human values. The scientist has made astounding discoveries and spectacular achievements, while the humanist has few discoveries to his credit and even fewer achievements. This has led to a retreat of the humanities before the physical sciences and it has opened a widening rift between them. Many tensions of the advanced societies are caused by this division, and the sense of alienation, of being only part whole, may often be traced back to this opposition between the human and the material fields of knowledge. These should be brought together again by a clearer understanding of their complementary function in civilization and culture.

The notion of self-division (Colin Wilson) in 20th century man is generally accepted. Many writers have tried their hand at the difficult definition of this idea, each from his particular angle of science, philosophy, psychology, history or social organization. All appear to agree that the remedy lies in a return to the concept and to the reality of whole man, total man (Fanon), complete man (Jung), undivided man, unitary man (Lancelot Law Whyte), unified man (Mumford), integral man (Alexandre Marc), integrated man (René Dubos). I believe that the basic factor of self-division is that the fundamental values are becoming 'corny' ideals. At best they appear to many people as nostalgic throwbacks or abstract utopias. They are being pushed out of the technicist society. 'In this century, in America perhaps more than elsewhere, the new social sciences collected statistics and interpreted them in norms, modes, medians and averages. Vast new accumulations of facts and ingenious applications of mathematics to social data brought new patterns of generalizations. These bred a deeper, "fact"-founded distrust of ideals.'[101] This distrust of ideals is primarily a rejection of the fundamental human values, which are nothing if not ideals that have no foundation in matter and quantity. There are many who believe that the student revolt stems from a reaction against this rejection. That this is so is not yet clear but, should it turn out to be true, there would be better hope for the future.

Man must be reunited in himself and this entails a deep rethinking of values and social priorities. By the reconciliation of science and humanism, knowledge immense and diverse becomes one again in the mind of complete man: a scientific mentality and a humanist attitude will together be the quality of those who enjoy and who enrich the heritage of knowledge and culture. The process naturally starts by education and instruction. The crisis of higher education, especially in America, started with the realization by students and faculties of the growing unbalance and deterioration in social relations. It is primarily in the educational field that the notion of complete man can find its direction, its impetus, and its fulfilment. There is no basic difficulty in working out a return to a unified approach to teaching and learning, because there is no real opposition between that part of knowledge that has monopolized the name of Science and the part that goes under the name of The Humanities. There is no possible conflict in knowledge, both theoretical and applied, of the material world (the constitution and the properties of matter), the living world (the biological conditions of vegetable and animal life) and the social world (the interactions of human beings).

The opposition and the conflict arise from the antagonistic positions taken by the specialists, because of one-sided instruction and insufficient general culture. The enthusiasm aroused by the brilliant results of specialized research, the consequent neglect of general knowledge in favour of segmentation and division, the increasing amount of learning required for professional studies, the rewards of technical specialization in a machine-orientated society, all this conspires to produce the present cleavage between physical sciences and human sciences (with various branches of biology and sociology in between, sometimes bridging the gap, but more often widening it by the desire of their own exponents to specialized independence). To review the reasons for the dissociation of knowledge is to show the way to reunification, by ensuring that all individuals will share a generous measure of general culture, an all-round and well-balanced grounding in the heritage of civilization. Thereby will be created an awareness of the oneness of knowledge, with the assurance that the members of a society will speak the same language and share the same values and priorities. Thus they will understand each other despite their professional specializations and they will be better able, because of their general culture, to understand the members of other societies.

And the cultured specialist will be a better specialist, the cultured technician a better technician. Besides the social benefit of a broad common culture, there will be the personal benefit that each individual will derive from his wider knowledge, the enhancement of his professional value by a deepened understanding of his own particular skill. Moreover, with the rapid evolution of applied science and constant development of new techniques, few men and women can expect to go on thirty or forty years (even if the period of actual work will come down to no more than forty thousand hours in a lifetime, as forecast by Fourastié) applying the specialized knowledge acquired in their student days. Training for new professions to replace those that become obsolete will also be a necessity in most people's lives. Adaptation to changing circumstances will require broadened outlooks and continuing study. An adequate grounding in general knowledge—culture in its widest sense—will allow men and women to adapt themselves without undue hardship or loss of fundamentals, and enable them to acquire the new skills that would be hard to master for narrowly specialized technicians.

For the prosperous nations, it is possible to augment the funds available for education and to lengthen the period of tuition, thereby providing time and money enough for both a balanced grounding in general knowledge and the specialization required for professional qualification. Tuition could now be prolonged further into adulthood without social censure or economic damage, especially as the average span of active life is wider than before, but this would aggravate the social and family strains due to deferment of young people's accession to independent wage-earning status. Instead of simply prolonging a continuous learning period, tuition could be interrupted for periods of wage-earning, and active life could later be interrupted for several periods of tuition. For instance, a system of training or articling or apprenticeship could provide for a period of three to five years in practical work after secondary education and before university enrolment. Arrangements could also be made for periods of tuition (say two periods, one in the forties and one in the fifties of a person's life) to give everybody (according to their academic or intellectual level) the opportunity to keep up with general culture and social change, as well as to be abreast of advances within their respective fields of work or specialization, or to enter new or related fields.

These suggestions for continuing education are not inspired by the idea of a mandarin-like organization, whereby learning obtains highest recognition at an advanced age, but rather by something like the refresher courses and examinations that are compulsory for diplomatic and military personnel in some countries. Also in the same line are the courses, seminars and study-groups organized by corporations for their personnel at various levels, except that they have little concern with general culture and social evolution. The 'popular universities' for people of all ages that are established in some countries appear as well to derive from the same idea. The notion that learning is confined to a limited period of people's lives, from which release is sought as soon as possible, should be replaced by the notion of a continuing process. A real change of perspective would integrate education and instruction into the lives of men and women. The cultural level of a nation would surely be thereby improved and, with better information and greater awareness, there would be a greater capacity for peaceful evolution and constructive change. It may not be out of place here to state that this notion has no relation to the indoctrination courses that are so industriously, and apparently so uselessly pursued in totalitarian societies. Continuing education when freedom of thought and expression are assured must help the operation of real democracy.

The aims of continuing education will be better served by development and change of present institutions than by creation of new institutions. Universities and colleges will have the greatest share in defining and applying the new perspective for closer integration of education and instruction with the social fabric. This will enable them to come out of their relative segregation and to improve for students of all ages opportunity and capacity for more responsible involvement with their local community, their national society, and the family of mankind. The nation must devote more of its resources to education, with less slant on research and more on general culture, less investigation and more education. Teachers, from kindergarten nurses to university professors, must keep in touch with fundamentals and they must acquire and preserve, despite their indispensable specializations, a unified outlook on knowledge. Only educators well grounded in the human values will restore society to sanity, so that dissociation of values and alienation of the individual may be resolved in a recaptured awareness of essentials and fundamentals. The policy outlined above should not be hard to carry out by the rich nations once it is understood and accepted by public opinion.

For the poor nations, education and instruction are the cardinal factor of social and economic progress. Because of their urgent need, emerging countries are tempted by accelerated programmes to speed up teacher training and illiteracy fighting. Most such programmes fail as basic education (which starts in the home) is inexistent or inadequate, teachers are insufficiently trained, and literacy is often lost in an illiterate environment. There is no alternative to a well-grounded system of education and it takes time, money and care to build it up on sound foundations. This is the field where tilling, planting and nurturing have to be the most thorough, where haste makes waste, and worse than waste. Programmes that are superficial or unsuited to the circumstances of a people, lack of balance between general education and specialized instruction, will retard social maturity and compound political problems. The high proportion of illiterates and the low level of education in the poor countries are of course part of the overall pattern of underdevelopment, but it is the level that commands most other factors of development, so that the spearhead of progress must be the school-room. Without technical and financial aid from abroad, most of the emerging countries would not have reached even their present educational level. Aid for education must come very high indeed in the priorities of international solidarity.

* * *

The time is ripe for bringing the scientist and the humanist together again. Science abandons its absolute rigidity, and the human and social sciences accept a more rigorous discipline. The distinction between mind and matter becomes so tenuous that they appear to meet in some hitherto unexplored region where the scientist and the humanist must cautiously advance hand in hand. The scientist must regain a sensitivity to the human values and the humanist a comprehension of the basic concepts of the physical sciences. Both must free themselves from the control of technique, the scientist by regaining his independence from the demands of technological application, and the humanist by asserting the value judgments and the moral issues that technique ignores. They must form their students to this unified outlook, wherein the human values are the foundation of society, and whereby the social purpose derived from these values becomes the responsibility of science and technology as much as of the social sciences and the liberal arts. Thus they may work together to plan the desirable future that will preserve civilization and culture.

13
Conclusion of Part Two

SUCH ARE THE MAIN FIELDS of application of the human values, the institutions and the activities of which they should be the essential motive and the paramount aim. Personal bias is hard to avoid, even when the intention is to abstain from singular opinions and value judgments. How much harder, then, must it be when the intention is to assert values and to define them for study and discussion. Inevitably there is a personal bias in these pages, though I have done my best to keep their contents objective and factual. An effort at simplification and synthesis has been made in order to bring into clearer relief the basic idea of the human values as the necessary and the only social ends, and to offset over-specialized analysis whereby the picture becomes blurred by magnification and disconnection of its details.[102] Relative importance of the parts cannot be grasped without an understanding of the whole. Without an overall view of social trends, the sense of perspective and proportion is lost. It then becomes a losing battle to retain any meaningful priorities among the varied solicitations encountered in daily life, between the sometimes contradictory, often discordant, and always insistent voices that drum these solicitations into people's minds.

Human values are readily apprehended as the ends of civilized society, but they do not have for all persons the same significance or the same applications. Besides, their significance in the modern context, their applicability to present problems, have become uncertain. The distinction between the fundamental and the subsidiary has become obscure and confused. Value choices and priorities were often unconscious in the past, but they must now be conscious and deliberate because of the new and potent influences that tend to deny or to ignore the fundamental values, and because of the increasing importance of the issues that depend on these choices. Thus it was necessary to explicate the meaning of the fundamental values as the perennial ends of civilization, to define their content in the light of existing conditions and foreseeable changes, to show their real significance for the present generations and their practical applicability to the problems of individuals and societies. They can best be summed-up in the following points:

1. *Basic premise of society*
A. The basic premise of society is the worth of a human being as an individual distinct from, and autonomous of, other human beings, as well as of social groups and institutions.
B. The purpose of the social order is the good of the individual, by development of his physical, his rational and his emotive capacities, by the exercise of his creativity, his desire for quality, his quest for perfection.
C. The good of an individual may be achieved only in society where, by awareness of his own individuality, he becomes conscious of the individuality and the worth of others, thereby giving reality to the principle of solidarity between human beings.
D. The freedom and dignity of each individual, to the fullest extent that is compatible with the freedom and dignity of other individuals, are the highest morality of society.

2. *Individual rights and duties*
A. The fundamental values shall never be denied or ignored for reasons of state (i.e. for the advantage of a social institution considered as an entity independent of its individual members) or for necessities of technique (i.e. for the requirements of scientific discovery and technological progress) however compelling the former or the latter may appear to be.
B. The basic rights of one or several individuals shall not be sacrificed, unless with their freely given consent, for the benefit of others, even if the numbers of those expected to benefit are very much greater than the number of those who are to bear the sacrifice.
C. Education at every level shall assert that the primary criterion of thought and action is the normative quality of right or wrong, moral or immoral, as derived from the fundamental values.

D. Education shall likewise assert that the duties of an individual are the counterpart of his rights, and that the object of social regulation of his duties and rights is to preserve the exercise of the same rights for every other individual, as well as to allow communal services to be suitably discharged.

3. *Social priorities*

A. Absolute priority shall be given to fundamental values in appreciating the ends and means of any social plan or action, however great or small be its scale and range.

B. The goal of any social plan or action shall be judged good or bad solely in the light of preserving freedom and justice, dignity and quality, for the individuals composing the society, without prejudice to other communities and societies.

C. No advantage or benefit expected from scientific discovery or technological innovation—however great the advantage or benefit may seem to be—shall be allowed to supersede in the smallest degree any of the requirements and implications of the fundamental values.

D. However worthy and desirable in terms of fundamental values social goals may be, they must be considered as absolutely unattainable if they cannot be attained by means that are equally worthy in terms of fundamental values.

4. *Solidarity of human beings*

A. The field of application of the fundamental values transcends each regional or national society and it shall comprise all mankind regardless of political boundaries and differences of race, language or religion.

B. The moral and institutional solidarity that binds individuals together within a regional or national society must gradually be extended to the relations between all human communities.

In such terms or in similar terms may be expressed the principles of a civilization that recognizes the fundamental human values as its social ends; the priorities of a society that is thereby animated by a sense of purpose and guided by a knowledge of its aims; the rules of a social order in which individuals are conscious of their individuality and are thereby made aware of the individuality of others, sensible of their worth and respectful of their rights; in which human beings may be saved from enmassment despite their great numbers, and thereby avoid alienation and self-division; in which men and women may improve in all that makes them human. . . . Expressed in this way, as a consistent whole, these principles are more like a credo and an act of faith than a set of regulations, and this is what they really are: a rejection of nihilism and despair, an act of faith in human beings and in their capacity successfully to come out of the present crisis. These principles should be inscribed on the walls of every parliament hall; they should be explained and exemplified in every school programme. The threats delineated in present trends stem from fading awareness, from equivocal in-tellectual attitudes and warped emotional tendencies, caused by the too rapidly changing circumstances of population and technological progress. It is therefore sanity of mind and of heart that must be sought in the first place, and they may be found only by regaining touch with the reality of the fundamental and permanent values.

* * *

These values may look uninspiring to eyes without sight; as guiding lights, they may glimmer only faintly through the mental smog of our time; but they are all we have left in this materialistic and existential age. It is well to repeat that we lack a new vision of the future, an image of a really desirable society. There is no gainsaying that we have lost faith and vision, that utopian thought appears to be dead. We hope to 'free up people psychologically for all kinds of new experiences out of which visions of the future may come' be-cause we need 'pictures of how human community might be struc-tured so as to be peaceful, hopeful and loving, pictures which con-vince us by realistic analysis that we could get from here to there' (Charles West). All very true, and eminently worth striving for. But what if the visions are not forthcoming? What if utopian thought does not revive? What if pictures of the desirable human com-munity remain absent? Have we then nothing on which to fall back while waiting for faith and vision and inspiration, nothing stable and true to help us to choose and to act now, hopefully to build a better future? This is the weakness of those who sail out in search of a high (and preferably original) ideal to guide mankind into the future, and fall into a trough of despair when they fail to find it. They forget that the basis for all ideals is not far to seek, and so they overlook the fundamental values and priorities that remain the necessary guidelines. If some cannot distill from them the high inspiration which they crave, at least all can find in them the sure criteria for thought and action.

They are indeed all we have left, and we are down to the rock, to the root. It depends on the living today to build again a worthwhile vision of the future, to make the tree flower once more with positive philosophical thought and constructive social action. But if we go on to wreck the foundation itself, to empty the roots of their remnant of life and potential, another civilization may come later, but our's will be extinguished in pain and suffering. To say—as many say and as I have so often heard objected—that the fundamental values, the principles of freedom and justice, of dignity and quality are stale and worn out, that there is no substance left in them to inspire and to guide a renewal of Western civilization, is to give in to the present nihilistic trend and to condemn that civilization to degradation and decay. If we do not arouse ourselves in time, the crisis of humanity will be resolved in the worst possible future.

To hold that the fundamental values are the essential motive and the paramount aim of civilization is to lay oneself open to the charge of being reactionary and old fashioned, hypnotized by the past, oblivious of the present, and blind to the future. That the charge is made shows to what extent Western civilization is exposed to reject the principles and the priorities that made its ascent possible. But the call to human values arises from awareness of the conditions of civilization in this age, not from a nostalgic reversion to an unspecified earlier age when the social order is presumed to have been more humane. Criticism of present trends is induced by fear of what the future can bring, not by a throwback to the ancient myth of a Golden Age, from which mankind has fallen and to which it aspires to return. There was no such golden age. The present age, despite its faults and its threats, its frequent and terrible denials of human rights, is the best of what is recorded in history. There were no 'good old days', save for the privileged few in every period. The old days were bad for the majority of people, as they are bad now for those who are subject to totalitarian rule or who labour in the throes of poverty and hunger. And the future can bring bad days for the whole of humanity if the human values are rejected or debased—as it is now clear that they can be—in the advanced countries.

It is also to invite the contemptuous accusation of idealism, of being utopian and unpractical. To claim for each human being a social and a material environment wherein his or her individuality may be fully respected, where the autonomy of the person and the dignity of human life may be affirmed in a sense of satisfaction and fulfilment, to claim this, say the self-styled realists, is to lag far behind the new realities of mass society, the requirements of efficiency, and the imperatives of continued scientific and technological progress. Freedom and justice, dignity and quality for each individual can no longer be (if they ever were) the principles of society in an age of technicist culture and expanding population. Justice alone will remain, but only in the sense of equality. 'Justice for All, Freedom for None'[103] expresses the attitude, regretful in some and prideful in others, of many intellectuals in the advanced countries. This is part of the new humanism, the 'Humanities of the XXth Century'[104] which all must learn to practise and to like under pain of alienation from the new society. Men's vision is indeed narrowing when their material instruments and their conceptual tools would enable them to see further and more clearly; their thought is contracting when the scope and range of their action are expanding.

One hears that fundamental values, true and good as they may be, are notions too vague to be significant, too general to be useful, too abstract to be realistic, too theoretical to be practical, too negative to be a guide for action. It bodes ill for the future that such opinions should influence the new generations. As remarked above, education has to keep a difficult balance between a grounding in tradition and a capacity for change, both of which are required for stability and improvement of society. The fundamental values are the necessary link between tradition and change because they are the permanent guiding lines for past, present and future. To claim for each individual freedom and justice, dignity and the chance to achieve some quality is to be realistic and practical, because there is no other criterion for making the best of this world, no other touchstone for the most favourable option on the future, no better guide to avoid its obvious dangers. The world has never been and never will be an ideal place; the human values will no doubt never be fully respected; but there has been in historical times an improvement, slow but certain, in men's conception of human dignity and human rights. This improvement is now threatened. The generations now living, the old and the young, can save it only by asserting those values, and thereby making the best of the possible futures that are before them.

Indeed, if idealism must be used in disparagement, if it has to be a sneer and not a salute, it becomes fair to say that the idealists are those who want to impose the cut and dried idea of an efficient organization unresponding to the needs and insensitive to the desires of individually differentiated human beings. These prophets of the new society are the unpractical and dangerous utopians, for they are out of touch with human reality, while the realists are those whose minds and hearts are firmly bound to the human values. . . . Enough of this wrangling! There are anti-civilization forces at work, and they must be resisted and neutralized by asserting the human values as social ends, and by acting now on the certain premise that a solution to the present crisis must necessarily intervene before long. There is a range of possible solutions from good to bad, a range of possible futures, and it should be everybody's concern to reach some consensus on the most favourable and desirable.

But the future does not stay open indefinitely. 'There is a continual dying of possible futures' (de Jouvenel) because choices are continually made that exclude them. The choices are mostly unconscious. They are left to happen by letting time pass, by allowing the conditions that made a choice possible to disappear. Thus there is a constant reduction of the options that are open to a society. The options are further reduced by short-term answers and stop-gap solutions to long-term questions and basic problems. This statement may be questioned by those who observe the accelerating progress of science and technique, and the expanding fields it opens up for human action, but it is none the less true. Science and technology do indeed open up new fields of action and thus new options for the future, but scientific discovery and technological innovations are not often such as to allow more scope for human values. In the sense of preserving human values as social ends, possible futures appear to be fast closing up. The longer the advanced nations wait in the present crisis without making conscious and deliberate choices, the less liberty of choice will there be until at last—not so far ahead—there will be left only the road that determinists and technicists are so industriously designing.

Examples of this closing up of options for the future are all around, alike in the developed countries and in the others: galloping urbanization of immense tracts of land and spreading death of living soil under asphalt and cement; frantic overcrowding of cities and deterioration of social relations; pollution of man's physical environment, of air and water, of his very body, his bones and his flesh, with the waste from his machines and the fall-out of his nuclear explosions; the premium put on material things and the priority given to material goals; the reduction of general knowledge in favour of early specialization; the decline of representative institutions and individual freedom; all these facts and so many others denote choices that are made, consciously or not, and that narrow down the future. In so far as they are not reversible (and some are fortunately still reversible) they reduce the options that remain open to preserve the human values.

*　*　*

The foundations of a tall building go deep into the ground, where they become invisible and soon forgotten. Yet they continue to carry the building and no modification, no addition or would-be improvement, may be carried out on it without reference to its foundations. If the foundation plans are lost, they must be found or retraced before any changes can be made on the building. The same holds good for the values and principles upon which a culture is founded. With passing generations and changing circumstances, the foundations—that are always taken for granted—fall out of sight. The fundamental values are pushed into the background. They insensibly become ignored or blurred in people's minds, while derivative goals and casual desires become the ever-changing focus of attention. When at last an opposition arises—as it must—between fundamental values and present goals and desires, a deep unbalance of society is created.[105] Unless clarity of mind and honesty of will combine to bring the fundamental values back into the focus of attention, social purpose is lost. The ends of society are forgotten or denied, and means are taken for ends without looking any farther. An unhealthy division, an alienation of its members grows within a society and disruptive factors, the anti-civilization forces that must be faced and overcome by each generation, are allowed unchecked to distract the minds of men and to undermine the foundations of humane society.

People speak nowadays of a rupture of traditional culture, a rejection of inherited values, a breakdown of morality. Much of this is true, as we have observed, but it must be qualified. Tradition is a body of beliefs and opinions, customs and precedents that are handed on from generation to generation. Tradition must be stable, or there is no continuity and no attainment, and it must also change, or there is no progress. Though beliefs that concern social order are more durable than customs that touch on superficial features of social relations, all tradition must evolve and sooner or later be transformed. But the fundamental values cannot be part of this movement, and change (by evolution or by revolution) cannot include them unless by a dangerous confusion of ideas. Should they be included in a breakdown—and present trends could make this come to pass—much more would be at stake than the loss of worthwhile or worn-out tradition. The whole of this book is an attempt to show just what is at stake, by proposing the explicit definition of the fundamental values as absolutes based on the autonomy of the human person.

Rigidity of course prevents any sort of progress, and ability for innovation and adaptation is a necessary condition for advancement, but the capacity for change must be guided and restrained by the priorities based on the fundamental values. Change must happen within the frame of those values or it must not be allowed to happen, because the frame allows for change without loss of fundamentals and degradation of culture. Moreover, change is necessary in order to uphold the fundamental values in changing circumstances, but if it ignores those values, it dissipates the substance and character of culture, and makes it no more than the clouds that are ceaselessly formed and unformed across the sky. Now, the capacity for change appears to be the only quality required by the technicist society, change without guide and without restraint, so that fundamentals are also carried away in its quickening current. A beneficial lack of rigidity and conservatism thus degenerates into a loosening of reflexive control in a culture that loses consciousness and awareness.

The advanced nations appear to be suffering from a psychosis of change, an aberration that derives in equal parts from the acceleration of technological innovation and from the materialism that prevents any countervailing influence. With technicists and the New Left especially the accent is solely on change, as if the world's sickness were due to people not discarding with sufficient despatch their values and priorities. This, we are told and retold, is 'the era of continuous progress . . . (where) even truth becomes out of date . . . (and) one thing alone is certain: change.'[106] Loose words, if not worse! There is a vertigo of change, a fashion for unlimited alteration of everything. Very many people appear to believe that change must overtake every element of social order, even the basic principles. For instance, 'the new situation requires . . . a new set of values';[107] 'no general theory of society could be constructed without a place for the security requirements of individuals for stability in fundamental values and for their consequent resistance to their change'.[108] In this and similar statements, the implication is that fundamental values must also change with changing circumstances. This points to a deep and a dangerous misapprehension. The fundamental values cannot change without entailing the destruction or debasement of civilization. That much talked-of complaint, alienation, derives from the threat to fundamental values, not from a threat to acquired situations that can and indeed must change with circumstances.

The problem is to work for change, even of time-honoured institutions and traditions, when it is required by changed circumstances, i.e. when institutions and traditions are no longer adapted to the present time and therefore no longer correspond to the principles and social goals for which they were previously established. When evolution (demographic and political, scientific and technological) reduces the relevance of institutions, it does not mean that the principles upon which they were based in earlier times have also lost their relevance. It means that a return to those principles must guide the changes required for these institutions to become adapted to the new circumstances. But people become attached to institutions, customs, privileges (which are only means or secondary goals) to the point of forgetting the principles, the fundamental values that are the ends of society. They will fight for their institutions, their customs and their privileges, even if they have become obsolete, in the mistaken belief that they are fighting for their fundamental values. Thus a part of society, generally the individuals forming a ruling or influential class, resists necessary changes, and this gives rise to social friction and political unrest. This is the sense in which some aspects of evolution and change are not fast enough in our time. Attachment to time-worn political and legal organizations, obsolete economic and social systems, out-of-date cultural patterns, is the source of ever-recurring difficulty for society to adjust to changing circumstances and to answer new challenges without losing hold of its fundamental values. Too slow evolution of worn-out institutions and traditions, too tardy surrender of unjustifiable situations and privileges can end up in a revolution that carries away everything, including the fundamentals.

Because of confusion between the fundamental and the secondary, there is resistance to the required or inevitable change of what is secondary, and lack of resistance to the always detrimental change of what is fundamental. Therefore the problem is also to refuse change, to react and to revolt against it when it imperils the fundamental values. To say that change must eventually overtake all values is tantamount to saying that no values are fundamental and essential for civilized society. But it is not possible to imagine by what the fundamental values could be replaced or into what they could be transformed while still maintaining a humane civilization. What principles other than freedom and justice, dignity and quality could conceivably be considered as fundamental for man in society? Charity and human brotherhood are also valid principles for society, and they are implied in the others. If change (the 'pervasive change' that self-styled progressists so light-heartedly welcome) should impoverish the substance of freedom, adulterate the meaning of justice, and drain away the content of man's dignity, it would obliterate civilization as we know it and want it to be. The only attitude that makes sense in the current agitation is to hold firmly to the fundamental values in appreciating the complex questions and deciding the vital issues that arise out of the present critical juncture in human affairs.

With these criteria to guide us, we may understand the implications of current developments. We may form worthwhile opinions on the traditions and the institutions that are up for discussion and contestation. We can then discern what reaches to essentials from what is really secondary and unessential, even though it may threaten established privilege and cherished custom. For example, property rights do not directly relate to essentials; they can change within very wide limits without endangering fundamentals. Change can also—and often must—overtake notions of state sovereignty, patriotic duty, work and leisure, parental and filial attitudes, without contradicting the basic priorities. On the other hand, there are issues where the fundamental values must be paramount in appreciating any sort of change; such are, for instance, freedom and availability of information, democratic process of government, independence and integrity of the judiciary, duty to human solidarity on the national and the ecumenical scale, in which the basic priorities must always be consciously and strongly defended regardless of whatever supposed benefits or facilities could be derived from a less uncompromising attitude. The most difficult value choices may well turn out to be those concerned with biological discovery and man's capacity further to control his body and his mind. Only with the fundamental values in the focus of attention may we hope to sort out the present confusion and to keep our bearings despite the acceleration with which the future seems to be descending upon us.

Certainly, when property rights are everywhere reduced by encroaching regulation; when monogamous bisexual marriage for founding a family is challenged by biological discovery and sexual liberation; when the meaning of patriotic duty and allegiance to the state is changing; when established religion and traditional morality are losing ground to atheism, fatalism, communism, materialism and plain nothing-ism; when physical and moral violence are spreading in all countries; when the individual stature of vast numbers of human beings is diminished as much by urban overcrowding and mass conditioning as by mass subjection to political totalitarianism; when contestation and dissent call in question every rule of ethics and propriety; people may well feel that their world is tumbling down. They may well think that there is nothing stable left upon which to attach some chain of continuity, some permanent touchstone of values and priorities. Before the century's end in the advanced countries, institutions and ideas such as state and nation, property and marriage, culture and education may develop into something very different to what the last fifty generations have accepted as good and true. 'What then will be left of civilization?', many will cry out in anguish. Everything that is essential will be left, if people remain aware of the fundamental human values.

Among those who reflect on Western civilization and human culture, who ponder the possible futures, worry about their threats and seek ways to avert their dangers, there are few guiding principles and basic priorities, little sense of purpose, no stable foundation or framework for the civilization that they want to preserve. While among those who are professed devotees of science and technique, who appear to be convinced that a new civilization can be designed, a new society organized on the sole foundation of continued technological and material progress, there is little coherent thought on the principles of their new civilization, no creative imagination in formulating values for their new society. Alike for those whose absorbing care is to preserve and those whose main concern is to innovate (and—we should add—those whose only purpose is apparently to pull down and destroy) the fundamental values, in the sense and with the content that this essay attempts to define, are the necessary guiding principles. They are perennial, true for every time and age. They are general, good for every people and every stage of social development. They are significant and practical and sufficient, providing the criterion applicable in first and last resort to every policy of ends and means, to every choice of options for the future.

Epilogue

REFLECTION AND RESEARCH during the second third of the 20th century exposed the main trends—demographic, technological, economic, ecological and cultural—the juncture of which constitutes the present crisis, and described the threats to all humanity arising out of these trends. As evolution of the crisis proceeds, many of these threats are being realized in painful experience. Aldous Huxley lived long enough to observe that his pessimistic forecasts were becoming fact even earlier than he had foreseen. Reflection on the immediate future (10 to 30 years) is no longer a question for prophetic insight or exceptionally acute observation, and research is now simply a matter of delving into detail and computing the speed at which undesirable developments will come if nothing or not enough is done to avert them. Continued technological progress is as certain as anything can be, while individual improvement and social betterment are not even probable, only barely possible. Everything points to a fall in human values. In retrospect, it will be said that the advanced nations knew full well the hazards of their road, and that the retarded nations laboriously followed after, with no thought of taking another road and no means of seeking another destiny.

For an individual or a community, there is generally a variety of possible futures, but seldom a variety of possible *and desirable* futures. Most often, there will be only one direction to take for a desirable future, and choice will be mainly that of means, to measure how near the goal may be approached and how high the aim should be. The term of possible future, that is coming into general use, is semantically irreproachable, as there is no sense in an impossible future, but it may not be psychologically the best. The mental procedure of first examining options, in order to ascertain the best or the least harmful to pursue, could have an inhibiting effect on decision and action, particularly if all options appear undesirable. Possible is the operative word, and its content is variable: what seems unfeasible for some will appear feasible for others; what would demand an impossible effort from one group could be well within the capacity of another group. As public policy must always settle for the broadest common level, the aim may be set too low.

Human energy has unlimited reserves, that can be tapped only when the aim is set high and the goal shines bright and desirable. I prefer Dennis Gabor's expression in the title of his path-finding book *Inventing the Future*. I am tempted to say 'let us plan for an impossibly desirable future, so that we may be sure that the utmost effort will be exerted to approach it'. More reasonably, the mental procedure would be 'let us first think of the desirable future, let us invent it in terms of the human values, and then examine the possible means to reach it or to get near to it'. There is a difference of perspective, and it is an important one. Great reformers set their aim very high, so high that people called them mad, but if they had set it lower they would probably have accomplished nothing. Christ's precept of love and charity from all men to all men has not been carried out, but if He had not set the aim so high, the genuine measure of improvement that has been achieved would not have been attained.

The lack of a coherent and inspiring vision of society is keenly felt in the present crisis of humanity, when it would be most needed to light the way to a desirable future. 'What thinker, what politician will re-invent political economy, not out of the confrontation of offer and demand ... but out of the definition of essential needs that do not pass by the market-place?'[109] 'Is policy being formed in the image of a relevant and appropriate model? Is it closely linked both to the pattern of the past, and to our heart's desire, or is it one which could only be related to the historical flow of events by coercive or revolutionary action? Is the model "true" ... in the ultimate sense that it serves to advance the social and political goals of the culture, or purposes more valid in absolute terms? Or is society adapting its institutions to a Pied Piper's myth which could lead into a jungle or a prison, or over the precipice?'[110] The jungle, prison or precipice: these are indeed the options open to humanity if present trends are not reversed. But there is now little awareness of the political and social goals of the culture, even less of purpose more valid in absolute terms.

There is hardly an articulate scientist (physicist or biologist, astronomer or geologist) or perceptive humanist (philosopher, historian, novelist, playwright or social observer), cultured economist or reflective administrator, who has not voiced grave concern for the possible, and possibly rapid, debasement of human values and degradation of Western culture. These men and women work in fields far apart but—in general terms—they all agree on the nature, the extent, and the urgency of the danger. As important is the fact that there are no voices to say that all will be well with human values in the technicist society, except a few light spirits flushed by nebulous dreams of planetary conquest and godlike supermen. I have not read a word in denial of the signs of danger, or heard a voice in refutation of the reasons for anxiety. Even science-fiction writers show their concern for the expected loss of human values in the portrayal of our descendants caught in the toils of technological progress on overcrowded Earth. *There is real consensus on the threat to human values and the confusion of social ends.*

But when it comes to consideration of what can be done to avert the danger, there is little agreement and no consensus. The pessimists appear to be in the majority. There are regrets and laments, but few denials of ideological and political systems that reject the primacy of the human values, few refutals of historical and technological views that contest the continued relevance of these basic priorities, few assertions that men and women can uphold their fundamental human principles against the combined pressures of technology and overpopulation. There is a breath of defeatism, an air of resignation to the worst. And yet the challenge is clear, and the answer must be given in full awareness and lucid consciousness.[111] It must be given by the present generation under pain of irretrievable damage, not because it was determined and fated, but because the present was allowed to drift into the future unchecked and undirected. As things are now, there is every chance that the damage will come to pass sooner than the most wide awake could think it possible.

The world needs an inspired thinker, a great reformer to give mankind a vision and a renewed purpose. In the absence of such a genius, can we not bring together the best minds of this generation— the men of thought and the men of action, humanists and scientists, politicians and businessmen—for the task of reaching a real value consensus, of shaping 'a political rationality which subordinates technique to consensual ends', of showing people the ends and the means of a desirable future? Such a co-operative intellectual enterprise, aided by the power of information and communications media, would have a decisive impact on public opinion. The issues at stake must be the object of study and discussion on a scale and a level commensurate with their importance to humanity. They must not be allowed to go by default, because men were not alert enough. The fundamental human values must be re-defined in terms of modern conditions and present challenges, reasserted as the only ends of society, the permanent foundation of civilization. Only by so doing can human beings hope to regain a sense of continuity in the midst of rapid change, of stability in the centre of incessant movement, of security despite violence and upheaval, of wholeness and integrity and fulfilment in their rise towards the future.

Notes

1. (p. 25) Haiti appears to be the epitome of despotism and tyranny for this age, the prime example of political depravation and social degradation. 'The systematic violation of every single article of the Universal Declaration of Human Rights seems to be the only policy which is respected and assiduously pursued in this Caribbean republic' (*Bulletin of the International Commission of Jurists*, No. 31, Geneva 1967, p. 28). But it is by no means the only country where human rights are denied and human values are rejected, by no means an exception in our times.

2. (p. 28) There is a trait of rigorous and sombre European logic that can push ideas and dogmas to their ultimate conclusions in unmitigated violence regardless of human considerations. With blind and incredible ferocity it appears at various periods, alike in the Latin, the Slav and the German nations. The excesses of church and state inquisitions into people's faiths and thoughts went as far in France, Italy and Spain as the 20th-century inquisitions of the GPU, the NKVD, the SS and such other dreary initials behind which the monstrous and insane reality was hidden for a time.

3. (p. 29) From the title of Robert Boguslav's stimulating book, *The New Utopians, A Study of System Design and Social Change*, Prentice-Hall 1965.

4. (p. 29) 'L'ordre est stable, statique; l'organisation est dynamique. Elle est une machine en mouvement qui ne tient pas compte, dans sa manière de fonctionner, de la vie humaine, de ses contingences, de ses accidents; une machine dont la fonction est de produire et qui, par conséquent, a toujours besoin d'être perfectionée. ... L'organisation est un produit du machinisme', Gonzague de Reynold, *D'où vient l'Allemagne, 1939*.

5. (p. 29) 'There seems to be no good reason why a thoroughly scientific dictatorship should ever be overthrown', Aldous Huxley, *Brave New World Revisited*, Chatto & Windus, London 1959, p. 164. Indeed, apart from external intervention, there is no reason at all.

6. (p. 30) There is something shocking in the title of an otherwise scholarly study, *The Origins of Totalitarian Democracy* by J. L. Talmon, 1952. To speak of a totalitarian democracy must be a contradiction in terms unless a debasement of the idea of democracy is accepted. It must weaken the significance of democracy in the context of human values. The confusion of words and meanings spreads at a bewildering rate. It would be an entertaining and perhaps a useful exercise in semantics to review the alterations and

confusions of philosophical, political and moral terms that appear to be a particular character of these times.

7. (p. 31) '. . . warfare as practised by man has no parallel in nature. That is to say that within the highly developed animal population of this earth, there is not now nor has there ever been similar destruction within a species itself. In fact, one has to go to the lowliest forms of animal life, such as certain kinds of ants, to find anything comparable to human warfare. It is a curious fact that mankind appears to justify the killing of his own kind by assuming that it is a "law of nature" ', Fairfield Osborne, *Our Plundered Planet*, Boston 1948, p. 23.

8. (p. 32) 'The nuclear weapon marks a turning point: either civilized society of European origin (the most rapacious race, that has prevailed over all the other races by destroying them or transforming them into its image) will change itself basically or human life, perhaps all life, will disappear from the face of Earth.' From the conclusion of Fausto Antonini's *L' Homme Furieux*, *l'Agressivité Collective*, translated from the Italian, Hachette, Paris 1970.

9. (p. 34) It is a matter for congratulation that the U.S. government has declared its intention to destroy some of the more repulsive weapons in its arsenal. Gas and germs are particularly repugnant but not more lethal than the various other modern means of killing. Is this a beginning, to be followed by the destruction of other weapons in America and in other countries, or merely an occasion to appear progressive and humane by scrapping unwanted or obsolete stocks?

10. (p. 34) And yet a hope that must come true if civilization is to survive. 'The epoch in which mankind was organized in armed factions—and the values and goals that moved them to wage war on each other—must at this point and will ever more be looked at as being as obsolete as tribalism, as condemnable as slavery, as irrational as trial by ordeal', Aurelio Peccei, in *The Chasm Ahead*, Macmillan 1969, p. 275. One improvement in attitude may be recorded in this connection: the 'right of conquest' which, as the ultimate result of contending forces, was until recently a principle of international relations, is no longer recognized as a legal and moral right. It is a far cry, for instance, from the Italo-Ethiopian war of 1935, when most governments of the advanced countries recognized Italy's right to the conquest, to the Israelo-Arab war of 1967, when no government speaks of Israel's right of conquest.

11. (p. 37) 'We live in a society the basis of which is materialism. In such a society, any activity which tries to influence youth towards idealism may become politically dangerous.' Thus spoke the judge of a Hungarian court in 1965 condemning Catholic ecclesiastics accused of subversion, and answering their defence that they fulfilled their duty as ordained priests. (*For the Rule of Law*, Bulletin of the International Commission of Jurists, Geneva No. 25, March 1966.) The judge applied the law of his country,

but it cannot be said that he respected the Rule of Law in so doing. It is right to call for a value-oriented jurisprudence, but dangerous to do so without defining what sort of value. After all, the law applied by the Hungarian judge was also value-oriented: it was based on a normative judgment (that materialism is good, absolutely) just as all laws are based on normative judgments. The problem is, what norms? Norms based on political power, social stratification, economic concentration, and other such transient situations? or norms based on some absolute, some ultimate values, such as the fundamental human values which form the thesis of this book?

12. (p. 37) From the prophetic words of Dubarle, quoted by Norbert Wiener. They were written in 1948 and they take on a more definite and ominous meaning as the years go by: 'We are running the risk nowadays of a great World State, where deliberate and conscious primitive injustice may be the only possible condition for the statistical happiness of the masses: a world worse than hell for any clear mind.' The operative words are not the 'great World State' (because present-day states are already great enough to have to organize 'the statistical happiness of the masses') but 'deliberate and conscious primitive injustice'. Injustice here concerns the individual's right to freedom, justice, dignity and quality. It is primitive because it touches the primary and fundamental conditions of civilization. That it may become deliberate and conscious is already clear in the tendencies of the new breed of social engineers.

13. (p. 39) For a humanist conception of the jurist's role in the technicist society, see *Le Rôle du Juriste dans la Société en Transformation* by Sergio Cotta, in Analyse & Prévision (Futuribles), Tome III, No. 4, Avril 1967, Paris. The author's conception of this role is placed on a high moral and ethical level, which includes very practical considerations.

14. (p. 41) Jacques Ellul, *The Technological Society*, Author's Foreword to the Revised American Edition, Alfred A. Knopf 1964, p. xxxii. The whole passage is worth meditating: ' . . . reality is itself a combination of determinisms, and freedom consists in overcoming and transcending these determinisms. Freedom is completely without meaning unless it is related to necessity, unless it represents victory over necessity. . . . We must not think of the problem in terms of a choice between being determined and being free. We must look at it dialectically, and say that man is indeed determined, but that it is open to him to overcome necessity, and that this *act* is freedom. Freedom is not static but dynamic; not a vested interest, but a prize continually to be won. The moment man stops and resigns himself, he becomes subject to determinism. He is most enslaved when he thinks he is comfortably settled in freedom.'

15. (p. 42) 'Man can choose: that is his greatness. He must choose: that is his servitude. He has chosen woe: that is his guilt.' To put this theological statement, attributed to Ruysbroek the Admirable, in the present context,

the last sentence could be recast as: 'He chooses wrong: that is his woe.'
The comparison with atheistic existentialism on freedom of choice is interesting: '. . . man is condemned to be free. Condemned, because he did not
create himself, yet is nevertheless at liberty, and from the moment that he
is thrown into this world, he is responsible for everything he does', Jean-
Paul Sartre, *Existentialism and Humanism*, Translation and Introduction
by Philip Mairet, Methuen, London 1948, 1966 reprint, p. 34.

16. (p. 43) 'We are insensibly biased toward a belief in determinism. The
belief that material events alone are real and condition everything else—
in other words, determinism—is the stuff of so much modern popular
thinking that it must be counted the most widespread belief of our day. For
at least a third of the human race—in Russia and China—it is not only
widespread but obligatory. Far beyond the totalitarian frontier, however,
popular determinism has its hold. . .', Barbara Ward, *Faith and Freedom,
A Study of Western Society*, Hamish Hamilton, London 1954, 1964 Edition,
p. 11. The unhappy consciousness of modern men is made up of a sense of
impotence turning into fatalism and a sense of defeat turning into despair.
The trends that led to this despairing fatalism are carefully analysed by
Judith Shklar in *After Utopia, The Decline of Political Faith* (Princeton
University Press 1957). The author traces the diverse European paths that
started from the optimism and self-assurance of the Enlightenment, and
converged—through Romanticism and Historicism and Socialism—in the
pessimism and broken spirit of this age. The increasing determinism of
philosophical and political thought is followed step by step, over the last
two centuries, along its Romantic, Christian, Marxist and Existentialist
roads. One regrets that the author, with her remarkable grasp of the subject,
did not attempt to present her own philosophical and political view or, at
least, to suggest a promising and possibly new approach to the problem.
She does not, however, evade the point, as she writes in the Preface that she
'shares in the spirit of the age to the extent of being neither able nor willing
to build an original theory of politics'. And she states in her concluding
phrases that 'the grand tradition of political theory that began with Plato is,
then, in abeyance. A reasoned skepticism is consequently the sanest attitude
for the present. For even skepticism is politically sounder and empirically
more justifiable than cultural despair and fatalism. For neither logic nor
history is in accord with these, and this even when no happier philosophies
flourish.'

17. (p. 43) Lewis Mumford, *The Transformations of Man*, 1956, Collier Books
Edition 1966, p. 143.

18. (p. 43) From the vigorous expression of Aurel David in *La Cybernétique et
l'Humain*, Gallimard, Paris 1965, pp. 162 and 168.

19. (p. 46) Paul Valéry, *Regards sur le Monde Actuel*, Editions Stock, Paris
1945, p. 178.

20. (p. 46) Aldous Huxley, *Brave New World Revisited*, p. 38.

21. (p. 48) Robert Theobald, *The Challenge of Abundance*, Mentor Books, New York 1962, p. 41.

22. (p. 48) For pertinent criticism of the present aims and methods of sociology, see *Invitation to Sociology, A Humanistic Perspective*, by Peter L. Berger, Anchor Books 1963; *Towards the Goal of Goals*, by Fred L. Polak, in Mankind 2000, Oslo 1969; *God and Golem Inc.*, by Norbert Wiener, Chapman & Hall, London 1964, Part VII.

23. (p. 50) *Essais de Morale Prospective*, Jean Fourastié, Editions Gonthier, Paris 1966. But this eminent economist and sociologist, in common with many others less eminent than he, starts off by laying so much stress on the 'radical mutation' of the human condition in our age, that he leaves little place for the fundamental human values in what he calls 'the new morality, the new humanism of the scientific society'.

24. (p. 56) 'Some writers have noted the displacement of "substantive reason", which evaluates the validity of goals, by "instrumental reason", which evaluates only the efficiency of techniques for achieving present goals. Many writers have commented on the tendency of academic ethical writers to deal more and more with the logical analysis of ethical propositions and less and less with substantive ethical questions: philosophers do not try to define the good life; rather, they construct treatises on the many senses in which the term "good" has been used. Even the popular manuals of ethics take on an increasingly instrumentalist character: how to get along with your neighbours; how to be successful; how to reduce your tension and guilts. (What if your neighbour is not worth getting along with? What if you have in fact committed a crime?) This technicism, it seems, pervades more and more areas of life: methodology replaces substance; why and what are replaced by how. Without stopping to examine it carefully, I would remind the reader of Spengler's warning that technicism is one of the marks of a declining society', John H. Schaar, *Escape from Authority*, 1961, Harper Torchbook Edition, New York 1964, pp. 307–8.

25. (p. 56) John Wilkinson puts this in more forceful terms: 'The how-to-do-it mould in the United States—in the schools of law and medicine and so on, as well as in American life in general—is based on a simple "philosopical" misunderstanding of the relationship between theory and practice . . . the basic reason seems to me . . . the vulgar American "pragmatic" conception of everything, which holds that the truth is what works—a blander version of the corrupt idea that the ends justify the means. Pragmatism, originally, did not hold this. It was a doctrine of meaning . . . concerned with, in Jefferson's phrase, "how to make our ideas clear". It was an attempt to say clearly and distinctly what one meant by an idea or theory, and then to determine if it were true or false. . . . But then there came a very big change in American thought. The practical consequences of an idea or theory came to be identified, not with meaning, but with truth. Whatever works, in other words, became the truth. This second, deformed, definition of prag-

matism is the one most Americans today would give. . . . The way to change this is to give the "practitioners" an understanding of that philosophy, including a standard of values, which precedes and lends meaning to the practical order of things and which they could then put into effect. If this were to come about, pragmatism in America would again assume its proper definition—a means of making one's ideas or theories clear, rather than an excuse for rascality', *Center Diary: 15*, Santa Barbara 1966.

26. (p. 57) Erich Fromm, *Foreword* to Edward Bellamy's Looking Backward, Signet Classics 1960, p. xiii. 'Cette Société où la chose a plus d'importance que l'homme', Henri Lefebvre, *Position: Contre les Technocrates*, Editions Gonthier, Paris 1967, p. 13.

27. (p. 57) Lecomte du Noüy, *La Dignité Humaine*, Brentano's, New York 1944, p. 73.

28. (p. 58) Norbert Wiener, *God and Golem Inc.*, p. 73.

29. (p. 58) The American answer to this question has been given, and it honours the congressmen who gave it despite the strong reasons that militated against their decision, not the least being national pride and the concern for employment. That they found stronger reasons in considerations of economy and ecology is a welcome change from unthinking acquiescence to technological progress. Even if their decision is later recalled, it will have marked the start of a better understanding of the many factors that combine to make up the quality of life.

30. (p. 59) 'We rush impetuously into novelty, driven by a mounting sense of insufficiency, dissatisfaction and restlessness. We no longer live on what we have, but on promises, no longer in the light of the present day, but in the darkness of the future, which, we expect, will at last bring the proper sunrise. . . . The less we understand of what our fathers and forefathers sought, the less we understand ourselves, and thus we help with all our might to rob the individual of his roots and his guiding instincts, so that he becomes a particle in the mass. . . . Reforms by advances, that is, by new methods or gadgets, are of course impressive at first, but in the long run they are dubious and in any case dearly paid for. They by no means increase the contentment or happiness of people on the whole. Mostly they are deceptive sweetenings of existence . . .', C. G. Jung, *Memories, Dreams, Reflections*, Recorded and Edited by Aniéla Jaffé, Translated from the German by Richard and Clara Winston, Collins and Routledge & Kegan Paul, London 1963, p. 223.

31. (p. 61) 'The powers of action generated by scientific advances are so great that the classical discussions on the ideals of the good life now take on very practical meaning. Mankind—that is to say we—shall find ourselves drifting aimlessly towards a state incompatible with the maintenance of the humanistic values from which we derive our uniqueness, unless we formulate

NOTES

goals worthy of the human condition, and are willing to take a stand at the critical time. This kind of freedom is the final criterion of humaneness. In the words of Paul Tillich, "man becomes truly human only at the moment of decision" ', René Dubos, *Humanistic Biology*, American Scientist, Vol. 53, No. 1, March 1965. Only one thing may be added to these very pertinent words, and that is: the critical time is *now* and the moment of decision is *now*.

32. (p. 64) 'It is a tragic fact that at the end of the 1960s there are more sick, more undernourished and more uneducated children in the world than there were ten years ago. . . . Despite all the efforts of developing countries, including endeavours by some to curb population growth, every half minute 100 children are born in developing countries. Twenty of them die within the year. Of the 80 who survive, 60 have no access to modern medical care during their childhood. An equal number will suffer from malnutrition during the crucial weaning and toddler age—with the possibility of irreversible physical and mental damage.' From the introduction of a report on *Trends in the Social Situation of Children*, U.N.O. Publication 1970.

33. (p. 65) *The Optimum Population for Britain*, Edited by L. R. Taylor, Academic Press, London 1970, pp. 159–60. This is the Proceedings of a symposium held in London on 25 and 26 September 1969. It is an original and stimulating publication, bringing together twelve authorized opinions and discussions on these opinions. I have not met any study like it, particularly in the importance it gives to human values—individual and communal—in evaluating optimum population. Ninety per cent of participants and visitors registered their opinion that 'the optimum population for Britain has already been exceeded'.

34. (p. 66) It may be relevant to ask 'can this or that nation learn to live the good life in the midst of material plenty?' and one answer could be that material plenty might not last the time required to learn to live with it. Answers could also be sought in history, with the examples of Sybaris, Rome and others; or in the internal strains and stresses of the Western World; or, more usefully perhaps, in an estimate of the power of the 'external proletariat', the have-not nations. But it is premature to consider whether mankind as a whole could learn to live with affluence and leisure, so premature that it may never be relevant, because the time may never come when all of humanity will have to adjust to plenty. And it is absolutely certain that it will not come in any foreseeable future.

35. (p. 66) Lyndon B. Johnson, quoted by *Time*, 3 November 1967. In the same sense: 'A vista of an enclave of privilege in an isolated West is not pleasant to contemplate. Wise and human political institutions do not thrive in beleaguered citadels' (Harold A. Thomas, Jr.).

36. (p. 66) cf. in *L'Empire Américain* by Claude Julien (Editions Bernard

267

Grasset, Paris 1968) interesting statistics on the proportion of available raw materials consumed by the U.S.A. The figures also show that part of the materials consumed which the U.S.A. have to import from other countries.

37. (p. 68) Jean Rostand, *Les Inquiétudes d'un Biologiste*, Editions Stock, Paris 1967, p. 85.

38. (p. 78) In particular, liberation of sex appears to be having little impact on marriage, which is rather being revalorized, both as a social institution and as a frame for individual fulfilment. At the time when revolt of the young is at its noisiest and rowdiest, when sexual relations before and out of marriage are commonplace, when there is increasing tolerance for sexual deviations, people are getting married younger and the rate of divorce is not increasing significantly. Because of earlier marriage and longer life, expectation of marriage life has increased. Perhaps the fact that economic considerations are no longer a basic factor in marriage arrangements and that choice of wife and husband is free from the compulsions of the past, has helped to consolidate the institution of marriage. True, it is different to what it traditionally was, it is no longer an alliance between two families, and family is reduced to its minimum form, but it remains the most vital social institution.

39. (p. 82) See *Le Robot, La Bête et L'Homme*, Rencontres Internationales de Geneve 1965, Editions de la Baconnière, Neuchâtel 1966, p. 189 et seq., for a thought-provoking comparison between poems churned out by a computer and poems by modern poets. A selection of cultured persons were asked to examine two such compositions and to determine which was the machine's. Four out of every ten guessed wrong. One quickly gets over the first shock of reading such word assemblages, often striking and colourful though meaningless, produced by a machine. One then realizes that the significant thing is not that a machine should produce a 'poem' as good as that of a human mind, but that a human mind should be set to work as if it were a machine, i.e. unconsciously and automatically. The automatic poet, electronic or human, will never produce a sonnet remotely like one of Shakespeare.

40. (p. 82) The following quotation from Albert Camus is appropriate in this context: 'The free artist is not the man of an interior disorder, nor is he the man of an imposed order. The free artist is he who creates his own order. The more wild and unchained that which he must express, the more will his rule be strict and the more will he have affirmed his freedom. If art does not restrain itself, it soon becomes delirious and is enslaved to shadows.'

41. (p. 85) Statistical information on crime in the U.S.A. staggers the imagination: continuous rise in serious offences, one crime per minute, 6,500 murders per year, 750,000 deaths by bullets since the turn of the century. . . . America is known as the land of records, and this appears to be one of the biggest.

NOTES

42. (p. 95) These slogans are found in *Traité de Savoir-Vivre à l'Usage des Jeunes Générations*, by Raoul Vaneigem, Gallimard, Paris 1967. This book, which is an all-out call for destruction of social order, appears to have been a source of inspiration for French student leaders and for 'advanced' groups in France and Belgium apparently affiliated to Chinese communism. There was no lack of generosity in the young people of Czechoslovakia who started, in that same year 1968, an indignant campaign in favour of better care for the aged (cited by Simone de Beauvoir in *La Vieillesse*, Gallimard, Paris 1970, p. 234).

43. (p. 101) cf. in Norbert Wiener's *The Human Use of Human Beings*, pp. 131–5, a penetrating analysis of this phenomenon.

44. (p. 106) 'Value' is generally used too loosely. The crucial difference between the fundamental values and the secondary or derivative is seldom made clear. For instance, in the 25 pages of *Some General Implications of the Research of the Harvard University Program on Technology and Society* (1969), Emmanuel G. Mesthene uses the following phrases: 'conflicts among our values', 'growing awareness that our values are in fact changing under the impact of technological change', 'values change through a process of accommodation', 'its (accommodation's) consequences for value changes', 'change in value systems', 'preparing the ground for change in its (society's) values', 'facilitating a change in values', 'require the emergence of new values', 'a system of values . . . appropriate to a society in which technology is so prevalent'. The author did not make it clear whether he had fundamental values in mind when he so frequently referred to value changes. Indiscriminate use of the word must blur the necessary distinction between what is fundamental (and therefore cannot change without regression of civilization) and what is derivative (and therefore must change with changing circumstances and fluctuating environment). The lack of definition is misleading, because the reader may infer that *all* values can and must change, even the basic and fundamental. Or he may infer that there are no fundamental values. In *How Technology will shape the Future* (1968), the same author writes that we will have to change 'from values to valuing, for it is not particular familiar values as such that are valuable, but the human ability to extract values from experience and to use and cherish them . . . (to guide us) in the reformulation of our ends to fit our new means and opportunities'. What ends are meant here? The short-term goals, which can be considered as means, or the perennial ends of civilized society, which may certainly be 'reformulated' but equally certainly not changed 'to fit our new means'. This is dangerous ambiguity, all the more because of the authority and distinction of the writer.

45. (p. 110) The expression of crisis is encountered more frequently, and with a mounting sense of urgency. 'I must underline the crucial character of the juncture . . . the present crisis which involves transition from an obsolete system to a future which has not yet taken shape. But I must insist on the fact of the crisis . . .' (Julian Huxley, *Science and Synthesis*, UNESCO 1967).

'There is only one crisis in the world . . . The trouble is that it is now coming upon us as a storm of crisis problems from every direction . . . multiple crises, a crisis of crises all at one time . . .' (John Platt, *The Center Magazine*, Vol. IV, No. 2, Santa Barbara 1971). It could be worth while to collect quotations from responsible writers, a sort of anthology of the crisis of humanity.

46. (p. 112) Fred L. Polak, *The Image of the Future*, 2 vols., Sythoff/Leyden & Oceana, New York 1961.

47. (p. 112) Barbara Ward, *Faith and Freedom*, p. 4.

48. (p. 112) Lewis Mumford, *The Transformations of Man*, p. 137.

49. (p. 114) Igor Bestoujev-Lada, *Les Etudes sur l'Avenir en U.R.S.S.*, in Analyse & Prévision (Futuribles) Tome V, No. 2, SEDEIS, Paris 1968.

50. (p. 114) Marxism appears to be turning into a system for underdeveloped pre-industrial countries. Its attraction is understandingly waning for the rich nations, while it is growing for the poor nations caught in the vicious spiral of underdevelopment and exploding populations. In this avatar, Marxism changes its basic premises (reliance on rural agricultural proletariat instead of urban industrial workers, acceptance of co-existence with other political systems instead of the earlier principle of utter incompatibility, use of nationalism as the door to communism instead of the original internationalism) but it still holds out to the unportioned and despairing everywhere the shining promises that it can never make good. These ever-renewed promises are the secret of Marxism's perennial attraction despite its manifest failures; the Marxist call would not resonate so strongly in men's hearts were it not tuned to the fundamental values and the dream of a better life for humanity. And no prophet has come out of the rich nations with a constructive vision of charity and justice for the world, to hold out the promises that the Western democracies could make good were they converted to an ecumenical conception of the human values.

51. (p. 117) Americans are only a little ahead of Western Europe, whose nations have the same values to guard and the same technology to adore and to fear. They are far ahead of Russia, where technology is advanced in certain fields only and where individual values are regarded as secondary to collective aims and the state religion. There is, therefore, little clash as yet between human values and technique in U.S.S.R. Russians and Eastern European nations have got less to lose and less to fear, as their totalitarian society is already bound in closed rigidity. There are signs that this rigidity is loosening. If the movement gains momentum, it will be of advantage to all of humanity, as Russians and their followers will have more to lose of human values and more incentive to defend those values in co-operation with America and Western Europe. Harvey Wheeler takes an apparently opposite stand in his deeply meditated *Democracy in a Revolutionary Era*

(Centre for Study of Democratic Institutions, Santa Barbara 1970). There, he appears to put his hope for a regeneration of democracy in the new countries and the developing nations (pp. 71–2). It looks as if one lost confidence in what one knew best and tried to regain it with an optimistic view of what one knew less well: he sees little self-regeneration to be expected from the advanced countries, caught in over-rationalized and technicized organization; I see little hope of regeneration from the new states, beset by poverty and over-population. May we both be wrong!

52. (p. 126) Julian Huxley, in the Introduction to the English translation of Teilhard de Chardin's *The Phenomenon of Man*, Collins, London 1959. A somewhat caricatural derivation from Teilhard de Chardin's notion of 'totalisation' may be found in *Les Dieux et les Rois*, by Jacques Rueff, Hachette, Paris 1968. The author sets out to present 'a quantum philosophy of the universe applicable not only to the physical sciences, but to all human sciences'. He speaks of the 'choice' of protons and electrons, the 'behaviour' of atoms and molecules, thus demonstrating the 'fundamental unity of the scientific interpretation of our universe' and proving the basic freedom of human beings. This is in line with a recent trend to deduce from theories on the structure of matter a new basis for asserting human autonomy. For instance, Heisenberg's principle of indeterminacy is seized upon to prove by unwarranted analogy the freedom of human beings. It is refreshing to note that scientists are giving up the absolute certainty of their measures and the rigidity of their deterministic laws, but it is depressing to observe humanists defending the autonomy of the person by reference to the random movements of the smallest known particles of matter. However, efforts at constructing a new metaphysics, at providing a new explanation of creation are all too few in these days of intellectual nihilism and philosophical sterility, and no such efforts should be disparaged.

53. (p. 127) For an example of this line of reasoning, see Aurel David, *La Cybernétique et l'Humain*.

54. (p. 128) Political and social morality are quite different from individual morality. The state, as the active organ of society, is generally considered, especially in its relations with other states, as unfettered by the rules that are recognized by human beings in their relations with one another. ' . . . la société peut faire le mal beaucoup plus facilement et plus souvent que l'individu. La moralité de l'individu est nettement supérieure à celle des sociétés' (Mohamed Kamel Hussein in MIDEO (Mélanges de l'Institut Dominicain d'Etudes Orientales), Tome 8, Cairo 1966). Apart from pure expediency, there is no justification for the organs of state and society to ignore the rules of individual morality; no justification for the individuals who speak and act for those organs to lie and to cheat, to steal and to murder, when they would refrain from so doing were they speaking and acting for themselves.

55. (p. 131) Norbert Wiener, *The Human Use of Human Beings*, p. 75.

56. (p. 133) India must be noted as the only 'non-advanced' country and one, moreover, facing the greatest difficulties, where liberty of thought and expression is recognized and practised, where the press is free and elections are free. It is said that only a minority in India is in a position to make use of this freedom, but this does not detract from the remarkable character of the achievement.

57. (p. 134) There is 'no reason for us to mistake civil rights for political freedom, or to equate these preliminaries of civilized government with the very substance of a free republic. For political freedom, generally speaking, means the right "to be a participator in government", or it means nothing', Hannah Arendt, *On Revolution*, Compass Books Edition 1965, pp. 220-1.

58. (p. 138) The title of a study that exposes the legal and economic aspects of social freedom, as well as the problems involved in maintaining a working democracy: *Planning for Freedom, The Public Law of American Capitalism*, Eugene V. Rostov, Yale University Press, New Haven 1959.

59. (p. 145) J. Bronowsky, *Science and Human Values*, 1958. Pelican Edition 1964, pp. 52 and 71.

60. (p. 151) ' . . . the all-comprehensive pretension of the social sciences which, as "behavioural sciences", aim to reduce man as a whole, in all his activities, to the level of a conditioned and behaving animal', Hannah Arendt, *The Human Condition*, 1958 (Anchor Books Edition 1959, p. 41). And more forcefully: 'The trouble with modern theories of behaviourism is not that they are wrong but that they could become true, that they actually are the best conceptualization of certain obvious trends in modern society. It is quite conceivable that the modern age—which began with such an unprecedented and promising outburst of activity—may end in the deadliest, most sterile passivity history has ever known', ibid., p. 295

61. (p. 153) What Jean-Francois Revel expresses as 'this fatal propensity to start off again from zero and, even more fatal, to stay there' in his interesting *Ni Marx Ni Jésus, De la seconde révolution américaine à la seconde révolution mondiale*, Laffont, Paris 1970.

62. (p. 156) Walter Seib, *The Intellectual Revolution*, in Scala International, August 1966.

63. (p. 156) 'It was like a negation of all things of heaven and earth, that can be called disenchantment or, if you will, despair' so that 'men throw themselves into cold enthusiasm, into great words, into the ugly sea of action without aim'. These words of Alfred de Musset in 1934 are echoed by many people in our day. It is not change and newness that we should fear, but the absence of aims that should be stable and lasting in the midst of change.

64. (p. 157) 'History itself . . . has no end and no meaning, but we can decide

to give it both. .... Historicism is born of fear, for it shrinks from realizing that we bear the ultimate responsibility even for the standards we choose. .... Like gambling, historicism is born of our despair in the rationality and the responsibility of our actions', K. R. Popper, *The Open Society and its Enemies*, 1945, Routledge Reprint 1963, Vol. II, p. 279. That men in society are responsible for their 'fate' as they are responsible for their freedom is a cardinal principle that should be taught and illustrated to every boy and girl. It is a far cry from this high conception of human dignity to the behavioural conditionment that aims to transform *homo sapiens* into *homo adfectus*. 'In social evolution, nothing is inevitable, but thinking makes it so', F. A. Hayek, *The Road to Serfdom*, 1944, Phoenix Books 1965, p. 48.

65. (p. 157) 'Totalitarianism need not be the wave of the future, by 1984 or any other date. If we succumb to regimes which order our lives and thoughts in these bleak ways, our fate will be recorded in history as suicide, not as the tragic consequence of inexorable forces. Neither the programmes we need to achieve economic stabilization and growth nor the necessities of our international position require us to abandon a philosophy that puts the liberation and self-development of the individual as the first of our social goals', E. V. Rostov, *Planning for Freedom*, concluding paragraph. It is refreshing and encouraging to read such words. They are too rarely found in the writings and sayings of responsible members of society.

66. (p. 157) 'To progress is to move towards some kind of end, towards an end which exists for us as human beings. "History" cannot do that; only we, the human individuals, can do it; we can do it by defending and strenthening those democratic institutions upon which freedom, and with it progress, depends. And we shall do it much better as we become more fully aware of the fact that progress rests with us, with our watchfulness, with our efforts, with the clarity of our conception of our ends, and with the realism of their choice', K. R. Popper, *The Open Society and its Enemies*, Vol. II, pp. 278–80.

67. (p. 160) 'For reasons of personality as well as professional perspective, many operations researchers and systems analysts have great difficulty in coping with the more ambiguous and less "logical" aspects of society. .... Crucial aspects of psychological and social reorganization have been pushed into the background simply because they cannot be handled statistically with convenience. .... Computers are especially useful for dealing with social situations that pertain to people in the mass. .... They are so useful in these areas that they undoubtedly will help to seduce planners into inventing a society with goals that can be dealt with in the mass rather than in terms of the individual . . .', Donald N. Michael, *Cybernation: The Silent Conquest*, The Fund for the Republic 1962. In his *Social Technology* (Basic Books, New York 1966) Olaf Helmer shows real concern for 'the obligation to conduct a continual analysis of moral values' (p. 38) in using the new forecasting and planning methods for social policy-making. It should be possible to exercise constant awareness of the issues at stake, so that the potential and easily established opposition between technique and human

values may be prevented, and technological means made to serve human goals and defend human rights.

68. (p. 161) E. V. Rostov, *Planning for Freedom*, p. 384.

69. (p. 163) 'A social order in which men make the decisions that shape their lives becomes more possible now than ever before; the unshackling of men from the bonds of unfulfilling labour frees them to become citizens, to make themselves and to make their own history', *The Triple Revolution*, a memorandum by the *Ad hoc* Committee on the Triple Revolution, 1964. It is indeed more possible than ever before to achieve such a social order but, as the memorandum also points out, 'a vision of democratic life is made real not by technological change but by men consciously moving towards that ideal . . .'.

70. (p. 164) *From Here to Where?* (Geneva 1970) is the title of an excellent report by David M. Gill on this exploratory conference. Several issues of *Anticipation*, edited by the Department on Church and Society of the World Council of Churches, include the key presentations which set the context for the debates at the conference. There are also four important volumes of essays prepared for the previous conference on Christians in the Technical and Social Revolutions of Our Time, held by the World Council of Churches in 1966. They are a valuable review of the problems that constitute the present crisis in human affairs.

71. (p. 165) Norbert Wiener, *The Human Use of Human Beings*, p. 186.

72. (p. 167) W. W. Rostov, *The Stages of Economic Growth*, Cambridge 1960, 1963 Reprint, pp. 66 and 99. Also see Milovan Djilas, *The Imperfect Society, Beyond the New Class* (Harcourt, Brace & World, 1969) for a close analysis of the myth of communist superiority and the reality of communist inferiority in social, political and economic organization. Andrei Amalric painted the picture of a society without hope in *Will the Soviet Union survive in 1984?* for which he was once more condemned to imprisonment.

73. (p. 169) Parkinson's 'laws' are witty and penetrating comments on the urge to organize with little regard or relation to social order and social purpose. A sinister example of this urge is the variety of information agencies that are established in totalitarian states for competitive spying on the people, for compiling endless lists of each individual's every act and circumstance and—last but not least—for collecting information on each other. They are cankers that waste much of individual energies and collective resources. It is disheartening to observe the advanced countries setting up centralized and computerized centres of information for vital statistics, criminal records, economic progress, taxation, health inspection and other plausible purposes. In the automated memory of these centres, analysis and dissection of every human being—to be known by his number rather than by his name—will be made possible in a vastly more efficient manner than by the police methods of less advanced countries.

74. (p. 172) There is a useful classification by Johan Galtung of the trends that transcend purely national indentification of men and women. He defines them as four basic types, namely subnational, crossnational, transnational and supranational indentifications. In *Mankind 2000*, edited by Robert Jungk and Johan Galtung, Oslo and London 1969.

75. (p. 176) *The Invisible Government*, David Wise and Thomas B. Ross, Random House, New York 1964. *The Game of Nations*, Miles Copeland, Weidenfeld & Nicolson, London 1969.

76. (p. 178) An indefatigable prophet of a united Europe is Denis de Rougemont. His *Lettre Ouverte aux Européens* (Albin Michel, Paris 1970) is an eloquent plea for his thesis.

77. (p. 184) See Report of the *Joint Committee on the Organization of Congress*, July 1966.

78. (p. 186) Information is generally good in the advanced countries, where the press fulfils a fundamental role. Everybody is aware of the pressures and influences that are brought to bear on it by political and financial interests, but this cannot be compared to enslavement of the press in totalitarian countries, where even the day's headlines may be prescribed and distributed among the several dailies that are maintained to preserve a semblance of differing opinions. The free press may and does criticize everything and everybody, while the other is simply the government's voice.

79. (p. 187) Looking down from the pinnacles of their specialization and their culture, some scientists and humanists appear to consider the 'common man' as a sort of moron of incredibly low IQ, incapable of understanding and imagination. But the common man is something quite different, much higher than this distorted image. Democracy could not have prospered anywhere without the common man. 'Common wisdom' (or common sense) has also become a term of disdain and commiseration. It is supposed to be insufficient for the comprehension of the complex issues of modern society. Advanced intellectuals appear to equate common wisdom with simple ignorance. Many of them would do well to acquire some of the common wisdom that they despise.

80. (p. 188) The important intellectual enterprise of Futuribles in France, under the able guidance of Bertrand de Jouvenel, appears to be concentrating its effort on thinking out the institutions to preserve democratic operation of government in the technicist and overcrowded society. Several institutions in the U.S.A. make this problem their principal concern. Thinkers and practitioners from many countries contribute to this research.

81. (p. 192) Genesis 3.16, which a Scottish doctor countered by invoking Genesis 2.21 where it says that Adam was put to sleep before a rib was taken from him to make into a woman. Quoted from H. L. Mencken, *Treatise on Right and Wrong*, Kegan Paul, London 1934, p. 42.

82. (p. 195) Donald J. Bogue, *The End of the Population Explosion*, The Public Interest, Number 7, Spring 1967, New York; and *The Demographic Moment of Truth*, Chicago Today, Winter 1967.

83. (p. 196) Annie Besant, Aletta Jacobs, Margaret Sanger, Marie Stopes are now household names. All men and women are indebted to them. Their bold journals, *The Malthusian* (1879), *The Woman Rebel* (1914), *The New Generation* (1921) contributed to the recognition of family planning as a necessary part of social service. Less than one hundred years ago, birth control was an obscene subject, to be condemned by the courts and denied the use of the post. Now there are well-established Associations and Foundations for Planned Parenthood, with some governments participating in the movement with official birth control programmes. The World Bank and the U.S.A. are interested in giving aid to several countries for establishing or developing birth control.

84. (p. 198) For a concise statement of the complexities and the possibilities of such a programme, see *The Role of Goals and Planning in the Solution of the World Food Problem*, Paper presented by Hasan Ozbekhan at the Mankind 2000 Conference, Oslo 1967.

85. (p. 200) This problem of the individual in an overcrowded society has exercised the sensitivity and perceptiveness of distinguished minds in many countries. Some are quoted in these pages. The best known and most detailed study on the subject is no doubt David Riesman's *The Lonely Crowd* (1950).

86. (p. 203) See *Toward a Social Report*, in The Public Interest, No. 15, Spring 1969: *I. The Idea of a Social Report*, by Daniel Bell, and *II. The Plan and Purpose of a Social Report*, by Mancur Olson, Jr. It would be interesting to work out something like the accounts of a company or corporation for, say, the United States of America at 31 December 1971, including the customary Balance Sheet and Profit and Loss Account. This would be a revealing and an instructive document, even if it can only be an approximation with many variables based on value appreciations and priorities.

The Balance Sheet would comprise numerical parameters for personal and social factors, such as the level of health and education, the epidemics of crime and drugs, the availability and quality of housing, schooling, transport, medical and social care, cultural recreation, conservation of beauty and prevention of ugliness, etc. However unreliable the estimate reached, it would be a useful and a sobering exercise for economists and politicians. Less interestingly but more accurately, it could be worked out as a purely economic and financial document which, instead of reflecting the flow of activity and production, would show the value of the current assets (stocks, etc.) and of the fixed assets (railways, post, telephone and telegraph, schools and hospitals, homes for the aged, as well as factories, ports and canals, power plants, etc.) together with the financial and economic debts and liabilities, and sufficient provision for fighting pollution and improving services. The 'national capital', as derived from the difference between liabilities and assets (even if the defence establishment is included as an asset) would probably result in much less than the expected wealth when divided *per capita*. It could be less than the *per capita* capital of Switzerland, where the fixed assets are in a better state of maintenance, repair and renewal, and where services are in incomparably better supply and availability than in U.S.A.

The Profit and Loss Account would be something very different from the GNP estimate which has become the object of national pride or dejection all over the world. The method of GNP computation would, in effect, be inadmissible for any company or corporation, and it would be set aside by the Auditors as false and misleading. The GNP computation contains a great many negative elements (that is, elements that result from disamenities and hardships, and the effort to remedy them) presented as positive production of services and goods, while the really positive elements (that is, elements that result from a better quality of life in its material and its moral aspects) have practically no place at all in it. A more realistic computation in the form of a Profit and Loss Account would lead to wiser policies than the present hypnotic fixation on GNP.

87. (p. 208) This happened when colonial powers took over countries which had already made a start in modern industry. Two cases in point are the British conquest of India in the 18th century and occupation of Egypt in the 19th century.

88. (p. 209) Only staple foodstuffs maintain their relative price as they continue to be in short supply because of population increase and because there are as yet no commercialized substitutes for cereals, meat and milk. But the flow is in the wrong direction: only special foods such as cocoa, and spices, tea and coffee come from the poor countries, while the staple foodstuffs are produced in greater quantities by some of the industrially advanced nations; these supply, for cash, credit or good-will an important part of the agricultural products required to ward off famine in the poor countries.

89. (p. 210) *L'Exode des Cerveaux* (Centre de Recherches Européennes, Lausanne 1968) contains interesting information on this subject. However, the statistics given apply only to immigration of graduates into U.S.A. and they do not include figures for the drain of graduates from developing countries into Europe, Canada and Australia.

90. (p. 216) Special mention must be made of aid in key fields, such as agriculture, education, health, by means of joint projects sponsored by some of the smaller European countries. The good results achieved by these projects have derived more from the care and concern devoted to them than from the funds provided.

91. (p. 219) There is a body of opinion to recommend budgeting the U.S.

space programme at one-half of 1 per cent of GNP, but there is nobody to recommend—to my knowledge—that aid to the unportioned part of humanity should also be continuously funded at a proportion of GNP which would stand in some relation to the direness of need, the urgency of danger, and the priorities of the American people.

92. (p. 219) For instance: 'The super-powers must face the utter bankruptcy of the theory of nuclear deterrence (Green, 1966) and start replacing the gross risks of continuing the arms race with the lesser (but still perhaps serious) risks of disarmament. Such a move is essential, not just to avoid the ultimate disaster of a thermonuclear war, but also to free the resources needed for an attempt to avoid a "crash" in the human population—an end to civilization as we know it through a combination of famine, plague and eco-catastrophe. The need for such a change has been clearly recognized on both sides of the Iron Curtain—it has been articulated recently by Academician Sakharov (1968) and Lord Snow (1969). Both feel that expenditures on the order of 20 per cent of the gross national product of the rich countries will be necessary for the next decade if the growing UDC–DC gap is to be closed, and such figures are probably unrealistically low if the entire problem of arresting environmental deterioration is to be tackled', P. R. Ehrlich in *The Optimum Population for Britain*, p. 159.

93. (p. 219) In *Development Assistance in the Seventies* (A Forward Look at Foreign Aid, Brookings Research Report 105) Robert E. Asher sets the target for U.S.A. at 1 per cent of GNP by 1975. This—I believe—is too low, both as a practical proposition and as a long-term target, and it may be influenced overmuch by the present juncture in American affairs. The author makes many important and constructive points; in particular: (a) Development aid is effective. (b) Aid should be predominantly multilateral. (c) Legislation should embody a five- or ten-year U.S. commitment to the development of the low-income world.

94. (p. 222) 'Under present conditions, no programme of hard work, spartan austerity, far-reaching social reforms, birth control, and unimpeachable administration that the underdeveloped countries may adopt, nothing of the sort—albeit necessary—can promise to redress this imbalance in the world economy, and set these countries really on the move', Aurelio Peccei, *The Chasm Ahead*, p. 179.

95. (p. 225) Lecomte du Noüy, *La Dignité Humaine*, pp. 51 and 52. ' . . . un des mythes les plus dangereux de notre époque: la création de personnes morales, sociales, politiques ou économiques dont l'existence finit par menacer les intérêts individuels qu'elles étaient primitivement supposées défendre . . . (cet être nouveau) cesse d'obéir aux lois morales que la société impose à l'individu . . . et se forge lui-même des lois contradictoires avec les lois des individus.'

96. (p. 227) This painful problem is analysed with lucidity and sympathetic

perception by Daniel Bell in *The Reforming of General Education*, Columbia University Press, New York 1966.

97. (p. 229) Volunteer service organizations are numerous in the advanced countries and they cover a wide range of services. They operate in their own countries and in foreign (underdeveloped) countries. At the same time as they give useful service, the volunteers acquire a deeper sense of human solidarity and a greater understanding of human unity in the variety of races, languages and cultures.

98. (p. 230) The quotations in this paragraph are from C. G. Jung, *Memories, Dreams, Reflections*, pp. 151, 240, 300 and 301. It is hard to conceive a world without consciousness to give it meaning; unbearable to imagine the works of men and women, their cities and their books, their pictures and their poetry, their toys and their gadgets still standing or lying about with no intelligence to ponder upon them, not even the dim understanding of a primitive bushman. Creativeness of men lies less in their actions than in their awareness that completes the work of creation by giving reality to the world around. That men may extinguish consciousness by a nuclear convulsion is a possibility present in everyone's mind. What is less present is that consciousness may also be extinguished by thoughtless submission to a technicist system of society. The last lines of Seidenberg's *Post-Historic Man* (1950) express this in dramatic phrases: (Man) 'will have passed through the transitional, historic phase of his evolution, and attained at length a post-historic stage. In the course of his development, he has been constrained from time to time to abandon his most cherished myths. Thus he has abandoned his animism; his Ptolemaic astronomy that assured his position in the centre of the universe; his faith in a hereafter that endowed him with eternal life; his belief in the supreme and infinite worth of his person that assured him a position of isolate dignity in an otherwise meaningless and impersonal world; and even his faith in a God whose attributes, under the impact of man's rationalistic scrutiny, became ever more abstract until He vanished in the metaphysical concept of the Whole. The shedding of these inestimable illusions may be merely stages in his diminishing stature before he himself vanishes from the scene—lost in the icy fixity of his final state in a post-historic age.' This terrible and despairing view is not an impossible picture. It is one of the possible futures from among which men must now make a choice. The same tragic sense is expressed, with more bitterness and less resignation, in the last pages of Ellul's *The Technological Society* (1954): 'It is apparently our fate to be facing a "golden age" in the power of sorcerers who are totally blind to the meaning of the human adventure. . . .'

99. (p. 232) Dennis Gabor, *Inventing the Future*, 1963. Pelican Books Edition 1964, p. 126.

100. (p. 236) Even thinkers of unmistakable independence of mind appear to bow to the prevailing fashion with definitions such as this: 'The author

cannot pretend to knowledge of the precise assumptions about human behaviour which, if formally elaborated, would yield a theory of society within
which economics would be one portion. He would however define the
ultimate theoretical goal of the social sciences in some such terms, while
admitting scepticism concerning the likelihood of its early achievement.
Progress towards that goal is likely to take shape when the fundamental
human motives are clarified and generalized by the maturing, in combination, of psychiatry, social psychology and sociology. From such a base, a
method might be developed for dealing with human and social behaviour,
in various circumstances, as a balancing among alternative human objectives
when confronted with the challenges and possibilities of different environment', W. W. Rostov, *The Process of Economic Growth*, Norton 1952, p. 35.
Always this apparent indifference to the purpose of society, which it should
reasonably be the goal of the social sciences to further. The rift is growing
between the human values, which nobody consciously denies as the ends of
society, and the social sciences, which appear to be as unconcerned with
those values as they are with the ends of society.

101. (p. 237) Daniel J. Boorstin, *The Image*, 1961. Pelican Edition 1963, p. 205.

102. (p. 243) Statistics, schedules and tables, graphs and curves have been
omitted as they can readily be found in reference compilations and specialized publications.

103. (p. 248) This is the title of a deeply pessimistic article by Roderick
Seidenberg in *Center Diary: 17*, Santa Barbara 1967.

104. (p. 248) *Les Humanités du XXe Siècle*, by Henri van Lier, Casterman,
Belgium 1965. This manifesto, as the author calls it, is an average example
of the uncultured optimism and curiously constricted thought of certain
European intellectuals, who see no solution for the future but an un-
hesitating, even enthusiastic acquiescence in the 'new humanism' of the
technicist and behaviourist society. But they are not representative of European thought at its best, which continues to be inspired by a high conception of the ends of civilized society.

105. (p. 251) The use of the term 'values' for secondary and subsidiary aims
and goals, even for trivial and transient desires, points to the extent of confusion between the fundamental and the secondary or derivative. It is an
instance of the inflation in the use of key words, and their consequent
depreciation. Every desire is a value, every change a revolution.

106. (p. 252) Georges Elgozy, *Automation et Humanisme*, Calmann-Lévy, Paris
1968, p. 16. The hysteria of change takes other unexpected forms. One of
the most frequent is a definite refusal of all tradition with an equally
definite refusal of any sign-posts on the road to the future. 'We must . . .
refrain from adopting any solution from the past. . . . We must confront
the situation (of America) with existential bravado—and become a nation

of ambiguity lovers' (William Pennell Rock, in Alienation: Yes; Patriotism: Yes. *The Center Magazine*, Vol. IV, No. 6, Santa Barbara November/ December 1971). But neither existential bravado, nor any kind of bravado, nor ambiguity in any form will help Americans to come out of their cultural crisis with something stable upon which to build a better future, some more fulfilling life for individuals and more satisfactory relations between them. This attitude is simply too easy and too lazy. In fact, the existentialist trend, the love of ambiguity, are main elements of the crisis; it is surprising (and unconvincing) to hear that they are the way to emerge from the crisis with a new identity for a new man. Without permanent fundamentals to guide us in the search for a better future, we will get nowhere and anything can happen. However, this feeling that anything can happen (and that anything must be better than the present) appears to excite and gratify many people, like so many leaves in the wind over which they have no control.

107. (p. 252) Aurelio Peccei, *The Chasm Ahead*, p. 281.

108. (p. 252) W. W. Rostov, *The Process of Economic Change*, Norton 1952, p. 41.

109. (p. 257) Daniel Chabanol, in *Analyse & Prévision*, Tome III, No. 5, SEDEIS, Paris 1967, p. 372.

110. (p. 257) E. V. Rostov, *Planning for Freedom*, pp. 6 and 7.

111. (p. 258) 'Thoughtlessness—the heedless recklessness or hopeless confusion or complacent repetition of "truths" which have become trivial and empty—seems to me among the outstanding characteristics of our time. What I propose, therefore, is very simple: it is nothing more than to think what we are doing', Hannah Arendt, *The Human Condition*, p. 6.

Index

Abortion, 194
Adaptation, 239, 251
Adjustment, 41, 48, 158, 159
Aesthetic, 98, 148, 227
Affluence, 66, 71, 72, 82, 85, 232
Africa, African, 65, 90, 128, 147, 170, 172, 173, 184, 194, 206, 215, 222, 232, 236
African Unity, Organization of, 173
Aggressiveness, 70
Agriculture, 65, 191, 197–8, 205, 216
Aid, 192, 211–22, 241, 278
Alienation, 87, 93, 105, 107, 140, 225, 227, 240, 246, 251
Amalric, Andrei, 274
America, American, 66, 110, 111, 117, 127, 146, 174–8, 189, 210, 213, 265
Anarchy, anarchist, 80, 83, 94, 138, 185
Anglo-Saxon, 35
Antonini, Fauste, 262
Apartheid, 132, 175
Apocalypse, 126
Arab, Arabs, 129, 205, 232, 262
Arab League, 173
Archaeology, 233
Architecture, 96, 97
Arendt, Hannah, 272, 281
Aristocratic, 102
Armament, arms, 33, 68, 207–8, 278
Armenians, 15
Art, arts, 16, 47, 81, 95–9, 205, 235
Asher, Robert E., 278
Asia, Asian, 65, 90, 127, 194, 222
Assassins, 128
Atheism, 193, 255, 264
Atlantic, 115, 210
Auschwitz, 28
Australasia, 133, 205
Australia, 189, 202, 277
Autocracy, autocratic, 129, 150

Authority, authoritarian, 25, 26, 80, 87, 132, 182
Automation, automated, 48, 54, 57, 66, 274
Awareness, 58, 61, 99, 103, 163, 229, 230, 232, 240
Ayn Rand, 126

Balkanization, 171
Basque, 169
Bazelon, David T., 139
Beauvoir, Simone de, 269
Beethoven, 28
Behaviourism, behavioural, 9, 19, 38, 48, 56, 58, 104, 272, 280
Belgium, 269
Bellamy, Edward, 266
Bell, Daniel, 276, 279
Bengalis, 15, 169
Berger, Peter L., 265
Bern, 169
Besant, Annie, 276
Bestoujev-Lada, Igor, 270
Biafra, 15, 169
Bill of Rights, 179
Biology, biological, 19, 33, 38, 49–52, 68, 122, 187, 254, 258
Birth control, 59, 139, 192–7, 220, 276
Bogue, Donald J., 195, 276
Boguslav, Robert, 261
Bomb, 32, 33, 80, 181
Bombay, 72
Boorstin, Daniel J., 280
Brain drain, 210, 277
Britain, British, 67, 113, 175, 178, 179, 210, 277
Bronowsky, J., 272
Buchenwald, 168

Caesarism, 184
Cairo, 72

Calcutta, 72
California, 75
Calvinist, 42
Camus, Albert, 268
Canada, 202, 210, 277
Capitalism, 23-5
Cassandra, 197
Catholic, 193, 262
Central American Common Market, 173
Chabanol, Daniel, 281
Change, 10, 19, 20, 88, 152-3, 155-6, 225, 250-5
Chicago, 72
Chile, 194
China, Chinese, 65, 113, 127, 133, 158-9, 169, 178, 194, 269
Christianity, Christian, 80, 106, 121, 125, 133, 155, 169, 177, 193, 194, 232, 257, 274
Church, 51, 228
Civism, civic, 185-8
Collectivism, collectivist, 25, 30, 42, 144, 158
Collectivity, 44-5
College, 91, 93, 224, 240
Colonialism, colonial, 77, 91, 147, 162, 172, 174, 208, 233
Common Law, 38
Communism, communist, 23, 25, 90, 113, 255,
Community, 17, 24, 71, 196, 199, 233, 245
Conditioning, conditioned, 42, 48, 56, 58, 136, 155, 159, 160, 273
Conformism, 41, 227
Consciousness, conscious, 9, 58, 99, 103, 229
Consensus, 51, 60, 84, 151, 228, 249, 258, 259
Conservatism, 79, 139-40, 157, 252
Constitution, 179
Consumption, 60, 66, 139, 201
Contraception, contraceptive, 193, 194, 197
Copeland, Miles, 275
Cosmopolis, 69
Costa Rica, 170

Cotta, Sergio, 263
Council of Europe, 181
Creativity, creation, 16, 45, 97, 100, 147, 279
Crime, 74, 84-6, 268
Crisis, 10, 29, 85, 109-10, 163, 204, 223, 246, 256, 269
Cuba, 176
Culture, cultured, 43, 102, 133, 229-34, 252
Cybernetics, cybernator, 15, 59, 66, 127
Czechoslovakia, Czech, 87, 93, 106, 114, 144, 269

Dachau, 168
Dante, 105
David, Aurel, 264, 271
Decentralization, 24, 37, 71
Déclaration des Droits de l'Homme et du citoyen, 179
Declaration of Independence, 179
Declaration of Rights, 179
Dehumanization, 87
Democracy, democratic, 10, 24, 25, 30, 83, 134, 168, 183, 185-7
Demography, 62-5, 191
Despotism, despot, 26, 28
Determinism, determinist, 40-3, 49, 122, 155, 163, 168, 183, 264
Dictatorship, dictator, 26, 30, 36, 90, 132, 134-5
Dignity, 29, 54, 60, 78, 145-7, 197
Dinkas, 169
Disaffection, 87, 88
Disarmament, 33, 34, 278
Discipline, 83, 225-9
Discrimination, 78, 88, 111, 144, 172, 228
Djilas, Milovan, 274
Doxiades, C. A., 72
Drugs, 47, 85, 111, 128, 146, 158, 228
Dubarle, Abbé, 263
Dubos, René, 237, 266

Earth, 33, 34, 45, 109, 129, 154, 172, 204, 230, 258

Eastern Europe, 24, 25, 92, 114, 184, 270
Ecology, ecological, 18, 65, 76, 129–30, 159, 163, 266
Economic Report, 202
Economics, economist, 23, 38, 172–4
Ecosphere, 75, 129–30, 163
Ecumenical, 204, 254, 270
Ecumenopolis, 72
Education, 57, 82, 102, 137–8, 205, 224–42, 244
Efficiency, efficient, 60, 71, 166, 248
Egypt, Egyptian, 92, 93, 161, 194, 232, 277
Ehrlich, P. R., 278
Electronics, 15, 49, 52, 128, 197
Elgozy, Georges, 280
Ellul, Jacques, 263, 279
Employment, 88, 207
England, English, 70, 75, 126
Environment, 72–6, 200
Egalitarian, 144
Equality, 113, 143, 144
Erie, lake, 75
Esthonia, 169
Ethics, ethical, 40, 56, 84, 104, 128, 155, 164, 255
Europe, European, 10, 24, 32, 36, 56, 72, 91, 116, 146, 161, 205, 261
European Commission of Civil Rights, 181
European Common Market, 178
European Convention for the Protection of Human Rights and Fundamental Freedoms, 181
European Court of Human Rights, 181
European Economic Community (EEC), 173, 178, 215, 222
Evolution, 42, 126, 168, 251, 253
Executive, 36, 37, 180
Existentialism, existentialist, 81, 125, 246, 264
Exploitation, 167–8, 206, 207, 208

Faith, 21, 59, 103, 104, 107, 112, 125, 136, 246

Family, 51, 197, 203, 224, 231, 254, 268
Family Planning, 191, 192–7, 220, 276
Famine, 10, 64, 65, 134, 145, 191, 202, 216
Fanon, Frantz, 237
Fascism, fascist, 27, 30, 141
Fate, fatalism, fatalist, 41, 56, 122, 142, 157, 163, 168, 264
Federalism, 169–74
Food, 59, 63, 197–8
Food and Agriculture Organization (FAO), 64
Fourastié, Jean, 50, 239, 265
France, French, 32, 94, 95, 103, 125, 141, 169, 175, 189, 210, 213, 261
Freedom, free, 10, 41, 130, 131–43, 150, 197
French Revolution, 28, 32, 179
Fromm, Erich, 266
Fulfilment, 60, 78, 105, 147, 156
Futuribles, 275

Gabor, Dennis, 257, 279
Galileo, 51
Galtung, Johan, 275
Generalist, 187, 236
Genesis, 126, 275
Genetic, 19, 50, 195, 197
Geneva, 33, 74, 93, 164
Germany, German, 87, 125, 141, 210, 261
Gill, David M., 274
God, gods, 16, 126, 142, 230, 279
Goethe, 28
Graeco-Roman, 153
Greece, Greek, 40, 47, 129, 161, 181, 205, 236
Green revolution, 65
Gross National Product (GNP), 60, 66, 213, 218, 219, 277
Guerilla, 31

Haiti, 261
Hayek, Friedrich A. von, 139, 273
Health, 144, 192, 206, 216
Hebrew, 40
Heisenberg, Werner, 271

Helmer, Olaf, 273
Hinduism, 194
Hippies, 80
Hiroshima, 32
Historicism, 273
History, 105, 233-4, 272-3
Hitler, Hitlerism, 27, 29, 168, 225
Humanae Vitae, 193
Humanism, humanist, 25, 49, 106, 110, 122, 258
Humanities, the, 97, 235-8
Hungary, Hungarian, 87, 262
Hunger, 10, 134, 191
Hussein, Mohamed Kamel, 271
Huxley, Aldous, 256, 261, 264
Huxley, Julian, 269, 271

Ibos, 169
I-Ching, 127
Idealism, idealist, 237, 248
Illiteracy, illiterate, 241
India, Indian, 90, 134, 170, 194, 272, 277
Indian (American), 147, 233, 236
Individuality, individual, 15, 16, 19, 24, 29, 48, 70-1, 95, 148, 182, 196, 231, 245
Industry, industrial, 34, 72, 75, 167, 192, 208, 216
Information, 51, 134-5, 138, 159, 185-8, 192, 207, 224, 240, 254, 275
Innovation, 56, 251, 255
Instruction, 102, 116, 235-41
International Bank of Reconstruction and Development (IBRD), 217
International Development Association (IDA), 217
International Finance Corporation (IFC), 217
Irak, 169
Islam, Islamic, 127, 194, 232
Israel, 262
Italy, Italian, 210, 261, 262

Jacobs, Aletta, 276
Japan, Japanese, 67, 75, 133, 166, 170, 189, 205, 210, 222
Jesus Christ, 106, 164, 257

Jews, Jewish, 15, 27
Jouvenel, Bertrand de, 249, 275
Judiciary, 37-8, 254
Julien Claude, 267
Jung, Carl Gustav, 101, 237, 266, 279
Jungk, Robert, 275
Jurassians, 169
Jurist, 38, 39
Justice, 113, 143-5, 150

Kahn, Hermann, 207
Karma, 146
Kelvin, William Thomson, Lord, 77
Kent State University, 87
Komsomols, 225
Kulaks, 27
Kurds, 169

Latin, 261
Latin America, 65, 90, 172, 176, 194, 209, 222, 232
Latvia, 169
Law, 35, 84, 180
Lecomte du Nouy, 266, 278
Lefebvre, Henri, 266
Legislative, 37
Leisure, 66, 99, 102, 103
Liberalism, liberal, 30, 117, 140, 168, 183
Liberation, 77-83, 106, 153, 268
Liberty, 16, 96, 133, 227
Literacy, literate, 87, 98, 205, 207, 241
Lithuania, 169
Liverpool, 147
London, 26, 29
Los Angeles, 72
Luxemburg, 170

Madison Avenue, 194
Magna Carta, 179
Malnutrition, 64
Mao Tse-Tung, 133, 158
Marc, Alexandre, 237
Marriage, 255, 268
Marshall Plan, 217
Marx, Marxism, Marxist, 25, 42, 114, 167, 168, 270

INDEX

Mass, masses, 46, 48, 80, 83, 86, 95, 105, 137, 139, 158, 161, 184, 232
Mass culture, 99–102, 230
Mass media, 52, 86, 96, 99–103, 136, 184
Mass society, 137, 248, 273
Materialism, materialist, 88, 103, 107, 246, 255
Mauritius, 171
McCarran Act, 29
McLuhan, Marshall, 52, 100
Mediterranean, 40
Megalopolis, 69
Mencken, H. L., 275
Mesthene, Emmanuel G., 269
Mexico, 69, 233
Michael, Donald M., 273
Middle East, 176
Military, 30, 56, 90
Morality, moral, 20, 40, 50, 76, 82, 104, 125, 128, 150, 155, 164, 192, 226, 244, 255
Moscow, 96
Mumford, Lewis, 34, 73, 101, 154, 237, 264, 270
Musset, Alfred de, 272
Mutation, 21, 265

Nagazaki, 32
Namibia, 172
Nation, national, 170–1, 183, 255
National Social Report, 202
Natural Law, 128–9
Nature, 18, 72, 128–9, 157, 262
Nazism, nazi, 27, 94
Near East, 184
Necessity, 122, 140, 150
Negro, 110–11, 178, 179
Nemesis, 146
Neumann, Erich, 126
New barbarians, 54, 234
New Delhi, 223
New Left, 79, 140, 252
New Orleans, 147
New York, 73–4
New Zealand, 189
Nigeria, 169

Nihilism, nihilist, 80, 227, 229, 246, 247
Nishapour, 28
North America, 116, 132, 201, 205
North Atlantic, 21, 133
Nuclear, 15, 33, 51, 67, 250
Nuers, 169

Objectivism, objectivist, 126
Olson, Jr., Mancur, 276
Ombudsman, 37
Optimum population, 198–203
Order, 168–9
Organization, 28, 42, 69–70, 98, 168–9
Osborne, Fairfield, 262
Overcrowding, 37, 63, 69, 72, 73, 76, 129, 161, 199, 255
Overpopulation, 10, 59, 62–76, 223
Oxford Provisions, 179
Ozbekhan, Hasan, 276

Pakistan, 194
Palestine, 161
Palomares, 75
Paris, 26, 72, 94
Parkinson, J. Northcote, 274
Parliament, parliamentary, 183–5, 246
Paternalism, paternalistic, 26
Peccei, Aurelio, 262, 278, 281
Permissiveness, 82
Philosophy, 23, 56, 125, 150, 164
Planning, planner, 121–3, 138–9, 220, 223
Platt, John, 270
Polak, Fred L., 110, 112, 265, 270
Poland, Polish, 87, 114
Police, 90
Pollution, 59, 72–6, 203, 250
Popper, K. R., 273
Portugal, Portuguese, 172
Positivism, positivist, 104, 126
Poverty, 62, 66, 85, 161, 162, 193, 223
Power, 25, 35, 49, 54, 172
Pragmatism, pragmatic, 56, 105, 126, 141, 168, 226, 265–6
Prague, 51, 96
Prejudice, 70, 162, 228
Press, the, 30–1, 51, 186, 272, 275

Privacy, 69, 71, 143
Private enterprise, 215–16
Progress, progressive, 45, 153–7, 166, 205
Property, 24, 85, 254, 255
Propriety, 255

Quality, 16, 60, 74, 147–8, 230

Race, racial, racism, 19, 70, 162
Radicalism, radical, 79, 139–40, 152
Rationalism, rationalistic, 18, 40, 88, 103, 107
Realism, realist, 104, 105, 183, 248
Reason, 141
Red Cross, 84, 160
Red Guards, 225
Regression, regressive, 41, 83, 84, 94, 152, 205
Relativism, relativist, 125–6
Religion, religious, 18, 103, 105, 107, 125, 127, 153, 162, 212, 255
Renaissance, 153, 205, 236
Representative Rule, 183–5
Repression, 89
Resources, 66–9, 166, 172, 199, 209
Responsibility of Power, 174–9
Restraint, 78, 227
Revel, Jean-François, 272
Revolution, revolutionary, 20, 42, 79, 141, 152, 163–4, 251, 253
Reynold, Gonzague de, 261
Rhine, 75
Rhodesia, 172, 175
Riesman, David, 276
Rights, 20, 24, 31, 174, 179, 181
Romania, 114, 191
Rome, Roman, 35, 37, 38, 127, 161, 205, 266
Ross, Thomas B., 275
Rostand, Jean, 268
Rostov, Eugene, 272, 273, 274, 281
Rostov, W. W., 274, 280, 281
Rougemont, Denis de, 275
Rueff, Jacques, 271
Rule of Law, 34–8, 262
Russia, Russian, 15, 24, 29, 113, 114, 133, 158, 166, 169, 177, 270

Ruysbroek, John of, 263

Saint Helena, 171
Saint Malo, 147
Sakharov, A. D., 278
Sanger, Margaret, 276
Sartre, Jean-Paul, 264
Savannah, 147
Scandinavia, 37, 113, 189
Schaar, John H., 265
Schiller, F. C. S., 101
Scepticism, sceptic, 40
School, 51, 224, 246
Science, scientist, 110, 238, 258
Science fiction, 112, 114, 154, 197, 258
Secularization, secular, 106
Seib, Walter, 272
Seidenberg, Roderick, 279, 280
Separation, 171
Sex, sexual, 54, 78, 85, 86, 158, 254, 268
Shakespeare, 268
Shklar, Judith, 264
Slav, 261
Slavery, slave, 129, 142, 145, 161, 162, 206
Snow, Lord, 278
Social Report, 202, 276
Social science, 44, 61
Social service, 188–90
Socialism, socialist, 23, 113
Sociology, sociologist, 8, 38, 40, 46, 47, 122, 224
Solidarity, 144, 147, 188, 211–13, 214, 245, 254
Sophistry, sophist, 56, 168
Sorbonne, 94
South Africa, 27, 172, 172, 206
South Korea, 194
Sovereignty, sovereign, 34, 171–2, 173, 181, 221
Soviet, 114, 167, 207
Spain, Spanish, 74, 169, 261
Specialization, specialist, 53, 135, 186–7, 236–41
Spengler, Oswald, 69
Spirit, spiritual, 18, 59, 76, 104, 150
Stalin, Stalinism, 27, 29, 77, 133

Starvation, 27, 64
State, 19, 27, 34, 51, 58, 133, 170, 181, 221, 255
Statistics, 29, 48, 141, 188, 237, 280
Stopes, Marie, 276
Students, 90–5, 234, 237
Sudan, Sudanese, 169
Superman, 19, 101, 258
Sweden, 170
Switzerland, Swiss, 113, 127, 169, 171, 185, 277
Sybaris, 266
System, systems, 27, 30, 56, 71, 148, 158

Talmon, J. L., 261
Taylor, L. R., 266
Technique, technology, 16, 58, 157–60, 164, 223
Technocracy, technocrat, 24, 80, 158, 163, 183, 185
Teilhard de Chardin, Pierre, 126, 270
Television (TV), 86, 98–9, 102, 231
The Triple Revolution, 274
Theobald, Robert, 265
Theology, 128
Third World, 25, 68, 91, 114, 174, 189, 193, 216, 232, 233
Tibet, Tibetan, 127, 169, 177
Tokyo, 69
Tolerance, 85, 116
Totalitarianism, totalitarian, 10, 15, 24, 25–31, 52, 79, 141, 146, 166, 168, 233, 255
Toynbee, Arnold, 101, 116
Trade, 221–2
Tranquillizer, 58, 227
Tribune, 37
Turkey, Turkish, 169, 194

Underdevelopment, underdeveloped, 64, 67, 90, 176, 207, 209, 215–17, 223, 278
Undernourishment, 64
Union of Soviet Socialist Republics (U.S.S.R.), 33, 34, 223
United Nations Conference on Trade and Development (UNCTAD), 223

United Nations Organization (UNO), 175, 180
United States of America (U.S.A.), 33, 37, 60, 66, 111, 167, 171, 206, 213, 222, 223, 262
Universal Declaration of Human Rights, 180
University, 93, 94, 210, 224, 240
Urbanization, 72–5
Utah, 75
Utopia, utopian, 29, 112, 237, 246, 249

Valéry, Paul, 264
Vaneigem, Raoul, 269
Van Lier, Henri, 280
Vatican, 192, 193
Vietnam, 93, 110, 136, 178
Violence, 83–90, 228, 255

War, 31–4, 68, 84, 90, 123, 129, 171, 220, 223, 225
Ward, Barbara, 264, 269
Warsaw, 96
Washington, D.C., 87
Western civilization, 17, 41, 48, 78, 115–17, 127, 149, 154, 231–2
Western culture, 89, 127, 153, 162, 231–2
Western Europe, 37, 100, 132, 161, 178, 201, 205, 213, 214
Wheeler, Harvey, 270
Whyte, Lancelot Law, 237
Wiener, Anthony, 207
Wiener, Norbert, 263, 265, 266, 269, 271, 274
Wilkinson, John, 265
Wilson, Colin, 237
Wise, David, 275
World Bank, 198, 217, 218, 276
World community, 204, 223
World Council of Churches, 164, 274
World War I, 112, 154, 167, 184, 209
World War II, 85, 149, 166, 176, 184, 209, 218

Youth, 32, 77, 85, 91–2, 138, 224, 227–9

Zen, 127